MARGERY KEMPE

GARLAND MEDIEVAL CASEBOOKS
(VOL. 4)

REFERENCE LIBRARY OF THE HUMANITIES
(VOL. 1468)

GARLAND MEDIEVAL CASEBOOKS
Joyce E. Salisbury and Christopher Kleinhenz
Series Editors

1. *Sagas of the Icelanders: A Book of Essays*
   edited by John Tucker

2. *Discovering New Worlds: Essays on Medieval
   Exploration and Imagination*
   edited by Scott D. Westrem

3. *Sex in the Middle Ages: A Book of Essays*
   edited by Joyce E. Salisbury

4. *Margery Kempe: A Book of Essays*
   edited by Sandra J. McEntire

MARGERY KEMPE
A Book of Essays

edited by
Sandra J. McEntire

GARLAND PUBLISHING, INC. • NEW YORK & LONDON
1992

H 2 5555 3120

Library of Congress Cataloging-in-Publication Data

Margery Kempe : a book of essays / edited by Sandra J. McEntire.
     p. cm. — (Garland reference library of the humanities ; vol.
1468. Garland medieval casebooks ; vol. 4)
  ISBN 0-8153-0378-5
  1. Kempe, Margery, b. ca. 1373. Book of Margery Kempe.
2. Christian literature, English (Middle)—History and criticism.
3. Mysticism—England—History—Middle Ages, 600–1500.
4. Women, Christian—England—Religious life—History.
I. McEntire, Sandra J. II. Series: Garland reference library of the
humanities ; vol. 1468. III. Series: Garland reference library of the
humanities. Garland medieval casebooks ; vol. 4.
PR2007.K4Z78 1992
248.2'2'092—dc20
                                              92-6437
                                                  CIP

Printed on acid-free, 250-year-life paper
Manufactured in the United States of America

CONTENTS

Acknowledgments   vii
Introduction   ix

THE WOMAN

Margery Kempe and Her Calling
   William Provost   3

"Understanding by Feeling" in Margery Kempe's *Book*
   Elizabeth Psakis Armstrong   17

Margery Kempe's Tears and the Power over Language
   Dhira B. Mahoney   37

The Journey into Selfhood:
   Margery Kempe and Feminine Spirituality
   Sandra J. McEntire   51

HER WORK

From Woe to Weal and Weal to Woe:
   Notes on the Structure of *The Book of Margery Kempe*
   Timea K. Szell   73

Voice, Authority, and Blasphemy in
   The Book of Margery Kempe
   David Lawton   93

Margery Kempe and the Critics:
   Disempowerment and Deconstruction
   Eluned Bremner   117

HER WORLD

Margery Kempe and King's Lynn
Deborah S. Ellis   139

Margery Kempe, St. Bridget, and Marguerite d'Oingt:
  The Visionary Writer as Shaman
Nanda Hopenwasser   165

Margery Kempe and the King's Daughter of Hungary
Alexandra Barratt   189

Bride, Margery, Julian, and Alice: Bridget of Sweden's
  Textual Community in Medieval England
Julia Bolton Holloway   203

Margery and Alison: Women on Top
Janet Wilson   223

List of References Cited   239
Index   255

ACKNOWLEDGMENTS

In particular I want to thank each of the contributors of this volume for meeting deadlines and adjusting to a rigorous schedule. As general editor, Joyce Salisbury has been unstintingly supportive in answering questions, particularly about computer shortcuts, assisting in many details of putting this project together, and sharing her warm and generous enthusiasm. The proofreaders at Garland deserve mention for their perceptions and efficiency. Last, I want to thank Rhodes College for providing me leave time in which to complete the major portion of work on this book.

INTRODUCTION

The rediscovery of *The Book of Margery Kempe* nearly sixty years ago marked the beginning of critically turbulent years which contrast profoundly the centuries of silence and obscurity which had preceded. Acclaimed and denigrated, Kempe has been subjected to a wide variety of interpretations which, on the whole, have been harsh and negative. Just who this woman was—lay/mystic, mother/spiritual virgin, experienced woman of the world/intimate of Christ—and what we as twentieth-century readers are to make of her as represented in her *Book*, have been and continue to be the central issues. From the first reviews to the essays in this volume, the controversy surrounding Margery Kempe remains alive. Indeed, this volume builds in large part upon the history of controversy: the dualistic thinking behind interpreting her, the patriarchal issues which must be examined, the attachment to personal or twentieth-century assumptions which fail to reveal much of relevance or value to understanding a fifteenth-century woman.

Even before the *Book* was written about, it was interpreted. The first translations of *The Book of Margery Kempe*, following upon the publication of the EETS edition of the manuscript by Sanford Brown Meech with the Introduction and Notes by Hope Emily Allen, presented Kempe's text in a visually disjointed manner. The English version placed all the chapters having to do with Kempe's revelations in an appendix; the American translation, also done by William Butler-Bowden, found this placement awkward and, while retaining the original order, "had all the chapters entirely devoted to mystical matters set in a smaller type to keep them distinct from the narrative text" (v). The publishers provide no explanation for this decision. Yet it seems to mark, in many ways, the assumptions and critical dilemmas that have surrounded *The Book of Margery Kempe*. This truncated presentation of Margery Kempe's *Book* systematically dislocates the central experience of Kempe's life and reduces her and her book to mere reflection of her readers' prejudices. Thus she can only be taken seriously when her tears, revelations, locutions, and emotions are set aside. As woman, as mystic, in effect, she cannot be taken seriously at all.

Kempe continues to be divided and dismembered by her critics, with some aspects of her life and spirituality found acceptable and others wanting. Even with the original ordering of the text restored in the EETS edition, critics seem to persist in reading her as Butler-Bowden did. Because she is not like other mystics, she is not a true mystic; because she is not like other women, she fails as a model of womanhood; because controversy swirls around her, she is a troublemaker, an egotist, a madwoman. Indeed, "most controversial" is the only issue about which critics agree.

Reflecting the divided and dismembered presentation of the *Book*, subsequent attempts to arrive at meaning, to interpret the contents of this *Book* are thus, too, disjointed. In essence, the unexamined assumptions behind years of critical response to Kempe's *Book* seem to have been that the *Book* cannot be read as a whole; as a whole it fails to become part of the canon; if it had, it would have endured, insists the logic. Further, the reasoning persists, since the paucity of manuscript evidence indicates a failure to be popularized in her own day, it was not taken seriously and, indeed, should be judged inferior and insignificant. This circular, self-serving argument both closes off any serious consideration of the *Book* and casts any new analysis into the guise of defensive reading (Kolodny 150).

The first critical reviews of the *Book* in the 1930's were by and large reactive and subjective. Except for Burns's essay in 1938 on Margery Kempe's spirituality of tears, there is little that is grounded on solid theological, spiritual, or cultural foundation. Evelyn Underhill asserted that there was "very little in Margery Kempe's book which can properly be described as mystical"; Dean Inge said she was "certainly queer, even in a queer age" (both cited in Burns 238–39); Graham Greene rejected the book as having religious significance but valued it as literature, as did John Squire. Thomas Coleman begs the question: "she is surely to be variously labelled as eccentric, neurotic and psychopathic; but none of these terms explains her" ("Margery Kempe" 499). Sigrid Undset deemed her a pronounced psychopath. And Herbert Thurston finds the subject a victim of "terrible hysteria and *exaltée* piety" and concludes that she is "no more than a neurotic and self-deluded visionary who had nothing about her of the spirit of God." He also asserts her queerness and "pronounced hysteria." The limited positive comments are reduced to such faint praise as that of Justin McCann who applauds her grasp of the Christian life while nonetheless calling her "eccentric and extravagant" (cited in Burns 241).

If the first generation of reviewers were by and large reactive and subjective in their assessments of Margery Kempe, the second generation of scholars is no less condemning in their conclusions even as they attempt to reassess her value. Writing roughly in the 1960's and 1970's, they are best represented by the expert in spirituality, Dom David Knowles. Knowles reaffirms the kind of assumptions behind the editorial decision to reduce or dislocate the spiritual revelations in the Butler-Bowden translations by asserting that "the marvels and visions and locutions, though never repellant and rarely silly, are the least striking part of her book; they give something of the same impression as do a series of banal conversations in an otherwise well written novel of adventure" (*English Mystical Tradition* 147). He also concludes that there clearly existed a "large hysterical element in Margery's personality" (146) and repeats that though "sincere and devout" she remains a "very hysterical woman" (147). The *Book*, finally, contains "little . . . of deep spiritual wisdom, and nothing of true mystical experience" (148). Only "improperly and accidentally" can she be classed among the other English mystics (149). It is the emotional behavior of such women as Margery Kempe that "contaminated" the "pure spirituality" of the Middle Ages (cited in Atkinson 204–05).

John Hirsh also damns Kempe by elevating the role of the second scribe. "Because of him, the reader is not overwhelmed by detail, and is shown the growth of a temperamentally static human being" ("Author and Scribe" 149). Hirsh concludes, ". . . the second scribe, no less than Margery Kempe, should be regarded as the author of the *Book of Margery Kempe*" (150).

Despite such patronizing appraisals, there were also positive responses to Kempe in this period as well. Colledge, Cholmeley, Thornton, Walkin, and O'Connell "recognized Margery's virtues, though without any agreement as to what they are" (Fries 228). Finally, however, these writers fail to come to an appreciation of Kempe's unique gifts or contributions to spirituality. Outside the parameters of acceptable behavior as a woman and as a mystic, Margery Kempe is seen as flawed and misguided.

It was not until the 1980's that a major shift occurred. As Paul Szarmach states:

> As in so many other disciplines during the last two decades
> the study of women in Medieval Studies and in Religious
> Studies has amplified those subjects by demonstrating
> relationships, influences, and achievements that were
> hitherto unknown or unappreciated—sometimes because of
> malign neglect. (Fries 10)

Thus the work of Goodman, Dickman, Weissman, Atkinson, Mueller, even when remaining ambivalent or hostile to Kempe, attempts to take Kempe seriously, to read her within a context of the complexity of her world, of the church in which she worships, of the cultural assumptions against which she is marked and measured. Goodman, though seeing the *Book* shaped by the clerical writer, and Kempe's spirituality tinctured by the *Revelations* of St. Bridget and the affective spirituality of her day, nevertheless reads her book as a representation of the "division of opinion between the conservative-minded burgesses and people of Lynn, encouraged by likeminded clerics, and a group of clerical radicals drawn together from various religious disciplines" (357). Dickman, too, contextualizes Kempe's spirituality within an English devotional ethos of popular religion. Her approach to spirituality is thus "practical, individualized, experimental, and worldly" ("English Devotional Tradition" 172). Atkinson's book *Mystic and Pilgrim* provides a strong reading of Kempe within devotional, secular, ecclesiastical, and textual contexts. Her book remains a fundamental starting place for reading Kempe and her *Book*.

It is solidly within this context of "relationships, influences, and achievements" that this volume continues. A diversity of issues continues to be raised here: spiritual, cultural, historical, textual. The themes of voice, authority, selfhood sound again and again. Feminist insights figure prominently. Old comparisons persist—Bridget of Sweden, Julian of Norwich, the Wife of Bath—while new ones emerge. The essayists in this book engage Kempe and her *Book* and appropriate new meaning from it, meaning that inevitably accords with the new sets of "critical assumptions and predispositions (conscious or not)" (Kolodny 153). Arranged loosely by three thematic sections, these sections are not meant to be divisive. Indeed, much that is presented in one section slips over into other sections as well.

The first section, "The Woman," includes four essays which consider Kempe as person, as seeker. Her inner, spiritual world is examined. In his essay, "Margery Kempe and Her Calling," William

Provost begins by contrasting our ability to know Margery Kempe, Julian of Norwich, and Alison of Bath. For the latter two, he argues, our understanding of them as whole personalities is confidently achieved. Not so for Margery Kempe. In order to come to some sense of clarity about Kempe, Provost turns to the medieval notion of vocation which is common to the three. The medieval, he reminds us, has an "exquisite perception" of being called individually and specifically. For Alison, "wif" encompasses the range and depth of her vocation; Julian is anchoress with pure and simple certainty. But Margery Kempe struggles with the vocation of wife while being drawn into heavenly things, a new, second vocation "not essentially in conflict with her calling as wife, but . . . hardly the usual, ordinary way of following out that calling." Hence the conflicts that ensue devolve around her acting or not acting as a wife. Finally, however, she is a complete person in her version of the mix of double vocation.

It is in the homeliness of her vocation that Elizabeth Armstrong focuses our attention in "'Understanding by Feeling' in Margery Kempe's *Book*." Unlike her contemporaries, Kempe did not reveal her sense of her calling in traditional representations of religious validity. She neither joins nor founds a religious order; she attracts no group of disciples, does not gather around herself manifestations of holiness. Instead, she is a plain, everyday witness to Christ. She reports experiences that arise "out of the smallest domestic details of life": the loss of a ring, the grasping in a vision of Christ's toes, the return to her senses and taking up her keys, but only to her own pantry. She is not transported into the realm of heaven, but heaven meets her in the earthly. Intensely exceeding the goals of such manuals of lay instruction as the *Meditations of the Life of Christ*, Kempe interiorizes them and recreates them as witness in the streets and churches. Finally, Armstrong looks at the several later expressions of this deeply personal sense of spirituality, among them a hymn of John Wesley and the prayers and conversations of the Pentecostal Holiness Congregation in southern Indiana.

Undoubtedly, the most troublesome and characteristic element in Kempe's spirituality is her tears. In "Margery Kempe's Tears and the Power over Language," Dhira B. Mahoney reexamines the significance of Kempe's tears as they define her and her role in society. While not enclosed in an anchor-hold, Kempe's tears function as an instrument of separation. "They are signs of the visionary experiences that she alone is privileged to witness, and that are denied to her ordinary contemporaries." This gift of tears mirrors the grace that she is unable to express in words; her sobs substitute for language and are, at the same time, language themselves. Her tears and sobs replace patriarchal language which will authenticate her experience. Thus are they a sign of her power, her link with the Other. When, at the end of her *Book*, she finally does speak, not only in dictation, but also in the composition of a prayer, she appropriates patriarchal language, the sentences rhetorically and syntactically formed.

Feminist theology and psychology inform my study, "The Journey into Selfhood: Margery Kempe and Feminine Spirituality." Feminine spirituality is characterized by the non-linear experiences of nothingness, awakening, and naming whereby a woman comes into unity with her own being, her world, and her God. As a paradigm for reading Kempe, this pattern elucidates her struggle as a woman, wife, and mother while at the same time includes the virginal sanctity traditionally demanded. Rather than sanctioning a dualistic either/or ideology, Kempe embraces all of the apparently contradictory elements of her call and in so doing moves into wholeness and female selfhood.

In the second section of essays, "Her Work," we move from the personality at the heart of the book to the *Book* itself. Timea K. Szell examines the tensions between Kempe's self-validation and the public's mistrust of her. "From Woe to Weal and Weal to Woe: Notes on the Structure of *The Book of Margery Kempe*" finds that Kempe interiorizes the contradictory impulses of her world. The narrative and structural tensions of the text reflect these impulses. Thus the narrative itself, achronological as it is, repeats a pattern of incidents of "partial or near loss and defeat or disempowerment" followed by restoration or recovery. This narrative structure replicates Kempe's own psychological experience and thereby, according to Freud, assuages her resulting anxiety.

Much of the controversy surrounding Kempe in her own day centered around the large questions of her orthodoxy. Her several trials and examinations indeed must be read within the context of heresy and blasphemy which the church authorities were anxious to stem. The subsequent preoccupation of Kempe's textual critics has been no less concerned with Kempe's heterodoxy. Thus David Lawton's article, "Voice, Authority, and Blasphemy in *The Book of Margery Kempe*," challenges the notion of Kempe as blasphemer. Lawton notes that the argument against Kempe is based on a misreading of her *Book* using tools more suited to literary texts. Contrasts with Chaucer and Langland provide evidence that Kempe's apparent blasphemy was not of the same order as that of Chaucer's Pardoner or of Langland's discussion on the Trinity.

Drawing on the theoretical principles of Luce Irigaray, Eluned Bremner examines the "blindspots" in Kempe's patriarchally inscribed text in "Margery Kempe and the Critics: Disempowerment and Deconstruction." Several twentieth-century critics reproduce the anxieties of the medieval contemporaries of Kempe. Hirsh, Thurston, Chambers, Knowles, and Colledge especially repeat the charge of hysteria. But by rejecting the sexual categories of her contemporary as well as more recent critics, Kempe refuses "to deny her sexuality in order to achieve a sanctioned role in the church." Taken seriously as a whole person, which therefore includes her outbursts, her tears, her public wailing, Kempe opens up the possibilities "for self-referential female speech within the text which the clerics and critics who speak for and classify her seek to close."

Hope Emily Allen's notes to the EETS edition have provided rich references to the texts and saints' lives which make up the textual community of Margery Kempe. In the third section, "Her World," several aspects of the wider context of Kempe's social and textual community are more carefully explored.

The home again comes into the fore in Deborah S. Ellis's essay, but here meant in the wider world of her town. In "Margery Kempe and King's Lynn," Ellis sets Kempe firmly within the context of her home in King's Lynn. Drawing on architectural history and the medieval *Red Register* to reconstruct the society in which Kempe lived, Ellis emphasizes the close interactions of the crowded and public space which Kempe inhabited. The map and key of the householders which she appends enliven the sense of the vibrant relationships that these people experienced.

Drawing upon anthropology, Nanda Hopenwasser explores in detail the resonances of ecstatic religion that Atkinson touched upon briefly. Hopenwasser shows that Margery Kempe, St. Bridget of Sweden, and Marguerite d'Oingt provided the bridge between the earthly and spiritual worlds and thus functioned in their societies in the same way that shamans function throughout the world to this day. Her essay, "Margery Kempe, St. Bridget, and Marguerite d'Oingt: The Visionary

Writer as Shaman," argues that such visionary writers and shamans "replicate sacred events of their cultures"; they "safely engage in the spiritual psychodramas which prepare them to serve as spokespersons for their otherworld communicants." Within this framework the visionary receives the gifts which mediate guidance and healing to others within their societies. Overcoming community resistance and gaining the acceptance of her message are "the final proof of spiritual power."

In "Margery Kempe and the King's Daughter of Hungary" Alexandra Barratt looks more closely at Margery Kempe's text and sees direct correspondences with the *Revelations* of Elizabeth of Hungary. Her close textual readings argue strongly that the parallelisms are more than coincidence and that Kempe must have orally absorbed, interpreted, and rewoven the *Revelations* of Elizabeth of Hungary into her own text. Thus any discussion of Kempe's textual community must include this woman as well.

Julia Bolton Holloway looks at the pilgrimage routes of St. Bridget of Sweden and finds that Margery Kempe followed her as a model; Kempe traveled the same routes, including as well those sites made notable by Bridget's presence. That Kempe would model herself on Bridget follows from the evidence of Brigittine influence in England which also influenced Julian of Norwich. Thus the revelations of the three form a textual community against which a "counterfeit" like the Wife of Bath, herself a pilgrim, might be contrasted.

Janet Wilson's semiotic approach to *The Book of Margery Kempe* in "Margery and Alison: Women on Top" utilizes the discourse of carnival to read Kempe as a marginal woman struggling to create space for women outside patriarchy. "Her eccentric conduct shows affinities with the categories of speech and spectacle" which Bakhtin identifies as carnivalesque. Differing in degree but not in kind from Margery Kempe, Chaucer's Wife of Bath also operates within the upside-down vision of domestic and social hierarchy. Both are figures of excess, "dislocating social boundaries and . . . disrupting society's norms." Over- and under-dressing, female preaching, and the melodramatics of piety, all inform the rejection of anti-feminist stereotypes that both women represent. Wilson concludes with a deconstruction of the stereotype of hysteria.

Each essay assumes that this woman and her *Book* are to be taken seriously. Each adds a piece to our more considered understanding of her and her world. Each urges careful reading and subjective distance from one's own social and religious assumptions. What we gain is a fuller and more completely focused picture of a vibrant, resilient, intelligent, resourceful, insubordinate, mystical, energetic, sexual woman.

In order to keep the repetition of citations to a minimum, all Middle English references are from the EETS edition by page number; translations where indicated by page are from Windeatt. A comprehensive bibliography follows at the end.

The Woman

MARGERY KEMPE AND HER CALLING

William Provost

Margery Kempe is troublesome. In her own time she was the source of much trouble to many of those around her: her fellow citizens of Lynn, her traveling companions, her husband, her son, her daughter-in-law, her amanuensis, and various of the ecclesiastic and civil officials with whom she had contact. And she is troublesome to us, modern readers of her book, as we try to comprehend the life and personality which that text offers us. The idea of the person she was develops for us a little in the manner of a Polaroid print, one for which we are never quite sure if the processing is complete—or maybe it is complete and the picture itself was taken a little out of focus; or maybe the subject in its real state was somehow a little out of focus. We read her book carefully, we respond as openly and honestly as we can, and still a lingering, troubling sense of incompleteness, of rough-edgedness remains. Who is this person about whom we know so much, on whom have such an abundance of factual detail and such an intimate perspective? Why can't we be more confident about how well we understand her, and about how well we like her?

In contrast, two of Margery Kempe's "contemporaries" cause us no such trouble, despite numerous and fascinating similarities between each of them and her: Alison of "biside Bathe" and Julian of Norwich. Concerning these latter two, it seems to me, we are a good bit more confident in our sense of recognizing whole, coherent personalities than we are in the case of the former. The experiment of reading the three texts, from whence the personalities emerge, through the particular comparative filter of vocation has seemed to me to produce some helpful focus for the "fuzzy" personality, Margery Kempe.

Presumably no justification is needed for such a "soft-core intertextual" approach as far as that approach deals with Margery's and

Julian's writings. The two women are so close in so many ways—time, geography, mystical experience, and the confirming fact of actual historical contact and conversation (Ch. 18)—that we naturally link and compare their works. Yet, despite their closeness, the effect of the linking and comparing is a strong sense of what would appear to be two very, even radically, different people. The medieval idea of vocation focuses at least one source for these radical differences, and offers a bit of clarifying perspective on the two characters.

But for Margery and Alison: here some defense of the approach is called for, most immediately because the latter is a fictional character, the creation of a shaping, artistic consciousness, and a male one at that. But in spite of this certainly basic and presumably significant difference, a common reaction of folks who do some reading around in late medieval English texts is (assuming they come, as most do, to Margery's *Book* after Geoffrey Chaucer's *Canterbury Tales*) like the reaction to a *déjà vu* experience. From my first encounter on with Margery's *Book* I have often found myself thinking "Chaucer *must* have read this!" Despite the fact that it is chronologically much more plausible, it did not (and does not) strike me as likely that Margery might have read or heard Chaucer.[1] But, whatever their existential disparity, chronological sequence, or actual source relationship may be, reading one against the other is instructive and so at least practically defensible, and perhaps theoretically so as well. Alison is an example of one of those consciously assembled hierarchies of signs that we used to be able to call a character and not feel we were being terribly silly or naive in doing so. Margery is, strictly textually speaking, a similar assemblage, though her assembler worked from different motives and for different ends. The differences between the two assembling consciousnesses and their relationships to their respective constructs—the Alison construct and the Margery construct—mean only that the constructs are different kinds of creatures; but both are creatures and hence comparable. While doing the comparing, we can focus specifically on some questions about what the two assembling consciousnesses were dealing with in relation to the idea of vocation as they shaped Alison and Margery.

Specifically, I want to begin from two facts: (1) the overwhelmingly and unambiguously positive impression we modern readers have of Julian, despite the depth, complexity, and often dramatically unsettling suggestiveness of her writing; and (2) the overwhelmingly favorable impression we modern readers have of Alison of Bath, despite what D.W. Robertson has taught us about the complex but totally negative valuation of the individual signs that constitute her character (*Preface to Chaucer* 317–31). Then I want to compare these two impressions with the exasperatingly troubled and blurred one we have of Margery, and consider all three under the light of the medieval idea of vocation.

For us moderns the concept of a vocation is not a concept we seem to require much. The term lingers around mainly for those few who consider some form of institutional religious life, but, for most, the matter is one of first (perhaps) determining our aptitudes and possibilities, then deciding how best to go about making our money and gaining whichever kind of power we most hanker after. Certainly the idea of an individual, personal calling from God to a particular way of life has little relevance to the proceedings. So the term with its quaintly old-fashioned suggestion of some Other's having a part, much less the significant part, in the decision and its day-to-day implementation is quite unnecessary. But we do seem to delight in defining our professions with exquisite terminological precision: Associate Professor of Later Romantic Prose/Lacanian. Our medieval ancestors, on the other hand, got along with less terminology—wife, clerk, prioress, ploughman—but had exquisite perceptions that they were indeed being called individually and quite specifically by God to a particular state in life. And despite a good bit of variety in actual profession—cloth maker, shipwright, fuller—the distinct types of vocation were not that many. The relatively straightforward "fit" of one's day-to-day activity with one's vocation was central to what we would call our ancestor's psychological equilibrium. The vocation was of God: hence simple, clear, whole. The process of living was no doubt, then as always, messy enough, but the underlying clarity of the sense of vocation provided a firm center.

However, as the High Middle Ages' economic/social descent toward the Renaissance proceeded, the matter of the specific occupation or profession one took up became more problematic and complicated as the possibilities increased. Under feudalism, the "fit" of vocation and occupation was—or must have at least seemed to be, in England around 1300 say—pretty simple. Under capitalism (even the early version) with its increasing occupational complexity, change, and variety, and with the emphasis and attention variety always attracts, such was not the case. As the fourteenth century drew toward its close, the perception of the slippage must have become more general and troublesome.

Chaucer certainly perceived it. Much of the liveliness we still feel in the *Canterbury Tales* comes from his considering various possibilities in the new mix between vocation and occupation. And that special point of liveliness, the character of Alison "of biside Bathe," is such a particularly powerful and clear character exactly because, unlike the developing tendencies in many of her premodernist contemporaries toward vocational indeterminacy and fuzziness, she is so precisely, vocationally specific. She is Wife: proud of it and, having thought the thing through carefully, fully willing to accept that that is what she is called to be by God, and whoever (especially clerks) might want to argue against it can go take the matter up with Him.

The word "wif," with the range of denotations and associations it has developed by late Middle English, will serve nicely as the referent of the vocation we are concerned with. It still at that time occupies some of the primary semantic range of "adult female, woman" which was its primary meaning in Old English. But it was also moving toward—indeed had even begun to do so in the Old English period—the meaning: "a woman who is a spouse and the mistress of a household." A quick check of the relevant entries in the *Oxford English Dictionary* (the *Middle English Dictionary*'s fascicles covering "W" are, alas, not yet available) makes it clear that this somewhat specialized semantic development was current and even dominant by 1400. This basic linkage of the original meaning and the vocationally oriented secondary one is by itself suggestive of the culturally dominant, perceived linkage: *Woman* is *Wife*, for most intents and purposes. Chaucer's typically playful exploiting of the possibilities of the semantic range is the basis of the lovely ambiguity we sense in, for example, the lines from the Nun's Priest's Tale: "As Chauntecleer among his wyves all/Sat on his perche" (VII, 2883–84) [As Chaunticleer among all his wives/Sat on his perch].[2]

But back to the particular wife we are presently considering: her profession we are told—though it seems quite insignificant—is cloth maker, and her avocation obviously is pilgrim, but her calling is Wife. The purity of her sense of her vocation is emphasized by the many aspects, often paradoxical, surrounding it and her: Wife though she has no husband; Wife though she's had five and reckons on at least three more; Wife from birth (at least that of reason, at about 12) to death and implicitly beyond since she's variously heaven, hell, and purgatory to those who are in orbit around her wifehood; Wife who by virtue of her calling is the staff of life itself: good, strong barley bread; Wife as Scripture itself affirms the calling, from the Song of Solomon to Christ's words to Paul's epistles (if one knows how to read the texts properly, and doesn't get the glosses of those modern troublemakers, the clerks, all mixed in with the original); Wife who embodies all the qualities of woman (Old English "wifmann"—"woman-person") as they are numerated in the misogynist literature of her day, and who shows in the wholeness of her being that all those negatives must add up to good, if one just knows how to add right. The term "Wife" itself and the vocational category and ideal it names take on new resonances and a new clarity as the result of Alison's *tour de force* performance. The character of Alison is a kind of literary optical illusion: a conscious, artistic assemblage of signs that, looked at one way, seems to be an idea, a grotesque exaggeration of the male abstraction Wife; but looked at the other way seems to be a real, vital, engaging human being who has considered her vocation carefully and pronounced it good enough. Like all optical illusions, the apparent ambiguity is the result of exceptionally vivid clarity. For Alison it is the clarity of her vocation.

Julian is of course much different, and the sense of her we derive from reading her text is not at all the result of the careful, artistic manipulation of signs that imply a character, whether contextualized by the idea of vocation or otherwise. But that sense is clear and whole, and in those respects similar to the sense we have finally of Alison. And, again, the concept of vocation can help explain something of that clarity and wholeness.

Julian is an anchoress, and the pure and simple certainty about and confidence in that calling is central to the impression of wholeness of character that comes from a reading of her text. The vocation of wife is much older than that of anchoress, but by the late Middle Ages, to be an anchoress is to follow an accepted, understood, clear, and rather frequent vocation.[3] Julian was perfectly at ease in her vocation, and would have been so, I feel certain, even if the twenty or so hours of dramatic mystical experience had never occurred in her life. That experience was the reason she wrote the two versions of her book and is hence the reason we have a text through which we come to know her. And the experience was certainly (how could such an experience be otherwise!?) an essential, memorable, and defining element of the character we meet in the text. Certainly it was powerful, with many parts of it causing her immediate confusion, pain, uncertainty, and even doubt. But for Julian the experience with all its specialness was finally a part of the whole she so confidently felt herself called to. I even suspect that what drew Margery to speak with Julian—her reputation as a simple, devout, wise, humble, accepting anchoress—would have drawn her even if Julian never had had her own mystical experience. And I think Julian's wise, simple advice to Margery about how one comes to a sense of sureness about one's own unique situation in life would have been the advice given from the quiet, withdrawn, contemplative life she had lived even if that life had not had its dramatic mystical vision. Surely they compared their experiences, since as Margery says, she spoke to Julian about her own "wondirful reuelacyons . . . to wetyn yf þer wer any deceyte in hem, for þe ankres was expert in swech thyngys" (42) [wondrous revelations . . . in order to know if there were any deceiving in them, since the anchoress was knowledgeable about such matters]. But Julian's advice as Margery recounts it (and many readers of both Julian and Margery have noted that Margery's recounting sounds very much like Julian's voice) draws not at all from the powerful, unsettling, dramatic images and ideas of her own revelations, but rather from the wisdom gained through contemplation of a life of clarity and wholeness. Her calling to that particular life seems to have comprehended all that she did and was: female (there is a clear, easy sense of sexuality in the *Revelations*, and not only in the marvelous understanding granted therein of the motherhood of God), mystic, theologian (despite the polite demurrals), celibate, recluse. There is no tension between the calling and the things she has done or the things that have happened to her—even the one greatest thing—day to day, through her long life. The clerks and the other males whose abstractions and definitions of what a particular life is *supposed* to involve have been no trouble for her; if she has had in any way to handle them, as Alison did, she has done so in the comprehending, accepting, loving way she seems to have done everything. Certainly the deep, joyful serenity that is finally the dominating feature of the visions—"but alle shalle be wele, and alle shalle be wele, and alle maner of thynge shalle be wele" (*Book of Showings* 405) [but all shall be well, and all shall be well, and all manner of things shall be well]—is a serenity given to one who can receive it and be at ease with it, one who has heard the call sent to her and whose life proves its validity. This is the essential Julian we come to know.

But Margery: so like Alison in her courage, persistence, struggling against the clerks; so like Julian in her troubling (to us and to her) visions, and the singular relationship with her Lord that the visions gave her; and yet so different from either, both in the muddled living of her life and in the muddled sense we have of her character and of what we think about her. And though it does not really eliminate any of the muddles themselves, considering that character from the perspective of vocation can help organize them in a somewhat more coherent way.

From our first view of her as her *Book* begins, she is struggling with the ordinary, assumed features of her vocation as wife. Married at twenty—what, one wonders, delayed her so long?—and soon pregnant, her great sickness, crisis of conscience, and first vision follow immediately on the birth of her child (6–7). She recovers and reclaims from her husband the sign of her vocation, "þe keys of þe botery" (8) [the keys to the pantry], but proceeds to live a life of vanity, and one in which she searches unsuccessfully for the *modus vivendi*, the day-to-day manner of living that will be the objective reality of her "goodwifery," since she does not yet know, as she says "veryli þe drawt of owyr Lord" (9) [truly the drawing of our Lord]. Brewing and milling fail, and she takes this as a sign of something essentially wrong with her way of living. She does penance, "and gan to entyr þe wey of euyr-lestyng lyfe" (11) [and began to enter the way of ever-lasting life]. Shortly the second supernatural revelation comes to her, the heavenly sweet melody she hears at night lying in bed with her husband, not the "revel and the melodys" of Chaucer's Miller's Alison and Nicholas in bed, but the true heavenly sort. The passage where she describes the event and its aftermath is interesting and instructive.

> Thys melody was so swete þat it þassyd alle þe melodye þat euyr mygth be herd in þis world wyth-owtyn ony comparyson, & caused þis creatur whan sche herd ony myrth or melodye aftyrward for to haue ful plentyuows & habundawnt teerys of hy deuocyon wyth greet sobbyingys & syhyngys aftyr þe blysse of Heuen, not dredyng þe schamys & þe spytys of þe wretchyd world. & euyr aftyr þis drawt sche had in hir mende þe myrth & þe melodye þat was in Heuen, so mech þat sche cowd not wyl restreyn hyr-self fro þe spekyng

þerof. For, wher sche was in ony cumpanye, sche wold sey
oftyn-tyme, "It is ful mery in Hevyn." & þei þat knew hir
gouernawnce be-for-tyme & now herd hir spekyn so mech of
þe blysse of Heuyn seyd unto hir, "Why speke 3e so of þe
myrth þat is in Heuyn; 3e know it not & 3e haue not be þer no
mor than we," & wer wroth wyth hir for sche wold not her no
speke of worldly thyngys as þei dedyn & as sche dede be-forn-
tyme. (11)

[This melody was so sweet that it surpassed all the melodies
that might ever be heard in this world beyond any
comparison, and it caused this creature, when she heard any
mirth or melody afterward, to have very plenteous and
abundant tears of high devotion with great sobbings and
sighings for the bliss of Heaven, not dreading the shames and
the despites of the wretched world. And always after this
drawing, she had in her mind the mirth and the melody that
was in Heaven, so much so that she was not able well to
restrain herself from speaking thereof. For, whenever she was
in any company, she would oftentimes say, "It is very merry
in Heaven." And they that knew of her behavior in earlier
times and now heard her speak so much of the bliss of Heaven
said to her, "Why do you speak so of the mirth that is in
Heaven; you know nothing of it, and you have not been there
any more than we"; and they were angry with her because she
was unwilling to hear any of the speaking of worldly things
such as they did and such as she had done in earlier times.]

In a nutshell (if not quite Julian's hazel nut), the significant elements of
Margery's calling, of her attempts to know and follow it, and of the
problems those attempts caused are all here. Margery's calling is to be
wife. She is continuing to work at that calling, and so far at least, the
implications of the earlier vision during her sickness do not seem to
have had any major effect on her working. She is at some point in the
process of producing the fourteen children she eventually has, and has
been attempting to help her husband materially. She is lying in bed
with him at the time the second mystical experience is given her. This
second experience she recognizes to be God's "drawt," a specific drawing
or pulling (she uses the word a number of times in her *Book*, most
recently before this in reference to her trying to run a mill and the horse
that won't pull for it, but on most or all of the other occasions in
reference to a divine drawing). The "drawt" is unambiguous,

compelling, and highly desirable. It becomes for her, in effect, a new and second vocation; or to put it another way in a rather clerkish-sounding phrase, she becomes vocationally bivalent. As she comes to learn gradually and with many troubles—and then eventually to show others around her—the new vocation is not *essentially* in conflict with her calling as wife, but it is hardly the usual, ordinary way of following out that calling; and it will require a lifetime of adjusting the one to the other. Like most out-of-the-ordinary ways, it creates suspicion, disbelief, and antagonism among many of the in-the-ordinary-ways sort of folk about her. It is probably going too far, but perhaps not a lot too far, to suggest that the continuance of the mystical experiences, over a span of many years in her life, may be a function of the adjustment problem. For Julian, a single sequence of revelations is recorded, contemplated for some twenty years, then recorded again, imagistically enhanced[4] but essentially unchanged. The day-to-day working out of her calling as anchoress was, though undoubtedly enriched, not imminently impinged on by the experience. Margery's was a different fortune.

An important point to emphasize about the differences between Margery's troubled and troubling life and Julian's serene one is that the matter of vocation rather than gender is what most sharply focuses the differences. Both are women and both experience some of the typical constraints of their day. Julian quietly plays down her learning and ability to understand, and assures her readers that she is not trying to preach or teach, since her sex is unsuited to such, as the clerks tell her. But she proceeds to show her great learning and powerful intellect, and to teach profoundly and preach cogently and so far as we can tell, runs into no difficulties in doing so. Her vocational clarity and simplicity are such that her actions are unexceptionable. Margery assiduously and repeatedly tries to avoid the appearance of teaching or preaching or of seeming to be a learned person, and is in constant trouble and even danger of life. The sort of trouble she runs into, though it appears in various guises, can be essentially attributed to her repeated encounters with the attitude summarizable thus: "You are not acting as the wife you are called to be is supposed to act." The trouble begins close to home, with her husband, over the matter of celibacy within marriage. Eventually, on the famous Friday of Midsummer's Eve, she gets him to agree to the matter (23ff.), working out a sort of compromise as married folk so often have to do on lesser matters. But they still must have the arrangement officially sanctioned by the Church, it being so

unwifely a request by ordinary standards. This sanction does not come
about for some time, and then only after Bishop Philip has ascertained
that her husband agrees (33ff.). Even then the bishop is unwilling to
grant her the ring and mantle which she has been told by the Lord to
request of him, because he is unwilling "to professe ӡow in so synguler
a clothyng wyth-owtyn bettyr avysement" (35) [to accept your
profession by such unusual clothing without better consideration].
Taking her request to the Bishop of Lincoln she is again turned down,
ostensibly on a technical matter of jurisdiction, but really, as she says,
"thorw cownsel of hys clerkys, for þei louyd not þis creatur" (35)
[because of the counsel of his clerks, for they did not love this creature].
It is not hard at all to imagine the quiet, learned, controlled voices of
some of those clerks: "But after all, my lord, she is a wife. Why should
God want her to dress as if she were something different?" The question
of clothing, especially her wearing of white, comes up at other times
during her life and travels, with the problem always being that for
God's reasons, which after all are not men's, she is specifically told to
dress so; but people, women and men of all ranks and not just the
clerks, say that that is not done by married women. In the first of her
several interviews with the Archbishop of York, the matter is framed
succinctly.

> At þe last þe seyd Erchebischop cam in-to þe Chapel wyth hys
> clerkys, & scharply he seyde to hir, "Why gost þu in white?
> Art þu a mayden?" Sche, knelyng on hir knes be-for hym,
> seyd, "Nay, ser, I am no mayden; I am a wife." He comawndyd
> hys mene to fettyn a peyr of feterys & seyd sche xulde ben
> feteryd, for sche was a fals heretyke. & þan sche seyd, "I am
> non heretyke, ne ӡe xal non preue me." (124)

> [At last the aforesaid Archbishop came into the Chapel with
> his clerks, and sharply he said to her: "Why do you go about
> in white? Are you a virgin?" She, kneeling on her knees
> before him, said: "No, sir, I am no virgin; I am a wife." He
> commanded his attendants to fetch a pair of fetters and said
> she must be fettered, because she was a false heretic. And then
> she said, "I am not at all a heretic, nor shall you prove me
> one."]

Though one gets the distinct feeling that eventually the busy and
efficient Archbishop develops a somewhat grudging respect for

Margery, here he shows himself quite unable to grasp the vocational complexity of the creature before him, and so leaps to the simplest conclusion that she must be a heretic. Margery, here and elsewhere, may be unsure of many things about herself and how she should follow her calling, but she has no doubt whatsoever about two things: she is a wife, and she is not any sort of heretic.

Later she is accused before the same man of trying to destroy the wifehood of another. The Archbishop's suffragan maintains that she had advised Joan de Beaufort, Lady Westmoreland to leave her husband (133ff. and note on 317). After some recorded clerkly obfuscation, and undoubtedly some more that did not get recorded but ran along the lines of "what will it all come to if we let a wife start telling wives to leave their husbands?" the Archbishop steps in and asks her exactly what she did say to Lady Westmoreland. Margery's answer is a rendering of the central doctrine of her Christian faith, couched in terms broad enough to cut across genders and vocations, referring as it does to a lady (wife) and a clerk (bailiff):

> "I telde hir a good tale of a lady þat was dampmyd for sche wolde not louyn hir enmijs & of a baly þat was savyd for he louyd hys enmys & forȝaf þat þei had trespasyd a-ȝen hym, & ȝet he was heldyn an euyl man." Þe Erchebischop seyd it was a good tale. (134)

> ["I told her a good tale of a lady who was damned because she was unwilling to love her enemies and of a bailiff who was saved because he loved his enemies and forgave the harms they had done against him; and yet he was considered to be an evil man." The Archbishop said it was a good tale.]

Even those problems she encounters which seem to stem simply from antagonism toward her and her actions because of her being a woman rather than because of her calling as wife are perhaps not quite so simple when they are considered a little more carefully. Richard of Caister, Vicar of St. Stephen's in Norwich, says to her with a tone of condescending mockery in his voice, "Benedicite. What cowd a woman ocupyn an owyr er tweyn owyrs in þe lofe of owyr Lord?" (38) [Bless us. What could a woman know that might take up an hour or two hours in the praising of our Lord?] Now what we know of this Richard seems to suggest that he was a good, honest, pious, cleric (see Hope Emily Allen's note, 276). Surely he must have known of Julian, and given a chance to hear her speak an hour or two of our Lord it is impossible to imagine him saying this sort of thing. It must have been his deep uneasiness as to what Margery was that troubled him and drew forth these words. Margery takes them in stride however, and in one of the many remarkable passages of her *Book*, pours out to him—and an hour or two would have passed easily in her doing so—a long, rather jumbled, emotional, and fervent statement of her condition, speaking of her whole life, her temptations and problems, her visions, her attempts to find corollaries and confirmation for the visions in the famous mystics of her day, her fears, everything. And the vicar is totally convinced. He believes her, supports her to the full extent of his power against those opposed to her, once speaking with a bishop on her behalf, and becomes her confessor, personally giving her Communion whenever she is in Norwich after this. He may not have put it quite this way to himself, but surely what has happened is that he has come to recognize the validity of her complex calling, and that was all it took for his basic compassion to assert itself.

For each of these three medieval women, Alison, Julian, and Margery, her own sense of person is primarily and essentially a function of her vocation, and the sense of person which we, modern readers of their texts receive, should derive from our understanding that calling and seeing the individual in its light. With Alison, the person is a conscious extension and exaggeration of the vocation wife. Julian is one of those rare humans for whom the sense of being and reason for being are so fully subsumed one into the other, that the wholeness and clarity of the person is completely evident, though—to her certainly and somewhat to us as well—the individualizing particularities of that person are quite unimportant. Margery is confusing for reasons similar to the ones that cause us so often to find our own contemporaries confusing. The "fit" of who and what she was, was not an easy, simple, clear one, and she struggled with it. Not that she, unlike most of us today, had any doubt about the primary essentialness of the "what" in the who/what mix; but rather that her particular version of that mix was so non-typical, non-standardized for her day, that it caused her to struggle constantly with others and with herself over it. We are not used to observing such struggles in our medieval ancestors, and the result is a certain uneasiness on our part as we see the obvious and somewhat unsettling evidence of them on her part. We at least subliminally recognize the struggles, but the idea of Margery Kempe involved in a lifelong attempt to do something as characteristically "modern" as striving to establish her personhood is an idea that we come to grips with slowly and with some trouble. At the end, though, a sense of completion comes to her and to us. Back at Lynn, her confessor fusses at her, sounding rather husband-like, for her unwife-like behavior in undertaking her last long journey without his permission—more, we sense, out of familiar habit and also because he has been worried about her than because he is seriously angry. Margery closes with the faintly ambiguous and maybe a little resigned-sounding comment which, nonetheless suggests balance, acceptance, and wholeness: "but owr Lord halpe hir so that sche had as good loue of hym & of oþer frendys aftyr as sche had beforn, worschepyd be God. Amen" (247) [But our Lord helped her so that she had just as good love from him and from other friends afterward as she had had before: praise be to God. Amen].

University of Georgia, Athens

NOTES

1. I have never been at ease with the common assumption that Margery Kempe was illiterate. She certainly would not have undertaken the huge task of writing her *Book* out herself, and so her references to having someone write for her can be seen as specifically referring to that task alone, or in some instances, perhaps, to the writing out of longish letters. And there is no doubt that many of her allusions to Scripture or to writings of her contemporaries could have come from preaching she had heard. But still, I think such an energetic, strong-minded, curious, and intelligent woman of her age would very likely have been able to read and probably to write as well, and I think that Margery Kempe indeed could.

2. All translations from Middle English in this essay are mine.

3. See, for example, the introduction to the Modern English translation of Julian's work, *Revelations of Divine Love*, by Clifton Wolters, especially 21–25.

4. The definitive treatment of the kind and degree of development of image patterns between Julian's Shorter and Longer versions of her showings is in Gayle Houston Miller's "Imagery and Design in Julian of Norwich's *Revelations of Divine Love*."

"UNDERSTANDING BY FEELING" IN MARGERY KEMPE'S *BOOK*

Elizabeth Psakis Armstrong

It seems to me that no scholarly trend in the last thirty years has been as fruitful as the diversity of interpretation that is now rescuing texts like Margery Kempe's from the misreadings and dissympathies that have been long visited upon them. The word "hysteric," once the consensus word for Kempe, is rarely used even by those readers still hostile to her, and we understand and can even celebrate the paradox of Valerie Lagorio's marvelous phrase "noisy contemplative" ("Defensorium" 29).[1] We see now how securely Margery Kempe is tied to certain traditions: her gift of tears is a link between her and many women in life and art from Mary and Magdalene on down the ages; she is part of the devotional way inherited and still evolving from that moment when Francis acted out his conversion before his father in Assisi.[2] Texts accessible to Kempe, like the *Meditations on the Life of Christ,* have been proved to be visible in her manner and method of devotion.[3] These studies, which show that Kempe, rather than being aberrant, is solidly rooted in medieval spiritual traditions, are more valuable to us than anything I write here. But they make it now fitting and proper to return her to her idiosyncrasies, to emphasize the ways she is profoundly different from any of the writers she knew, Richard Rolle, Julian of Norwich, Walter Hilton, Saints Bridget of Sweden and Catherine of Siena. I will explain my sense of the revolutionary nature of her work by discussing two issues which still inspire controversy: her fondness for expressing her experience in the most common and domestic terms and the degree (or even the existence) of her triumph over clerical authorities. I want also to imply that we can sort out our responses to Kempe more comfortably and fairly if we can move away from the topics which have most occupied scholars—her potential heresies, her specifically Lollard connections, the arguments about how much of a mystic she is. I am, of course, not alone in seeing a truly revolutionary spirit in Kempe; it will become clearer that I am working along the lines especially of Maureen Fries, Susan Dickman, Elona Lucas, and Hope Phyllis Weissman who also do not minimize, as some scholars do, the kind of opposition Kempe sets up to clerical authority.[4] My final goal, however, is to illuminate the difference she makes in her own age by showing how some of the ideas and themes most powerfully written in *The Book* are flourishing in the still radical, if very widespread, expressiveness of modern Protestantism. To see Kempe from this perspective frees us from the explicit interpretative limits imposed by labels like "para-," "quasi-," or "pseudo-"mysticism.

A word that recurs in many writings about Kempe is "unique." And though most mystics are unique because their experience seems to bring them to a pitch of living that demarcates them from people who live less energetically, Kempe's *Book* is unique also in a simpler way. It is the only surviving complex text of her age's folk religion which shows us how instructional texts, like *Meditations on the Life of Christ*, worked out in one laywoman's devotional practice. Her *Book,* Susan Dickman writes, "represents a distinctive step, individual and radical . . . in the late medieval search for an effective, personal faith" ("Margery Kempe and the English Devotional Tradition" 160). Margery Kempe's *Book* is first-hand witness to that amazing popular rise of devotion in the fourteenth and fifteenth centuries, and its greatest degree of uniqueness as an English text is not that it was written by a middle-class wife and mother or that it is autobiographical (though those facts are astounding), but that it is the only one not written by one of the traditional kinds of teachers—clerics like Walter Hilton or Nicholas Love or recluses like Richard Rolle or Julian of Norwich. *The Book* is written without a shred of theological scholarship behind or in it, and is independent of any devotional institution or organization.

However, Kempe was not textless, as we now know. She knew about St. Bridget of Sweden, visiting her house in Rome, hearing how she was considered by some an oddity—she laughed too much—and, though she does not say in so many words, she must have loved Bridget for being as married a woman as she herself was. She undoubtedly knew Richard Rolle and like Rolle, Bridget, and St. Catherine of Siena she celebrated the manhood of Christ; she mentions Hilton. And it seems very likely that simply their existence encouraged her own devotions. But if these touches of influence are obvious, just as obvious are the differences and the absence of significant textual borrowings. Clarissa Atkinson's comment that Bridget's life was more important to Kempe than Bridget's writing seems generally true (175). The mere presence of biographical or devotional similarities does not seem to carry over in any dynamic way to a similarity in the tone, style, or perspective in the texts. Hilton, for instance, is part of the long and large tradition loosely based on monastic rituals of confession and expiation. These texts describe the road to salvation by explaining the practices and purposes of penances and self-analyses; the temptations of the world and the sinful weakness of the will are always in the foreground of the message. These texts are addressed to a particular person, or a small group of people, and though they make gestures to a larger audience, they keep their focus on the secluded, solitary soul who is confronting his individual sin in private. This is also true of gentler texts like Thomas à Kempis's *The Imitation of Christ*. Kempe's *Book* finds no model in this spiritual handbook tradition. The mode of discourse she chooses, third-person narrative, precludes an overtly pedagogical mode of discourse: like the Wife of Bath, she tells stories, and the stories are not directed to teach some other sinner the road to salvation but to describe her own passage that way. There were many women on the continent during the fourteenth and fifteenth centuries living full and emotionally adventurous spiritual lives.[5] But the only words we have of some of them—Mary of Oignies and Dorothea of Montau, for instance—were written by men in the hagiographic tradition or dictated to men who wrote the text out in Latin. Texts whose first writing was in the vernacular, either via dictation, like Catherine of Siena's or via direct composition, like Bridget of Sweden's, are also very different from the text Kempe writes. *The Book* has hardly anything in common with the rigorous, didactic rhetoric that marks Catherine's and Bridget's addresses to the Church and its erring clergy. In fact, their texts are centered in God's voice whose rhetoric of argument and admonition takes precedence over the dialogue between the writers and God; these writers present themselves almost exclusively as mouthpieces for God's word.

The content of Kempe's story, though reminiscent of hagiographic tradition, has little in common with that genre's familiar topics. Kempe never becomes connected in any way with any religious institution; she joins no monastic order, not even one of the lay divisions as Catherine of Siena, a third-order Dominican, did;[6] nor does she follow St. Bridget by founding a new order; though she tends the sick and the poor, those labors are secondary to her practice of meditation. The people who defend her never coalesce into a group of disciples. No one appears to write her life, as Thomas Camperis, Jacques de Vitry, and Raymond of Capua did for Angela Foligno, Mary of Oignies, and Catherine of Siena. We owe the existence of her *Book* to her own determination to publish, a decision she reaches after rejecting the advice of both Jesus Christ and one of her confessors to write it. The superficialities of holiness—heroic penances and parades of miraculous events—that attend the lives of holy women do not gather around Kempe, though there are some humble manifestations of such power now and then, for example, the snowstorm that her prayers call up to put out a fire (Ch. 67). Her saintly attributes, since they were not signaled in the traditional ways just listed, must have been shadowy to the people around her who found her acts of devotion objectionable. Indeed, Maureen Fries's essay describes the nature of both medieval and modern objections to Kempe's social and religious anomalies, concluding that in her own times and ours, her *Book* has been fit to a Procrustean bed (234).

Over the course of their "dalliance," Christ teaches her how to be the everyday, plain witness he wishes her to be. She shows us thoughts and acts with a candidness that is devoid of the kinds of heroisms bestowed by biographers upon saintly lives—there really are no Francis-like gestures of sublime renunciation; no secret, terrible penances like Mary of Oignies's; no lifelong trials of sickness and starvation like, among many, Catherine of Siena's. The one time Kempe thinks about how martyrs usually die, she prays, if that is to be her fate, for the "soft death" provided by a very sharp and swift ax (30). The memorable images of her suffering and persecution have no other source than her own experience. We see her standing in the Archbishop's court, concealing her trembling hands inside her sleeves (Ch. 52); or abandoned by her tour group in foreign lands (Ch. 27); or trying to catch up with a guide who is both surly and embarrassed by her oddness (II, Ch. 5); or looking for a lost ring under a bed (Ch. 31); or being bitten by "vermin" (II, Ch. 6); or finding that traveling companions have cropped her dress to a ridiculous shortness, a medieval rendition of short-sheeting a bed (Ch. 26). No matter how much other mystics are sincerely conscious of their humility, none of them, as far as I know, report experiences that arise as these do out of the smallest domestic details of life, utterly devoid of dignity. The way of her spirituality seems not to invest the literal with allegory, but to equip the spiritual with the real. We find out, for instance, that the loss of the ring is disturbing to her because she *bought* it to commemorate her spiritual wedding. There are many such rings among female mystics, but they are bestowed by Christ and remain invisible to all but the bride. In another of her visionary experiences, she is able to grasp only Christ's toes, perhaps the most unsophisticated image of humility ever recorded (Ch. 85). As St. Teresa knows, talking about one's humility is chancy because it can so easily go over into pride in the narration of one's exquisite and heroic forbearings, a danger Teresa chooses to meet by humor and by blatant and brief interjections about her own wretchedness. It is the solid literalness of Kempe's experience that keeps her narrative naturally modest.

Roland Maisonneuve, responding to the embarrassment created in readers by these apparent naiveties, has most evocatively solved the problem in one way by describing Kempe as one of God's Fools, a kind of mystic recognized better in the East. His essay carefully outlines the historical theme and its exemplifications, and sets it firmly in the Christian tradition starting with Paul: "Hath not God made foolish the wisdom of this world? For . . . in the wisdom of God the world by wisdom knew not God, it pleased God by the foolishness of preaching to save them that believe" (1 Corinthians 19–21); "We are fools for Christ's sake . . . weak, despised, reviled, persecuted . . . we are made as the filth of the world, and are the offscouring of all things unto this day" (1 Corinthians 4:19–13). The implications of this were worked out over time, leading to the mystics' wish to be "totally transformed into Christ's fools, [performing] very bizarre actions which puzzle or scandalize" (3). The basic idea is simple—to exemplify the distance between the believer and conventional social behavior is to define the difference between earth and heaven, between God's love and the world's. Maisonneuve shows us how Kempe fits into this large pattern, but I think there needs to be some adjustment to consider how the way Kempe plays the role is different from Francis's, the greatest and most well known of God's Christian Fools, in part because she does not have Francis's grand gift for drama. Being forced to walk abroad in a ludicrously short dress is clearly not of the same emotional element (not bizarre enough?) as Francis removing his clothes to stand naked preaching before a stunned crowd and finally moving them from amazement and ridicule to tears of understanding. Reading back from the end to *The Book's* first chapter, we can see that Kempe's idea about the divine and the human is implied in that most memorable story of her childbed illness. Its emotional range from the poignant to the mundane, firmly set in the realm of her ordinary life, makes it an epitome of everything she was to write later. Christ comes to her in her woman's ordinary need, not in one of the traditionally mysterious bouts with illness many saints experience. Christ simply sits on her bed and utters one sentence: "Dowtyr, why hast þow forsakyn me, and I forsoke neuyr þe?" (8) [Daughter, why have you forsaken me and I forsook you never?]. Although he exits in a grander way which recalls portrayals of ascensions, the immediate effect of the visit is domestic. Kempe becomes "stabled in her wits" and immediately takes up the keys to her kingdom—the pantry—and so steps sane again into housewifery. The twenty years of daily communication between Kempe and Christ continue in this mode of familial intimacies, which Christ again and again describes, sometimes in a language faintly contractual:

> For, whan þow gost to chyrch, I go wyth þe; whan þu syttest at þi mete, I sytte wyth þe; whan þow gost to þi bed, I go wyth þe; &, whan þu gost owt of towne, I go wyth þe. Dowtyr, þer was neuyr chyld so buxom to þe fadyr as I wyl be to þe to help þe and kepe þe. . . . Whan þow stodyst to plese me, þan art þu a very dowtyr; whan þu wepyst & mornyst for my peyn & for my Passyon, þan art þow a very modyr to haue compassyon of hyr chyld; whan þow wepyst for oþer mennys synnes and for aduersytes, þan art þow a very syster; and, whan thow sorwyst for þow art so long fro þe blysse of Heuyn, þan art þu a very spowse & a wyfe, for it longyth to þe wyfe to be wyth hir husbond. (31)

> [For when you go to church, I go with you; when you sit at your meal, I sit with you; when you go to your bed, I go with you, and when you go out of town, I go with you. Daughter, there was never a child as obedient to a father as I will be obedient to you. . . . Daughter, when you study to please me, then are you a true daughter, when you weep and mourn for my pain and my Passion, then are you a true mother having compassion on her child; when you weep for other men's sins and for adversities, then you are a true sister; and when you sorrow because you are so long from the bliss of heaven, then are you a true spouse and a wife for it is fitting for the wife to want to be with her husband.]

During the marriage ceremony God not only repeats the traditional promise: "I take thee, Margery, for my wedded wife," but further pledges: "dowtyr, þer was neuyr childe so buxom to þe modyr as I xal be to þe" (87) [daughter, there was never child so obedient to a mother as I shall be to you]. When she hesitates during the ceremony in fear because as she explains, she "could no skill of the dalliance of the Godhead," God takes her "by the hand in her soul" (87).

These are the kind of touches of godliness Margery Kempe prefers, and they all go the other way—not she in heaven's realm, but God in hers:

> Sche was so meche affectyd to þe manhode of Crist þat whan sche sey women in Rome beryn children in her armys, 3yf sche myth wetyn þat þei wer ony men children, sche schuld þan cryin, roryn & wepyn as þei sche had seyn Crist in hys childhode. . . . And, 3yf sche sey a semly man, sche had gret peyn to lokyn on hym. (86)

> [She was so much affected when she saw women in Rome bearing children in their arms, if she found out that they were male children, she would then cry, roar, and weep as though she had seen Christ in his childhood. . . . And if she saw a handsome man, she took great pains to look on him.]

Christ habitually calls her "daughter," as he does Saints Catherine and Bridget, but what he has to say to Kempe does truly suggest the domestic tone of a father speaking to a beloved daughter. In Catherine's *Dialogues*, the word is often simple preface to the continuing, lengthy, homiletic discourses Catherine receives and passes along. But with Kempe, Christ never forgets that he is speaking to a particular daughter, and his speech to her is colloquial and familiar: "A, dowtyr, how oftyn-tymes haue I teld þe þat thy synnes arn for3oue þe & þat we ben onyd to-gedyr wyth-owtyn ende?" (50) [Ah, daughter, how often have I told you that your sins are forgiven you and that we are joined together without end?]. Another time, he chooses an image from the kitchen: "Dowtyr, . . . þu art so buxom to my wille & cleuyst as sore on-to me as þe skyn of stokfysche cleuyth to a mannys handys whan it is sothyn" (91) [Daughter, you are most obedient to my will and you stick to me as persistently as the boiled skin of the stockfish sticks to a man's hands]. Talking to her about the way her uncomfortable life on earth will become a blissful life in heaven, he says,

Tyme xal come whan þu xalt holdyn þe ryth wel plesyd, for it
schal be verifyed in þe þe comown prouerbe þat men seyn, "He
is wel blyssed þat may sytten on hys wel-stool & tellyn of
hys wo-stool." & so xalt þu don, dowtyr, & al þi wepyng & þi
sorwe xal turnyn in-to joy & blysse. (82)

[Time shall come when you shall be right well pleased, for it
shall be verified in the common proverb, "He is well blessed
that may sit on his well-stool and tell of his woe-stool." And
so shall you do, daughter, and all your weeping and your
sorrow shall turn into joy and bliss.]

Christ has, in short, all the time in the world to do nothing more than
reassure her over and over again, to bolster her up when she is
overcome with doubts and fears about her worthiness, to build up her
faith in him. Sometimes these re-conversion experiences are modeled on
events in the Gospel, the time, for instance, when caught in a storm at
sea, she must be convinced that God's power extends from land to sea:
"Why dredist þe? Why art þu so aferd? I am as mythy her in þe see as
on þe londe. Why wilt þu mistrostyn me?" (230) [Why are you so
afraid? I am as mighty here in the sea as on the land. Why will you
mistrust me?].

To ridicule and find wanting this concreteness, this triviality
which Kempe purveys in her text is to reject the text's center in
triviality as emblematic of her spirituality. She takes Franciscan
spirituality a little lower than perhaps even Francis would wish, though
the presence of God in stockfish and stools and bought rings and toes is
only a step away from such small, worldly presences in nobler texts,
such as the herring scales and hazel nut in Julian. Of course, this
incarnational center has had a varying presence through the centuries,
sometimes flourishing and sometimes submerged, but Kempe's
proximity to the Protestant era lends a special aura to her re-creation of
it. Her spirituality suggests a connection to Luther's comment on
medieval paintings of Mary—the old artists were wrong, he thought,
because they depict her so that "'there is found in her nothing [lowly] to
be despised, but only great and lofty things;' what they should have
done was, as she herself had said in the Magnificat, to show 'how the
exceeding riches of God joined in her with her utter poverty'" (qtd.
Pelikan 161).

Many scholars who are by no means scornful of Kempe's text
still have trouble accepting its essential nature. For instance, they are

disappointed in the way the text confronts the authority of the Church, finding it and Kempe not as seriously feminist as they would wish. Sarah Beckwith and Sheila Delany, reading from a feminist/Marxist point of view, each find Kempe backing away from a full discovery of decadence in the patriarchy. David Wallace concludes an excellent essay on the kind of peculiarities I am discussing here—on her "quotidian devotion," her "extraordinary conflations of religious and worldly motifs"—by observing that Kempe, though she "repeatedly confounds clergy's critique of her personal devotional practices," does not really succeed in breaking away from the clerks. Although she "aspired to be self-directing," she "requires a clerk to record her dictation and speaks . . . as a third person 'creature.'" These failures to divert the line of authority to the individual, Wallace says, reveal that "Margery's triumphs over clergy, however exhilarating, do not amount to a triumph over clerical discourse" (185–86).

But where do we see Kempe seeking such a triumph? She always refuses in her confrontation with clerks to discuss the texts they are interested in. When she stands before an open (and we assume Latin) Bible while one of those richly dressed clerks points to Paul's admonition about preaching women, her response is not to discuss Paul's content but to adjust the charge to her own vocabulary: I do not preach, she says, because I do not mount a pulpit and what I say is not preaching because I simply "use communication" (126). Another time when she faces the mockery and hostility of another cleric, she turns away his charges by directing her own charges to him via a little parable about defecating bears and the kind of priest which Chaucer calls "shiten shepherde" in *The Canterbury Tales* (GP 504). I think a case can be made that these encounters do indeed suggest that Kempe is victorious over clerks because she manages to substitute clerical discourse with her own modes of discourse. It is not simply that no clerk can find a heresy in her speech; much more significant is that no clerk succeeds in condemning her engagement with divinity or her way of communicating that engagement publicly.

Several times she is able to expose clerical error in the midst of their attempts to find error in her. In Chapter 13 an old and acclaimed monk, in an obvious attempt to encourage her to do the forbidden thing, to preach, asks her "What kanst þow seyn of God?" (27) [What can you say of God?]. She replies by "rehearsing a story of Scripture." Since she does not record the story itself, we focus on the apparently unprovoked rage the telling elicits from the old monk, whose malevolent response is, "I wold þow wer closyd in an hows of ston þat þer schuld no man speke wyth þe" (27) [I would you were closed in a house of stone so that no man could speak with you]. She coolly reminds the monk that he is supposed to "maintain" not condemn God's servants. At this point a young monk intervenes by sarcastically observing that since she could not naturally have the knowledge of scripture she has just exhibited, she must be possessed either by the Holy Ghost or the Devil. Her response to this is not to explain her visionary education or to defend her right to quote scripture, but to tell a little story about a man who took pleasure in the kind of gratuitous hostilities which the monks have just visited upon her. This man, she says, always met spite and scorn, when they were given freely, with laughter because his practice was to keep himself humble by paying people to chide him. She makes this man's situation precisely like her own, he, the earnest Christian, the scorners, great men of consequence: "On a day he cam a-mong many gret men as now ben her, god saue ȝow alle, and stod a-mong hem as I do now a-mong ȝow, despysyng hym as ȝe do me" (28) [One day he came among many great men like those here now, God save you all, and stood among them, as I do now among you, despising him as you do me]. She tells this story, turns, and begins to walk out of the monastery (having met them on their own ground), and the monks follow her "crying vp-on hir, 'þow xalt be brent, fals lollare'" (28) [crying upon her, "You shall be burned, false Lollard"].

It may be useless to analyze the monks' words since they are clearly speaking out of rage and frustration here. But it may be that, because she meets their challenges with story, not with a direct rebuttal, they find themselves at a loss for an effective reply. There is no short way for them to have at her because a reply would demand that they interpret the story in a way hostile to her, reply, that is, at some length and coolness. They cannot simply challenge the story's theme because that is couched, of course, in a biblical truth known to everyone. Neither in this interview nor any interview with authorities of the Church does she ever breathe a word of Lollard heresy, not a word about the efficacy of a bad priest's celebration of the Eucharist (though she has much to say about bad priests) or about transubstantiation. If she is a Lollard, she is one in the most fundamental way, in her knowledge of scripture and her confidence in her personal knowledge of God. What she does with a hostile audience, as she explains herself, is that she "leyd Scriptur a-geyn hem" (235) [laid Scripture against them].

This kind of triumph over clerical discourse does what mystics always implicitly did and which Protestants fully articulated in their own debates: Margery Kempe is *Gottesgelehrte*, not *Scriftsgelerhte*.[7] She is one of many females taught directly by God rather than by texts, a pedagogy that is both safer and stronger than the Wife of Bath's attempt to formulate a parallel exegesis to the clerical one. St. Teresa of Avila also becomes "Gottesgelerhrte" when Church authorities deprive her of certain texts and Christ promises to fill the gaps: "Don't be sad," he says, "for I shall give you a living book" (26). Even texts as doctrinally orthodox as Heinrich Suso's *Büchlein der Ewigen Weisheit* or Thomas à Kempis's *Imitation of Christ* imply a one-to-one relationship between a teaching Christ and a student human which is largely silent about worldly ecclesiastical agency—the Catholic doctrine that priests represent Christ in their priestly duties is not prominent in such texts, except in the occasional admonitions about attending to the orthodox sacraments that surface among the intimate dialogues between divine teacher and human student. Kempe, too, takes advantage of this tradition. During her continental pilgrimage, when the only sermons she is able to hear are spoken in German, she is struck by "sodeyn sorwe & heuynes . . . for lak of vndersondyng, desyring to be refresched wyth sum crumme of gostly vnderstandyng" [sudden sorrow and heaviness . . . for lack of understanding, desiring to be refreshed with some crumb of ghostly understanding], and asks Christ for help. Christ forthrightly says to her: "I xal preche þe & teche þe my-selfe" (98) [I shall preach thee and teach thee myself]. Even granting her fears and her wish to remain orthodox, the constant reporting of her experience might just as logically indicate her own sense of its newness, how, in the ways I suggested earlier, she is fundamentally different from the holy women she knows in texts. She does, after all, clearly exceed the goals of instruction to lay folk intended by texts like *Meditations on the Life of Christ* which meant only to intensify the moral and ethical precepts of Christianity and to enhance the observance of the sacraments. The most dynamic thing Kempe does to those meditations is to bring them out of private rooms and silence to the church and the street, to re-create them as public witness to God's love. In all her public religious observances, it is her own responses that fill the public space; her tears and shrieks at the Eucharist, her interruptions of sermons from her solitary occupation of an amen corner make every institution of the Church's observation a part of her personal rituals of observation.

Although public acts of great daring were recorded in the Middle Ages, Francis's among them, Kempe's behavior is more like religious displays of a much later date. Mrs. Hester Thrale's witty and dismissive reaction to Christopher Smart's behavior in eighteenth-century London might echo fourteenth-century Norwich's response to Kempe:

> The famous Christopher Smart, who was both a wit and a scholar . . . would never have had a commission of lunacy taken out against him, had he managed [to keep his eccentricities private], for Smart's melancholy showed itself only in a preternatural excitement to prayer which he held it as a duty not to control or repress—taking *au pied de la lettre* our blessed Saviour's injunction to pray without ceasing. So . . . he went on to call his friends from their dinners, or beds, or places of recreation, whenever that impulse towards prayer pressed upon his mind. (qtd. Sherbo 115)

Margery Kempe and Christopher Smart are obviously similar in being *"au pied de la lettre"* and being oblivious to social proprieties. Much of Kempe's demonstrations would not be out of place at the religious meetings of the kind we would call "revivals" that began in the eighteenth century. Charles Wesley's journal describes a scene which would comfortably admit Kempe:

> In the evening we met, a troop of us, at Mr. Sim's. There was one Mrs. Harper there, who had this day . . . received the Spirit . . . but feared to confess it. We sung the hymn to Christ. At the words, "Who for me, for me hath died," she burst out into tears and outcries, "I believe, I believe," and sunk down. . . . We sang and prayed again. I observed one of the maids run out, and following, found her full of tears, and joy, and love. I asked what ailed her. She appeared quite overpowered with his love. (115)

Certain prevalent themes describing concourse with Christ, the intimate care and concern he feels for any kind of human difficulty, are also prominent in Kempe and some Protestant hymns. Many hymns temper the old penitential way, as she does, simply by coupling sins with griefs. Jesus bears both—the serious sins and the griefs that are sometimes incidental to life in the world: "What a friend we have in Jesus," the hymn sings, "All our sins and griefs to bear,/What a privilege to carry/Everything to God in prayer" *(The Methodist Hymnal* #551). The presentation of Christ as friend and confidant borders on emotions that embarrass many readers of Kempe. A modern hymn set in a waltz tempo has become famous for such a borderline portrayal:

> I come to the garden alone
> Where the dew is still on the roses,
> And the voice I hear falling on my ear,
> The son of God discloses.
> And he walks with me and he talks with me
> And he tells me I am his own
> And joy we share as we gather there,
> None other has ever known.
>
> *(Unity Song* #165)

I do not mean to say that such a spirit of intimacy was not abroad earlier than the fourteenth century and earlier than Francis. It is, after all, in its celebratory mood, the spirit of the Psalms where humans talk to God about anything, as Augustine does, with the full conviction that God is listening though he does not answer. But the flavor of Kempe's experience of God, its emotional simplicity, is most like the emotionalism of Charles Wesley's hymns, especially the hymn of which John Wesley apparently could not totally approve:

> (1) Jesus, lover of my soul,
> Let me to thy bosom fly,
> While the nearer waters roll,
> While the tempest still is nigh;
> Hide me, O my Saviour, hide,
> Till the storm of life be past;
> Safe into the haven guide,
> O receive my soul at last.
> (2) Other refuge have I none,
> Hangs my helpless soul on thee;
> Leave, ah, leave me not alone,
> Still support and comfort me.
> All my trust on thee is stayed;
> All my help from thee I bring;

> Cover my defenseless head
> With the shadow of thy wing.
>> (*The Methodist Hymnal* #462)

Like Kempe, and unlike Bernini's Ecstasy of St. Teresa, Wesley sets the amorous implication in love's comfort and safety, rather than in physical ecstasy. John Wesley need not have worried, if that was the source of his hesitancy about this hymn.

That Kempe's spirituality may have some counterpart among modern Catholic worshipers is suggested in a study of her by John Hirsh. The devotional practices he witnesses in certain Catholic charismatics suggest that they may be feeling the same kind of impulse Kempe felt to express informally, extra-liturgically, without benefit of clergy, their own experience of God. Hirsh finds in Kempe and in the Catholic charismatic testimony the same themes: Christ's intimate concern with each human's particular problems, the power and absoluteness of his love. But Kempe's spirituality, though it includes the kind of experience Hirsh reports among Catholic charismatics, goes far beyond them in the emotional intensity of the personal relationship she and Christ share. Hirsh's comparison is attached to a theological and rationalist *apologia* of what he calls "paramystical" devotions, and that perspective makes Kempe (and perhaps the charismatic groups) seem much tamer and much more sophisticated than I think she is.

The recent work of Elaine J. Lawless on the Pentecostal Holiness congregations of southern Indiana gives us a spiritual model much more relevant to Kempe's. Lawless's exposition of the feminist implications of Pentecostal worship makes a most suggestive analogue to Kempe:

> The Pentecostal religious service is male dominated and male manipulated. Yet women can and do participate freely and openly in carefully regulated segments of the religious services. Their active participation and the exhibition of their spiritual powers are desired because there is a generally held belief that women are naturally able to conjure spirits and commune with God. All Pentecostals, both male and female, long for the moment in the service when all propriety can be abandoned and persons are set free to express themselves in an uninhibited manner. This moment of freedom is largely created by the women and is, to be sure, coveted by the women. (111)

What the women do in Johnson's Creek Church is very like what Margery does or wishes to do—they testify to the great emotional bonds between them and God. They do this by taking advantage of their Church's ritual allowance for such testimony to be spoken from the congregation at a time always placed just before the preacher's sermon. The simplest form of the testimony is that a member of the congregation rises and says what she feels about Christ, what God has done for her:

> I know he's never going to try me
> Or try to pull me down.
> He's going to work with me
> And he's going to put his arms close around me.
> But I know tonight
> That my blessings tonight
> Are going to pull me through next week
> I'm going to be safe. (122)

Sometimes, inspired by the communal devotions, the witness will speak in tongues, fall on the floor, and cry copious amounts of tears and cause other women in the congregation to do so as well. Sometimes this part of the service will go on for hours to the resentment of the male preacher. The similarities between the Johnson Creek women and Kempe might be put this way: deprived like them of a full and public expression of faith, Kempe can be seen trying to gain some authority of her own when she shouts her own rendition of God's word. Like them, her performance is both fervid and circumscribed:

> For a brief time in Pentecostal testimony services, the power of the speaking women threatens male authority. . . . The women create a situation in which they exhibit their own natural powers. . . . From her pew [if not from the pulpit], the Pentecostal woman can stand and speak; from that position she and the members of her sister group are able to transform the service through their verbal powers. They gain control through verbal art—shortlived control, to be sure, but a masterful illustration of the power of words. (108–09)

Another Johnson Creek woman takes a delight in shame and being "peculiar" similar to Kempe's acceptance of these modes of witness:

> I think shouting is great and people on the outside don't
> understand that because they haven't already received the real
> joy, and they don't have their eyes set on the eternity that we
> have a hope for. . . . People don't think a thing about going
> to a ball game and screaming and yelling. They think that's
> all right. . . . We're nuts for Jesus and we are happy about it.
> You know when I sing and when I testify, everybody looks at
> me. And they think I'm kind of peculiar, but you know
> something? I'm not ashamed of Jesus, because this is the Lord
> that I sing, that I testify for, that I stomp my feet for. (67)

A general description of Pentecostal faith by Troy D. Abell might serve
to sum up its striking relevance to Kempe's experience:

> I am writing about a people and their God; about the guilt and
> frustration and unworthiness caused by sin . . . about the joy
> and ecstasy of praising God with all of one's mind and desire
> and, yes, one's body; about talking to God in an unknown
> language and interpreting the message hidden in the
> otherwise unintelligible sounds [of glossolalia]; about
> dancing in the spirit and running the aisles until one falls to
> the floor—exhausted and unconscious. (5)

These are, of course, only analogues, but they can inform our
response to Margery Kempe because they suggest that the devotional
rituals of Pentecostal women are one kind of completion to the
revolution which began in Kempe's time. Like these women in
southern Indiana, Margery Kempe both succeeded and failed in securing
a space for herself in the institutional practices of worship, and that
seems more complex than the Marxist/feminist sense of a simple
political failure. One Holiness woman describes her experience of
taking her rightful place in the worship of God this way:

> Sometimes I'm called to a church and I run into a hard spirit at
> first. I say, "Relax, I don't call myself a preacher. Let the men
> do that; it's all right. But you have got to give me the right to
> be a handmaiden of the Lord and he has poured out his spirit
> unto me and he has called me into his work and I'm here." (82)

"*I'm here*," a phrase of basic feminism! Most of the time, Kempe also
makes her presence and existence felt as a fact, but she also receives a
kind of apology from St. Paul himself, whose texts were the most well

known and authoritative bar to women as preachers. It is Christ, not the "creature," who mentions:

> I sent onys Seynt Powyl vn-to þe for to strengthyn þe & comfortyn þe þat þu schuldist boldly spekyn in my name fro þat day forward. And Seynt Powle seyd vn-to þe þat þu haddyst suffyrd mech tribulacyon for cawse of hys wrytyng, & he behyte þe þat þu xuldist han as meche grace þer-a-ȝens for hys lofe as euyr þu haddist schame er reprefe for hys lofe. (160)

> [I once sent Saint Paul to you to strengthen and comfort you that you should speak boldly in my name from that day forward. And Saint Paul said to you that you had suffered much tribulation because of his writing, and he promised that you should have as much grace as ever you had shame or reproof for his love.]

Like the Pentecostal women, medieval women always used what they were allowed to use, the power of their visionary spirituality, though they secured that validation with apparently more difficulty than the women of Johnson's Creek Church. We can also recall St. Teresa's agonizing and protracted effort to convince her confessors of the divine source for her experience. It is interesting how visionary women have a way of overwhelming or at least interfering with sermons and sacraments—St. Teresa's nuns had to take hold of her body to keep it from levitating during the Eucharist; Mary of Oignies's tears inundate the celebration of the Eucharist, as Kempe's sometimes do. That the means of that access is presented as involuntary does not invalidate the possibility that these women intend to secure a greater participation than tradition allows.

I'm not sure that Margery Kempe was as conscious as St. Teresa of making a difference, but sometimes a phrase will imply a full consciousness of the nature of her struggle with authority. This sentence, for instance, about those "great clerks" and the "creature's" tears: "Sum gret clerkys seyden owyr Lady cryed neuyr so ne no seynt in Heuyn, but þei knewyn ful lytle what sche [Mary *and* Margery?] felt, ne þei wolde not beleuyn but þat sche myth an absteynd hir fro crying yf sche had wold" (69) [Some great clerks said our Lady never cried so, nor did any saint in Heaven, but they knew very little what she felt, nor would they believe that even if she wanted to, she might not have abstained from crying].

Margery Kempe, like Teresa, felt the gender rift between passionate woman and rationalist man. At the end of *The Book* where she is adding things she forgot in the main narrative, she gives us the interpretative key to her text: "Also, whil þe forseyd creatur was ocupijd a-bowte þe writyng of þis tretys, sche had many holy teerys & wepingys . . . and also he þat was hir writer cowde not sumtyme kepyn hym-self fro wepyng" (219) [Also, while the foresaid creature was occupied about the writing of this treatise, she had many holy tears and weepings . . . and also he that was her writer could not sometimes keep himself from weeping]. Though many women wept tears of devotion, only Margery Kempe has left such a poignant and instructive link between feeling and writing, between the writer's and the reader's emotions.

University of Cincinnati

NOTES

1. For other work on Kempe and the general tradition of mysticism see Clarissa Atkinson, *Mystic and Pilgrim*; Janel M. Mueller, "Autobiography of a New 'Creatur'"; Karma Lochrie, "*The Book of Margery Kempe*: The Marginal Woman's Quest for Literary Authority"; Sue Ellen Holbrook, "Order and Coherence in The Book of Margery Kempe."

2. Sandra McEntire, "Walter Hilton and Margery Kempe: Tears and Compunction," and "The Doctrine of Compunction from Bede to Margery Kempe"; Susan Eberly, "Margery Kempe, St. Mary Magdalene, and Patterns of Contemplation."

3. Denise L. Despres, "The Meditative Art of Scriptural Interpolation in *The Book of Margery Kempe*" and *Ghostly Sights: Visual Meditation in Late Medieval Literature*.

4. Elona K. Lucas, "The Enigmatic, Threatening Margery Kempe"; Maureen Fries, "Margery Kempe"; Susan Dickman, "Margery Kempe and the Continental Tradition of the Pious Woman." Dickman's essay makes the strongest statement: "In her singularity, isolation, and individuality, Margery Kempe represents a medieval, English middle-class version of one of the most important feminist movements in history" (166). Hope Phyllis Weissman, in "Margery Kempe in Jerusalem: *Hysteria compassio* in the Late Middle Ages," explains how, though Kempe did not "escape the

system," she succeeded in "affronting it," by her "self-created oxymoron of a married virgin" (217).

5. For bibliographic information and overview of continental women mystics, see Valerie Lagorio, "The Medieval Continental Women Mystics: An Introduction."

6. Susan Dickman in her 1984 essay believes that the lack of evidence about tertiaries in England indicates that the institution simply did not exist there, at least for women.

7. Scholarship on this topic is extensive. For a start on discussion relevant to Kempe, see Peter C. Erb, "Pietist Spirituality: Some Aspects of Present Research," and Leonard Trinterud, "Origins of Puritanism."

MARGERY KEMPE'S TEARS AND THE POWER OVER LANGUAGE

Dhira B. Mahoney

When Margery Kempe, fifteenth-century gentlewoman of Bishop's Lynn, Norfolk, was brought before the Archbishop of York to be examined for heresy, her behavior moved him to complain, "Why wepist þu so, woman?" (125) [Why do you weep so, woman? (163)]. *The Book of Margery Kempe* recounts many such dramatic incidents when its author would exasperate her contemporaries by her uncontrollable weeping and loud cries, sometimes accompanied by bodily convulsions. Her fellow townspeople sought to ban her from attendance at public sermons and even from communion, and her fellow pilgrims refused to have her join them at meals. She was accused of fakery, of self-dramatization, sometimes of being an epileptic (Ch. 44). Why indeed, did she weep so? This essay will attempt to answer the Archbishop's question, by exploring the various significances of Kempe's tears, in the light of her attempt to define herself and her role in society, as woman and creature set apart yet remaining in the world.

As Sarah Beckwith has observed, "Margery was a religious woman who refused the space traditionally allotted to religious women—the sanctuary (or imprisonment) provided by the anchoress's cell or the nunnery" (37). The nunnery is certainly the most concrete example of that imprisonment, physically enforcing the separation of its inhabitants from society with its walls, its vows and veils (Bynum, *Holy Feast* 280); but the anchor-hold was equally set off from society, being essentially an enclosed place; the anchorite was often literally walled up, with only a window to the outside world, or a "squint" into the church so that she could see the altar and hear the office. Surviving rites of enclosure reveal that the idea of the ceremony was to imply a premature burial; the cell was "visualized as a tomb or grave in which the inmate was buried alive" (Anson 170). However, as recent studies, particularly Ann Warren's, have brought out, that very enclosure and removal from the world was simultaneously a source of great power. Precisely because of their marginal nature, their austerity and holiness, their freedom from worldliness, anchorites acquired what C.J. Holdsworth describes as "'a permanent condition of sacred outsiderhood,' a status felt to be full of power which could flow out into the world" (204).[1] The holy man or woman was an intimate of God, in touch with the Other; he or she could function like a lens to concentrate and refract the spirit shining through.[2] As different kinds of historical record attest, the power of a recluse's prayers was widely recognized: wills often contained bequests to anchoresses, accompanied by specific requests for their prayers (Warren 253, 259). Anchorites were also known for their powers of prophecy, and were regularly sought out for their advice by nobles and royalty. Richard II and Henry V both consulted recluses at Westminster Abbey (Knowles, *Religious Orders* 2.219–222, 367–368), while the double crowning of young king Henry VI in England and France was at least partly prompted by the prophetic dreams of a famous early-fifteenth-century recluse in York, Dame Emma Rawghtone (*Pageant* 93–94). Thus, although cut off from human intercourse, on the margins of society, recluses could acquire surprising power and influence within it. As Warren has observed, "the recluse was both a commonplace daily presence and a likely heavenly dweller" (279).

Kempe certainly knew many recluses, both famous and less well known ones. She visited Dame Julian of Norwich, and many of her confessors were male anchorites. Yet, for whatever reason, when her call to religion came, she did not choose this avenue of religious life; she chose to live in the world while not of it. She sought to find a role in society which could fulfill a function similar to that of the anchorite without the actual enclosure, a role which would exercise a similar power. She needed, therefore, to find physical markers that would perform the same function as enclosure, that would announce her separation from society, her holiness, and her link with God. One of such markers is the desire for celibacy. As Peter Brown suggested in his plenary lecture at Kalamazoo in 1986, sex and marriage are social obligations, and a vow of celibacy is the first step in the withdrawal of the body from society. Kempe takes that first step in her denial of sex to her husband and refusal to share food with him on Fridays; later, she searches for a more public sign in the wearing of white clothes. Yet she never wishes to give up her married status in legal terms: she is still John Kempe's wife of Lynn (Chs. 46, 51). What she does is to maintain her role of the separated soul in defiance of traditional assumptions about what is appropriate for a married woman, in face of the men who tell her, "Damsel, forsake þis lyfe þat þu hast, & go spynne & carde as oþer women don, & suffyr not so meche schame and so meche wo" (129) [Woman, give up this life that you lead, and go and spin, and card wool, as other women do, and do not suffer so much shame and so much unhappiness (168)].

Continence and white clothes are effective markers, non-verbal signs, of separation, but a more striking instrument of separation for Kempe, because more dramatic and more disruptive to those around her, is her tears. They also become a source of power, an alternative to the kind of power an anchoress might achieve by her holiness and seclusion. Kempe's first recording of her tears comes in Chapter 3, and they are presented explicitly as the first step of her entry on "þe wey of euyr-lestyng lyfe" (11) [the way of everlasting life (45)]. They come in response to an auditory experience, of heavenly music "so swet & delectable, hir þowt, as sche had ben in Paradyse" (11) [so sweet and delectable that she thought she had been in paradise (46)]. As scholars have pointed out (Windeatt 313, n. 8; Atkinson 63) these early fits of simple weeping should be distinguished from Kempe's later manifestations of emotion, the loud involuntary crying, often accompanied by convulsive thrashing or writhing of the body, which appears first on her trip to Jerusalem, at the Mount of Calvary (Ch. 28). As her narrative points out, "þis was þe fyrst cry þat euyr sche cryed in any contemplacyon. And þis maner of crying enduryd many 3erys aftyr þis tyme . . ." (68) [this was the first crying that she ever cried in any contemplation. And this kind of crying lasted for many years after this time . . . (104)].[3] Yet even the simple tears are from the start an instrument of separation. They are signs of the visionary experiences that she alone is privileged to witness, and that are denied to her ordinary contemporaries. Furthermore, though Kempe makes a distinction between her weeping and her "cries" when she first introduces the latter, once she has introduced them, her narrative begins to present both behaviors in the same breath, as a standard doublet: "Þan fel sche down wepyng & crying . . ." (167) [then she fell down weeping and crying (206)]; "þe sayd creatur . . . brast owt wyth a lowde voys & cryid ful lowde & wept ful sor" (166) [the said creature . . . burst out

with a loud voice and cried very loudly, and wept very bitterly (206)].
Tears and cries are inseparable, a single manifestation of her
particularity, a "specyal ȝift þat God hath ȝouen þe" (99) [special gift
that God has given you (136)].

Kempe's tears express her experience of heavenly grace,
experience that is "so hy a-bouen hyr reson & hyr bodyly wyttys . . .
þat sche myth neuyr expressyn it wyth her word lych as sche felt it in
hyr sowle" (3) [so high above her reason and her bodily wits . . . that
she could never express it with her words as she felt it in her soul
(34)].[4] Thus her tears are beyond language; her sobs substitute for the
words she cannot find. But they are also, at the same time, themselves
language. Being illiterate and dependent on male scribes, the only words
that are available to Kempe are patriarchal, the language authenticated
by the male ecclesiastical establishment. Though urged by her
confessors, even by the Bishop of Lincoln (Ch. 15) to have her story
written, she resists for more than twenty years. Even when she is ready
to use the patriarchal language, the process of persuading scribes to
record it correctly is incredibly difficult. In the meantime, her tears and
her cries are her public language, an individual expression of
separateness through bodily action in defiance of the prohibitions of
custom and the ecclesiastical system. Her inarticulate tears for Christ's
sufferings become her voice in a world which, as Elizabeth Petroff
points out, "would deny that voice" (39).

Weeping for Christ's crucifixion allows Kempe to link herself
with a potent tradition, that of the many thirteenth- and fourteenth-
century continental female saints and mystics who also distinguished
themselves by uncontrollable weeping as well as excessive bodily
penances. Women such as Marie of Oignies and Angela of Foligno
provide powerful models on which Kempe, perhaps quite consciously,
patterns her life and behavior. Indeed, Hope Emily Allen suggests that
it was the reputation of the continental female mystics that enabled
Kempe's confessors to support her in her unconventional behavior
(*Book*, Prefatory Note lv); certainly her second scribe records the fact
that his initial reservations about Kempe dissolved when he read about
Marie of Oignies and Elizabeth of Hungary and noted the similarity of
their weeping to Kempe's (Ch. 62). What is particularly significant
about the behavior of these continental female saints is that they
deliberately underwent self-imposed torments to relieve the pain of
souls they had seen languishing in purgatory. As Caroline Bynum has

shown, such women were suffering by substitution; they acted on the assumption that their pain could help to reduce the universal pool of suffering (Bynum, *Holy Feast* 127, 171, 234–35). Elizabeth of Schönau and Christina of Stömmeln would even focus on specific souls suffering in purgatory and set themselves a program of bodily tortures until told in visions that the souls had been set free (McNamara). Kempe does not undergo such dramatic bodily penances, but she deliberately suffers the scorn of her contemporaries as a kind of purgatorial persecution (Ch. 63), and on many occasions mortifies her flesh by putting herself in the service of the most lowly and unpleasant human beings, such as indigent widows, lepers, and finally her incontinent husband (Mueller 166). Her tears also have a power similar to those of her saintly models. Kempe weeps not only for her own sins, but also for those of humanity: "sumtyme for hir owyn synne, sumtyme for þe synne of þe pepyl, sumtyme for þe sowlys in Purgatory, sumtyme for hem þat arn in pouerte er in any dysese, for sche desyred to comfort hem alle" (20) [sometimes for her own sin, sometimes for the sin of the people, sometimes for the souls in purgatory, sometimes for those that are in poverty or in any distress, for she wanted to comfort them all (54)]; (see also Ch. 65). She is told directly by Julian of Norwich, and in visions by St. Jerome and by Christ himself, that her tears are drink to the angels and torment to the Devil: "He is wroth wyth þe, for þu turmentyst hym mor wyth þi wepyng þan doth al þe fyer in helle; þu wynnyst many sowlys fro hym wyth þi wepyng" (51) [He is angry with you, because you torment him more with your weeping than all the fire in hell does; you win many souls from him with your weeping (87)]. Christ tells her that when those who have scorned her pass out of this world he will inform them that he ordained her to weep for their sins (Ch. 64).[5]

Kempe's tears are a sign of her power, her link with the Other. She has, as it were, a direct line to God. Christ speaks to her in her soul, and the divine conversations and communications (her favorite word for them is "dalyawns") result in the uncontrollable upsurge of love that finds relief in tears:

> Þan was hir sowle so delectabely fed wyth þe swet dalyawns of
> owr Lorde & so fulfilled of hys lofe þat as a drunkyn man sche
> turnyd hir fyrst on þe o syde & sithyn on þe oþer wyth gret

wepyng & gret sobbyng, vn-mythy to kepyn hir-selfe in
stabilnes for þe vnqwenchabyl fyer of lofe whech brent ful sor
in hir sowle. (98)

[Then her soul was so delectably fed with the sweet converse
of our Lord, and so fulfilled with his love, that like a drunk
she turned herself first on one side and then on the other, with
great weeping and sobbing, powerless to keep herself steady
because of the unquenchable fire of love which burned very
strongly in her soul.] (135)

Though her tears and cries are embarrassing to her contemporaries, and
even, frequently, to Kempe herself, they are also the source of her well-
being, her very identity. When she is deprived of the ability to shed
tears for a day or even half a day she considers herself "bareyn" [barren]
(199) and in despair. Furthermore, the cessation of tears affects her
ability to pray: "hir thowt it was no sauowr ne swetnesse but whan
sche myth wepyn, for þan sche thowt þat sche cowde preyin" (199) [she
thought there was no savor or sweetness, except when she might weep,
for then she thought that she could pray (240)]; when she cannot weep,
it is as if the current has been switched off. Thus her tears are explicitly
associated with her prayers.[6] Tears lead to prayer; they are two ends of
the same continuum, and frequently spoken of together in one locution.
On one occasion Christ tells Kempe: "Dowtyr, I haue many tymys seyd
to þe þat many thowsand sowlys xal be sauyd thorw þi preyerys, &
sum þat lyn in poynt of deth xal han grace thorw þi meritys & þi
preyerys, for þi terys & þi preyerys arn ful swet & acceptabil vn-to me"
(186) [Daughter, I have many times said to you that many thousand
souls shall be saved through your prayers, and some that lie at the point
of death shall have grace through your merits and your prayers, for your
tears and your prayers are very sweet and acceptable to me (226)].

Thus the association between tears and prayers is constantly
confirmed, an association which points to Kempe's power. And
Kempe's prayers are extremely powerful. When the parish church of St.
Margaret is threatened by fire, Kempe's prayers bring a snowstorm out
of a clear sky. During this process her weeping and crying are tolerated,
even requested, by the congregation which had formerly complained of
them (Ch. 67). It is a genuine miracle, as her confessor tells her,
granted by God in direct response to her praying. Similarly, her prayers
are responsible for curing the woman suffering from postpartum
madness (Ch. 75), and she is asked by many people to be present and to

pray for them at their deathbeds: "for, þow þei louyd not hir wepyng ne hir crying in her lyfte-tyme, þei desiryd þat sche xulde bothyn wepyn & cryin whan þei xulde deyin . . ." (172–73) [for, although they had no love for her weeping or her crying during their lifetimes, they desired that she should both weep and cry when they were dying (213)]. Such references demonstrate that not only to Kempe herself, but to those who call on her help, her tears and prayers are interchangeable, or rather, interlocked; together they combine to express and channel God's spirit to her and through her. Incident after incident demonstrate that she has power, the power to foretell the future, the power to save souls, the power to cure illness and to cause miracles.

Thus, though Kempe's tears are themselves inarticulate, their explicit link with her prayers translates into an equation whereby tears equal prayers which equal power. Paradoxically, even power over language. Kempe's accounts of her many pilgrimages constantly emphasize the difficulties of communication in foreign lands, but as her self-assurance and self-validation grow, she learns to overcome these difficulties. In Rome, her prayers enable her to communicate with her German confessor, who speaks no English (Ch. 33). After thirty days of prayer at her direction, he is able to understand her though he cannot understand the English that other men speak. This facility is tested and demonstrated in a bizarre scene at the dinner to which he has been invited in response to her companions' complaints that she is confessing herself to a foreigner. The German priest sits silent and unhappy at the meal while Kempe and others talk in English, until Kempe, "in party to comfort hym & in party er ellys meche mor to preuyn þe werk of God" (97) [partly to cheer him up and partly, or much more, to prove the work of God (134)], tells a little homily in English; when the priest is asked whether he has understood, he responds in Latin with "þe same wordys þat sche seyd be-forn in Englisch, for he cowde neyþyr speke Englysch ne vndirstondyn Englisch saue only aftyr hir tunge" (97–98) [the same words that she said before in English, for he could neither speak English nor understand English except from her tongue (134–35)]. It is Kempe's special link with God that enables her to overcome the barriers of national language to the amazement of her persecutors. Prayer transcends the barriers of language, but it is *through* language that, in this incident, she able to demonstrate that power.

Similarly, prayer enables her to surmount barriers of communication in the writing of her book, the story of which is told in the Proem, well known but worth repeating. Her first scribe, an Englishman who has lived in Germany, dies before its completion. When she takes the manuscript to the second scribe, he cannot decipher the language or the script of her first amanuensis: "for it was neiþyr good Englysch ne Dewch, ne þe lettyr was not schapyn ne formyd as oþer letters ben" (4) [for it was neither good English nor German, nor were the letters shaped or formed as other letters are (35)]. He puts off reading it for four years because of slanders being spread about her, until, attacked by remorse, he resolves to try again: Kempe brings the book back to him, promising that she will pray to God to "purchasyn hym grace to reden it & wrytyn it also" [gain him grace to read it and to write it as well]. The priest, "trustyng in hire prayers" [trusting in her prayers], begins to read the book, and finds that "it was mych mor esy, as hym thowt, þan it was be-forn-tym" [it was much easier, as he thought, than it was before]. When he starts to transcribe, however, his eyesight fails him, so that he cannot see to make his letters or even mend his pen, and even spectacles do not help. When he complains to Kempe she encourages him to persevere, and think of God's grace. On his return to the book, he finds he can see as well "as euyr he dede befor þe day-lyth & þe candel-lygth boþe" (5) [as he ever did before both by daylight and by candlelight (37)]. The implication is unmistakable: Kempe's prayers have given him the power to surmount the physical and perceptual barriers that have interfered with the inscribing of her voice. Though forced by circumstance to have that voice mediated, it is her energy, determination, and finally her spiritual power that enable the instrument of mediation to function. Her prayers have power over meaning, signification. When the scribe himself learns to weep at what she dictates, when Christ and the Virgin also endorse her book (Ch. 88), her validation is complete.

Many readers find themselves inclined to stop Kempe's work with Book I. It is aesthetically satisfying and provides a fitting sense of closure to finish with her success in finding her voice, and with God's validation for the writing. Book II, in contrast, seems to be tacked on, short and repetitive, with no clear structural principle. However, there is a principle, if we observe the text closely enough. To recognize it we need to examine another of Kempe's favorite terms: "felyngys." Wolfgang Riehle, in his analysis of the terminology of Middle English mystics, interprets this word as "the ability . . . to experience God through the powers of the soul" (112); Riehle mentions also that on one occasion Kempe equates it specifically with "contemplacyons" (25), which suggests that the term could be glossed as "the experience of divine communication." However, Kempe also couples the term quite frequently with "reuelacyons;" as, for example, in the Proem, where she speaks of being urged to "don hem wryten & makyn a booke of hyr felyngys and hir reuelacyons" (3) [have a book written of her feelings and her revelations (35)], or in Chs. 23–25; in these passages "felyngys" is clearly equivalent to prophecies or foreknowledge of the future, which are the result of her visions and conversations with God. Sometimes this foreknowledge is expressed as "how sche felt in hir sowle" (59) [how she felt in her soul (95)]; (see also 57). At the end of Book I she explicitly describes the early doubts and distrust she has had of those feelings: "sche had no joye in þe felyng tyl sche knew be experiens wheþyr it was trewe er not" (220) [she had no joy in the feeling until she knew by experience whether it was true or not (261)]. The scribe also wishes to test the truth of Kempe's revelations: "the prest whech wrot þis boke for to preuyn þis creaturys felyngys many tymes & dyuers tymes he askyd hir qwestyons & demawndys of thyngys þat wer for to komyn" (55) [the priest who wrote down this book, in order to test this creature's feelings, asked her questions many different times about things that were to come (90)]. Both Kempe and her scribe must be sure that the source of her "felyngys" is divine and not demonic. At specific moments in Book I Kempe narrates incidents that validate her prophecies (Chs. 23–25, 70–75); similarly, the gradual strengthening of the scribe's faith in Kempe's power is almost contrapuntal with Kempe's own self-confirmation.

Thus "felyngys" seems to be Kempe's term for the link with God that allows her to prophesy, the metaphysical knowledge that results from her tears and prayers, authority and endorsement for which she has been searching increasingly throughout Book I. If we view Book II in the light of this theme of growing validation, it gains a new significance, for it is actually structured to demonstrate the theme. Kempe embarks on her journey on the Continent impulsively, without getting permission from her confessor—in fact, defying his instructions, solely because she is "comawndyd in her hert" (226) [commanded in her soul (270)] to go. She survives her pilgrimages intact, despite all her tribulations and persecutions, her physical infirmities, her constant fear of rape, because she trusts her feelings in growing spiritual independence. Although she needs traveling companions or male escorts for physical protection, she is essentially on her own in spiritual terms, cut off from her usual support network of male ecclesiastics.[7] Nor, unlike her earlier pilgrimages to Rome and Jerusalem, does she search for substitutes for those ecclesiastics: her sense of her link with God is strong enough that she does not need their confirmation. When she returns home to Lynn she has to placate her confessor who is angry at her disobedience, but she has survived; she has proved the truth of her feelings. As David Lawton points out elsewhere in this volume, Kempe is not so much searching for her voice as for authority for that voice, authority which in Book I she gets from her confessors and clerical supporters. Her travels in Germany and Poland in Book II show her that she does not need either their authority or their mediation; her authority comes directly from God (II, Chs. 2–3). Indeed, Christ tells her, "Dowtyr, I browte þe hedyr, & I xal bryngyn þe hom a-geyn in-to Inglond in saf-warde. Dowte it not, but leue it ryth wel" (233) [Daughter, I brought you here, and I shall bring you home again to England in safety. Do not doubt it, but well believe it (277)].

Book II, then, develops on a clear thematic principle, that of Kempe's growing self-confidence and self-affirmation; but it ends oddly, with her prayer. Barry Windeatt observes that "Margery's dictation of her recollections ends . . . characteristically and authentically without any formally contrived or artistic sense of climax. She has simply ceased to speak" (15). Many readers would agree. However, on reflection, we may see that the ending of the *Book* is surprisingly appropriate. Much of Kempe's life has been spent in fighting the charges that she has usurped the male prerogative of preaching. This is made explicit in the scene of the examination by the Archbishop of York, who tries to extract a promise from her that she "ne xalt techyn ne chalengyn þe pepil in my diocyse" (125–26) [will not teach people or call them to account in my diocese (164)]. She refuses, citing the Gospel as authority that gives her leave to "spekyn of God" [to speak of God]. When a cleric invokes St. Paul's injunction against preaching by women, her answer is, "I preche not, ser, I come in no pulpytt. I vse but comownycacyon & good wordys" (126) [I do not preach, sir; I do not go into any pulpit. I use only conversation and good words (164)]. She is not preaching, only conversing, repeating the good words, telling holy stories.[8] One is driven to ask, what is the difference for Kempe between preaching and telling holy stories? In her discussion of this episode, Karma Lochrie points out that the charge of lay preaching was specifically aimed at Lollards at the time, and argues that Kempe was drawing a distinction between preaching and teaching in order to invoke the defense that the latter was not only allowed, but the duty of every Christian (42–47). I suggest that a further connotation is implicit here: that for Kempe preaching is associated with learned men; it implies rhetorical training, the employment of formal rhetoric, the patriarchal language. The fourteenth-century treatises of the *ars praedicandi* such as that by Robert of Basevorn (Murphy, ed.) clearly indicate the training and education that is required for writing sermons. Kempe, the unlettered woman, has not only been denied such learning, but constantly dissociates herself from it.[9] Indeed, it is a particular source of pleasure to her that she can hold her own before the Archbishop of York against her accusers, "so many lernyd men" (128).

It is significant, then, that although she has resisted through much of her life the adoption of patriarchal language, Kempe finally finds the confidence to appropriate it for herself in her prayer at the end of Book II. Though in conventional narrative terms there is indeed no climax to Book II, its ending is highly fitting, for it is an account of Kempe's own form of prayer, presented here not in the third person like the whole of the rest of the work, but in an assured first person, speaking directly to God. Compared to the colloquial language and the rhythms of living speech that so characterize the rest of the work, the prayer is formal and rhetorically effective.[10] One passage is an extended periodic sentence, most uncharacteristic of the rest of the work (251– 52). The appeals to God are presented in repeated parallel structures, using the scheme of anaphora: "As wistly as it is not my wil . . . to worschepyn no fals deuyl . . ., so wistly I defye þe Deuyl, & al hys fals cownsel . . ." (248) [As surely as it is not my will . . . to worship any false devil . . ., as surely I defy the devil and all his false counsel (293)]; "I cry þe mercy, blisful Lord, for þe kyng of Inglond & for alle Cristen kyngys. . . . I cry þe mercy, Lord, for Iewys, & Saraȝinys, & alle hethen pepil . . ." (250) [I cry you mercy, blissful Lord, for the King of England, and for all Christian kings. . . . I cry you mercy, Lord, for Jews and Saracens, and all heathen people (294)]. The rhetorical formality is demonstrated most effectively if we lay out two consecutive sentences to show their syntactical and rhetorical structure:

Haue mend, Lord, of þe woman þat was takyn in þe vowtre
         & browt be-forn þe,
  and, as þu dreue a-wey alle hir enmyis fro hir
      & sche stod a-lone by þe,
    so verily mot þu dryuyn a-wey alle myn enmijs fro me,
       boþ in bodily and gostly,
     þat I may stondyn a-lone by þe
      & make my sowle ded to alle þe joyis of þis world
       & qwyk & gredy
          to hy contemplacyon in God.
Hafe mend, Lord, of Laȝer þat lay iiij days ded in hys graue,
  &, as I haue ben in þat holy stede
      þer þi body was qwik & ded & crucifijd for mannys synne
  & þer Laȝer was reisyd fro deth to lyfe,
as wistly, Lord,
     yf any man er woman be ded in þis owr be dedly synne,
     yf any prayer may helpyn hem,
       here my preyerys for hem
      & make hem to leuyn wythowtyn ende. (253.15–29)

[Remember, Lord, the woman who was taken in adultery and
brought before you, and as you drove away all her enemies
from her as she stood alone by you, so truly you may drive
away all my enemies from me, both bodily and spiritual, so
that I may stand alone by you, and make my soul dead to all
the joys of this world, and alive and greedy for high
contemplation in God.

Remember, Lord, Lazarus who lay four days dead in his grave,
and as I have been in that holy place where your body was
alive and dead and crucified for man's sin, and where Lazarus
was raised from death to life, as surely, Lord, if any man or
woman be dead in this hour through mortal sin, if any prayer
may help them, hear my prayers for them and make them live
without end.] (297)

These are the rhythmical cadences, the rhetorical schemes, that
Kempe has learned through her extensive oral education, through
hearing so many sermons, and through having devotional works read to
her (see Ch. 58). But it is also the patriarchal language, the formal
rhetoric of male ecclesiastics. Whereas in Book I Kempe dissociated
herself from the patriarchal language, which to her was suspect because
it was the symbol of the male ecclesiastical establishment that wished

to exclude or at the very least control her, in Book II her spiritual independence from her male support network provides the assurance and strength that allows her finally to appropriate the male rhetoric for her own. No longer do her tears and body language need to be a substitute for the patriachal language, or a shield against patriachal attempts at control. Now she can take her place beside the male ecclesiastics, as a utilizer of formal rhetoric herself. Nor does this new self-assurance in any way diminish the importance of her tears: the current that begins in God's "dalyawns" and ends in tears and prayer is undimmed. In her final prayer she specifically asks that she continue to be visited by the "welle of teerys" with which she can not only wash away her own sins, but also the sins of all other Christian souls, alive or dead (249); and she appeals to God for mercy for all those that trust in her prayers (253–54). Thus Kempe's work ends by simultaneously emphasizing and demonstrating her role as intercessor for humankind, with a prayer which is both a model for others and a validation of itself. Kempe's final prayer not only alludes to her continued link with God, but is itself an enactment of that link, a demonstration of her power.

Arizona State University

NOTES

1. The internal quotation is from V.W. Turner, *The Ritual Process* 103.

2. I owe this perception to a conversation with Caroline Walker Bynum, 1984.

3. The cries seem to last for a period of ten years (see Ch. 57) or perhaps longer (Atkinson 63); the weeping continues to the end of Kempe's life.

4. See also 201, especially lines 34–38.

5. Atkinson points out Kempe's role as an intermediary between God and "repentant sinners" (64), but does not mention the concept of suffering by substitution.

6. This point is also made by Atkinson: "[F]rom earliest times, tears were connected to prayer: John Cassian was one of the first to define compunction as a necessary part of effective prayer" (58). See also the fine analysis of the doctrine of compunction of the heart and the grace of tears in

Sandra McEntire, "The Doctrine of Compunction from Bede to Margery Kempe," and "Walter Hilton and Margery Kempe: Tears and Compunction." It will be apparent that my focus is less on Kempe's relation to the orthodox mystical tradition than on her highly individual fashioning of her role in society. The impulse that drives Kempe is complex and somewhat problematic; tears signify her link with God, the current that begins with "dalyawns" and ends in prayer.

7. Anthony Goodman writes persuasively of this network, the influential regulars and seculars of Lynn, which he suggests were a group of "clerical radicals drawn together from various religious disciplines" (357; see 353–57).

8. Even Kempe's use of the vernacular for telling holy stories and good words is potentially heretical. The clerics complain that her knowledge of the Gospel demonstrates that she has a devil within her (126). As Margaret Aston has shown, the devotional interest of lay people in books and religious writings in the vernacular was a threat to "ancient clerical assumptions" that the highest mysteries of the faith should be couched in Latin, ultimately accessible only to the learned (131). "For lay people to prove themselves capable of theology, direct auditors of God, was to change the world" (132). The idea that reading religious writing in the vernacular was heretical, and that its availability was offensive to stability and order, lasted well after the Reformation, when Hobbes was to write sourly, "After the Bible was translated into English, every many, nay, every boy and wench that could read English, thought they spoke with God almighty and understood what he said" (qtd. *Story of English* 110).

9. Rhetorical skill and facility with language may also have had associations for Kempe with deceptive persuasiveness, with "glosyng" and hiding the truth. As Jill Mann shows, the association of friars with a persuasive and deceptive tongue was a familiar theme for medieval satirists (37–40). Kempe's antagonists are frequently friars (see Ch. 54, Chs. 61–62), though it must be admitted that the Carmelite friar Alan of Lynn was a supporter (Chs. 9, 61).

10. I should note that Robert Stone's analysis of the style of Kempe and Julian of Norwich brings out the surprising extent to which both women use rhetorical schemes such as anaphora, anadiplosis, antimetabole, parallelism, antithesis, and other devices such as alliteration. However, though Stone touches on syntax and inversion of normal word order, he does not analyze it in detail, and therefore does not note the particular rhetorical formality of the prayer. It is significant that the two longest sentences from the *Book of Margery Kempe* included in his list of examples of balanced clauses (142), sentences which show the most intricate combination of balance with other rhetorical features, are from the prayer.

THE JOURNEY INTO SELFHOOD: MARGERY KEMPE AND FEMININE SPIRITUALITY

Sandra J. McEntire

Margery Kempe and her *Book* have challenged nearly a half century of critical interpretation. Her character, reliability, eccentricity, as well as the *Book*'s social and historical interest have all come under scrutiny. She has also been subjected to a wide variety of responses with regard to her spirituality. Seen variously as unconventional, mediocre, mad, sensational, monotonous, hysterical, abnormal, trivial, and even morbid, Kempe seems to have little to recommend her. More recently, however, Margery Kempe and her spirituality are being reexamined both from within the traditional conventions of contemporary medieval spirituality[1] as well as from the stance of feminine spirituality.

One attempt to determine a tradition of feminine mysticism and Margery Kempe's place within it has been undertaken in Ute Stargardt's essay "The Beguines of Belgium, the Dominican Nuns of Germany, and Margery Kempe." As a result of her contextual reading, however, Margery Kempe still fares poorly. Solidly within a tradition which faults Kempe for her failures to meet a standard outside of her possibilities, Stargardt continues the rejection of the spirituality of Kempe and other continental mystics, identifying her and her struggle as arising from "lifelong feelings of inferiority," "inadequacy" (298), and a "repressed sexual appetite" (299). Furthermore, due to her "superficiality" and "falsification of mystical ideas" (300) Kempe represents the "ultimate decay of continental feminine mysticism" (301). Although Stargardt examines continental women equally critically, she fails to provide a useful understanding of spirituality which might be applied not only to Kempe, but to other women as well.[2]

Some recent work of feminists and theorists begins to assist us in our understanding of what might constitute a feminine spirituality. The work of feminist writer and theologian Carol Christ provides a model for a spirituality which is uniquely feminine. In her book, *Diving Deep and Surfacing*, Christ delineates three distinct elements in a woman's spiritual journey which distinguish it from that established by male experience. That pattern has traditionally been identified by the three stages known as the purgative, illuminative, and unitive and are essential in the process of an individual experiencing what we know as conversion. Christ, however, indicates that woman's spiritual experience is different from this essentially linear progressive process and does not fit precisely the parameters of conversion experience. Rather than seeking to turn away from the world and the flesh, women, she says, seek "a wholeness that unites the dualisms of spirit and body, rational and irrational, nature and freedom, spiritual and social, life and death . . ." (8). A woman's spiritual quest thus concerns her "awakening to the depths of her soul and her position in the universe" (8). The social implications of her quest concern her struggle "to gain respect, equality, and freedom in society—in work, in politics, and in relationships with women, men, and children" (8). In listening "to her own voice and coming to terms with her own experience" a woman opens herself to "the revelation of powers or forces of being larger than herself that can ground her in a new understanding of herself and her position in the world" (9).

Christ delineates three elements in women's spiritual quest. Starting from where they are, "it begins in an experience of nothingness":

> Women experience emptiness in their own lives—in self-hatred, in self-negation, and in being a victim; in relationships with men; and in the values that have shaped their lives. Experiencing nothingness, women reject conventional solutions and question the meaning of their lives, thus opening themselves to the revelation of deeper sources of power and value. (13)

Although analogical to the "dark night of the soul," this experience of nothingness must be distinguished from negative mystical experience associated with Pseudo-Dionysius, which "taught the practice of 'vacating' or suppressing the self as part of an elaborate preparation for a mystical access which would not register in sensory perceptions at all" (Partner, "Reading the Book of Margery Kempe" 34–35). Since "men are not conditioned to think of themselves as worthless" the experience of nothingness "often has a different quality for women than for men" (Christ 17).

> Men are not conditioned to think of themselves as worthless. For them the experience of nothingness often comes after they have taken their place in the world of male power and joined the traditional hierarchies that support men's dominance in family and society. . . . Women, in contrast, live in a male-defined world in which culture has, for the most part, denied them access to power. The ordinary experience of women in patriarchy is akin to the experience of nothingness. Women never have what male mystics must strive to give up. (17–18)

Thus must women come to terms with the nothingness that their world and culture inculcate within them.

The experience of nothingness is followed, second, by an awakening "in which the powers of being are revealed" and which "ground her in a new sense of orientation in the world" by which she overcomes her self-negation and self-hatred (13). "Awakening often occurs through mystical identification" sometimes with nature or in community of other women or, as in Kempe's instance, with a divine being. "'Awakening' suggests that the self needs only to notice what is already there. Awakening implies that the ability to see or to know is within the self" (18).

Third and finally, awakening is followed by "a new naming of self and reality that articulates the new orientation of self and world achieved through experiencing the powers of being" (13). It is important for a woman "to name her experience through words. When one woman puts her experiences into words, another woman who has kept silent, afraid of what others will think, can find validation" (23). Ultimately, a key theme in this new naming is the revaluing of what it means to be a woman:

> Women learn to overcome the "false naming" and devaluing of traditional women's activities like mothering and nurturing. They begin to name women's activities as sources of insight, to name women's valuing of nurturance as a power

of life which women may use to transform culture. . . . Far
from being trivial, the new celebration of women's bodies,
powers, solitude, and connections to each other is the
beginning of the end of centuries old patterns of self-hatred
and self-negation. (24)

This pattern of nothingness/awakening/naming is not exclusively linear
and the elements may overlap and repeat in circular patterns throughout
a woman's life.

Sometimes awakening precedes awareness of the experience
of nothingness, and mystical insight can intensify a
woman's experience of the nothingness of conventional
reality. It should not be assumed that a woman can ever be
through with the experience of nothingness. As long as she
lives—and especially in a male-centered society—the
experience of nothingness will reappear. The moments of
women's quest are part of a process in which experiences of
nothingness, awakenings, insights, and namings form a
spiral of ever-deepening but never final understanding. (14)

This ever deepening understanding is both like the union of the
traditional conversion topos and also different in that it contains
characteristics distinct to woman's experience. A woman's naming
brings her first and foremost into union with herself, her identity, her
place in the world. Like the circles formed in a pool of water when a
pebble is dropped, her sense of self reverberates throughout her
universe, and, when connected with a divine being, her identification
with godliness increases as well.

I do not mean to replace the purgative, illuminative, unitive
pattern with new terms, but to argue that, while the end may be
essentially similar in both patterns—union and integration—the very
process itself is distinct. The traditional pattern is based on clear
progressive stages; it is essentially linear, as Hilton's "Scale"
symbolizes and replicates. Its object is the rejection of the self, the
perfection of abstract Self. For the pilgrim seeking conversion, union
represents the dislocation of all that is bodily, earthly, material. Union
is supposedly pure(r) heightened spiritual reality. The pattern of female
spirituality, however, does not divide a woman from herself, but
integrates her in her very self, including everything that enters her
sphere. She strives not so much for perfection but for completion. For

woman's spiritual journey, union includes all that is homely and earthly as well as the mystic and visionary. It includes her essential nature and the contradictions that have been imposed upon her by her society and culture. Woman integrates it all in one coherent whole and in so doing is complete.

Similar to the spirituality of Carol Christ, the study of psychologists Belenky, Clinchy, Goldberger, and Tarule in *Women's Ways of Knowing. The Development of Self, Voice, and Mind* seems to provide corresponding and complementary insights. In this book, the authors, "show how women's self-concepts and ways of knowing are intertwined . . . and describe how women struggle to claim the power of their own minds." (3). The first way of knowing they describe is that of silence. It is primarily passive, deprived, "dumb." Women in this experience perceive words as weapons "used to separate and diminish people, not to connect and empower them" (24). Silent women "do not cultivate their capacities for representational thought" (25). Thus in their relationships to authorities they feel "passive, reactive, and dependent" and "see authorities as being all powerful, if not overpowering" (27).

Change occurs when a woman moves from "passivity to action, from self as static to self as becoming, from silence to a protesting inner voice and infallible gut" (54). This move "away from silence and an externally oriented perspective on knowledge and truth eventuates in a new conception of truth as personal, private, and subjectively known or intuited" (54). The psychologists identify this as "subjective knowing."

> As a woman becomes more aware of the existence of inner resources for knowing and valuing, as she begins to listen to the "still inner voice" within her, she finds an inner source of strength. A major developmental transition follows that has repercussions in her relationships, self-concept and self-esteem, morality and behavior. . . . Women become their own authorities. (54)

Heeding the "still small voice" is the "hallmark of women's emergent sense of self and sense of agency and control" (68).

As in Christ's spiritual model, the psychologists note that the process of the emerging self is not smooth or perfectly linear. "Subject to an extraordinary range of emotional pushes and pulls—anxiety, anger, insecurity, guilt, depression, exhilaration" (76)—once a woman begins to think and know, she begins to act. Acting brings with it "increased experience of strength, optimism, and self-value" (83). Nevertheless, the woman is not free of conflict. Authorities attempt "to inflict their opinions in areas in which the women believed they had a right to their own opinions" (88).

Finally, in the category identified as "constructed knowledge" women discover that "all knowledge is constructed, and the knower is an intimate part of the knowing" (137). Thus women develop a narrative sense of the self—past and future. It is a time of "passionate knowing" where feeling informs abstract thinking (142–43). Once finding a voice, a woman "wants to be heard" (146).

It seems to this writer that the correspondences between the spiritual model and the psychological observations are profound. Carol Christ's "experience of nothingness" parallels the psychologists' "silence." Similarly, "awakening" relates to "subjective knowing" and "naming" to "constructed knowledge." I would argue that these correspondences provide us with a template which might be used more appropriately as a means of interpreting the feminine spiritual journey in general and Kempe in particular than the traditional, patriarchal model of conversion represented by the purgative, illuminative, and unitive ways that has been imposed—not entirely comfortably—on Kempe.[3] This combined model provides us with a language for interpreting some of the more problematic aspects of her self-representation, and implicates in a far broader way the range of her experience. Whereas many writers conclude in their analyses that Kempe was an inferior mystic (if mystic at all),[4] I believe we should begin from her deep sense of inferiority and glean insights into this woman's and perhaps other women's spiritual struggle and journey.

Kempe begins her book with a description of her self-negation, the loss of herself, her reason. She tells us of her postpartum illness: "sche dyspered of hyr lyfe, wenyng sche mygth not leuyn" (6) [she despaired of her life, believing she might not live]. Consequently, she sends for her confessor who too hastily reproves her. His authoritarian, linear response confirms her fear, self-doubt, and dread. His words "separate and diminish" (Belenky 24) her from herself. As a result, she tells us, "þis creatur went owt of hir mende & was wondyrlye vexid & labowryd wyth spyritys half ȝer viij wekys & odde days" (7) [this creature went out of her mind and was amazingly disturbed and tormented with spirits for half a year, eight weeks and odd days (41)]. Partner notes that "in the interior logic of her memories . . . everything followed from marriage: sexual initiation, pregnancy, sickness, pain, fear of death, madness. . . ." ("Reading the Book" 39). But it is also important to recognize the two elements in the moment: her own rejection of childbirth and motherhood and the reproof of the paternal authority over her hidden sin. These two elements cement her sense of despair of the value of her life, her sense of nothingness and marginality.[5]

The tension between her dissatisfaction over traditional female roles and patriarchally determined behavior is repeated again and again throughout her text. Although in bearing fourteen children, she is caught in "the reproduction of Motherhood" (to borrow from Chodorow), she has also interiorized the traditional norm of virginity as the ideal for female sexual identity.[6] For her sexual experience and the contemplative life are mutually exclusive possibilities. She says to Christ:

> For becawse I am no mayden, lak of maydenhed is to me now gret sorwe; my thynkyth I wolde I had ben slayn whan I was takyn fro þe funtston þat I xuld neuyr a dysplesyd þe, & þan xuldyst þu, blyssed Lorde, an had my maydenhad wyth-owtyn ende. (50)

> [Because I am no virgin, lack of virginity is now great sorrow to me. I think I wish I had been killed as soon as I was taken from the font, so that I should never have displeased you, and then, blessed Lord, you would have had my virginity without end.] (86)

This sense of despair of her sexual identity alienates her from herself. Hence she struggles against the physical expression of her relationship with her husband, which she finds "very peynful & horrybyl" (14) [very painful and horrible], and seeks to live chastely. Her struggle with her bodily identity reasserts itself throughout her life.

> She tells how, after her conversion, she wears a hair shirt under her girdle, concealing it so effectively that even her husband is unaware of its existence; she fasts conscientiously; she wakes at two or three in the morning in order to spend hours in prayer; later she desires to kiss lepers

as a sign both of her affection for and identification with the
diseased and the discarded and of her cavalier attitude toward
her health. Through such behavior the material body is
sacrificed in a kind of martyrdom, and Kempe can transcend
the "faults of female nature." (Smith 73)

The unobtrusive, quiet, good woman role of wife and mother is
repressive and unacceptable to Kempe. Although she conforms in many
ways, her book represents her years of resistance to these norms.

The illness of her madness ends with the first of her mystical
revelations when Jesus appears to her:

owyr mercyful Lord Crist Ihesu . . . aperyd to hys creatur
whych had forsakyn hum in lyknesse of a man, most semly,
most bewtyuows, & most amyable þat euyr mygth be seen
wyth mannys eye, . . . syttyng upon hir beddys syde, lokyng
vpon hir wyth so blyssyd a chere þat sche was strengthyd in
alle hir spyritys, seyd to hir þes wordys: "Dowtyr, why hast
þow forsakyn me, and I forsoke neuyr þe?" And anoon, as he
had seyd þes wordys, sche saw veryly how þe eyr openyd as
brygth as ony levyn. . . . And anoon þe creatur was stabelyd
in hir wyttys & in hir reson as wel as euyr sche was beforn.
(8)

[Our merciful Lord Christ Jesus . . . appeared to his creature
who had forsaken him, in the likeness of a man, the most
seemly, most beauteous, and most amiable, . . . sitting upon
her bedside, looking upon her with so blessed a countenance
that she was strengthened in all her spirits, and he said to her
these words: "Daughter, why have you forsaken me, and I
never forsook you?" And as soon as she heard these
words, she saw truly how the air opened as bright as any
lightning. . . . And presently the creature grew as calm in her
wits and her reason as she ever was before.] (42)

This moment marks the beginning of her awakening to her new self,
one identified with the godhead and including within her increasing
power and self-assertion. Indeed the major portion of the book from this
point on represents the awakening she experiences, the movement into
subjective knowing marked by identification not only with Christ, but
also with the godhead, the Virgin Mary, and other saints. This moment,
recollected and transcribed twenty years after the event, also foreshadows

the new sense of herself she will later name, a daughter in union with Christ.

Kempe's awakening and subjectivity to new spiritual possibilities are grounded not in repression and punishment of her body, although she falls into this behavior on occasion, but in spiritualizing and affirming female bodily nurturing. This identification with female roles is contextualized within a community of women saints who model and affirm her femaleness, albeit within traditional roles. Her first mindful reflection on Mary results in a vision of St. Anne pregnant:

> And þan anoon sche saw Seynt Anne gret wyth chylde, and þan sche preyd Seynt Anne to be hir mayden & hir seruawnt. & anon ower Lady was born, & þan sche besyde hir to take þe chyld to hir & kepe it tyl it wer twelve ȝer of age wyth good mete & drynke, wyth fayr whyte clothys & whyte kerchys. (18)

> [Then at once she saw St. Anne, great with child, and then she prayed to St. Anne to let her be her maid and her servant. And presently our Lady was born, and then she busied herself to take the child to herself and look after her until she was twelve years of age, with good food and drink, and fair white clothing and white kerchiefs.] (52–53)

Childbearing, midwifery, white garments: the images attest to the preoccupation these issues have for Kempe. Both as spectator and as participant, Kempe attends birthing moments twice more, first with the birth of St. John the Baptist: "& þan Seynt Iohn was bor, & owyr Lady toke hym vp fro þe erthe wyth al maner reuerens & ȝaf hym to hys modyr" (19) [And then St. John was born, and our Lady took him up from the ground with all reverence and gave him to his mother . . . (53)]. And again she assists in the birth of Jesus:

> And þan went þe creatur forth wyth owyr Lady to Bedlem & purchasyd hir herborwe euery nyght wyth gret reuerens, & owyr Lady was receyued wyth glad cher. Also sche beggyd owyr Lady fayr whyte clothys & kerchys for to swathyn in hir Sone whan he wer born, and, whan Ihesu was born, sche ordeyned beddyng for owyr Lady to lyg in wyth hir blyssed Sone. . . . Aftyrward sche swathyd hym. (19)

[And then the creature went forth with our Lady to Bethlehem
and procured lodging for her every night with great reverence,
and our Lady was received with good cheer. She also begged
for our Lady pieces of fair white cloth and kerchiefs to swaddle
her son in when he was born; and when Jesus was born
she arranged bedding for our Lady to lie on with her blessed
son. . . . Afterwards she swaddled him.] (53–54)

These contemplative scenes of birth and midwifery suggest Kempe's
need to integrate what has been painful and oppressive in her own
experience. She awakens to a new sense of female sexuality which
includes the acceptance of her body's sexual expression. Indeed, as
Caroline Walker Bynum asserts, Kempe embraces her femaleness as a
sign of her spiritual expression (*Holy Feast* 263). Subsequent visions
continue the identification of a maternal and nurturing Kempe with the
virgin at the crucifixion and with Mary Magdalene after the resurrection.

The struggle of her sexuality and her desire for a spiritual identity
is deeply interiorized. As a result of her identification with Christ, she
discovers that her loss of virginity is of no consequence to him. She
says to Christ: "Lord, I am not worthy to heryn þe spekyn & þus to
comown wyth myn husbond. Nerþelesse it is to me gret peyn & gret
dysese" (48) [Lord, I am not worthy to hear you speak, and still to
make love with my husband, even though it is a great pain and great
distress to me (84)]. She repeats the message of the patriarchy: "Lord
Ihesu, þis maner of leuyng longyth to thy holy maydens" (48–49) [Lord
Jesus, this manner of life belongs to your holy maidens (84)]. Jesus,
however, assures her, both replicating the patriarchal position and
subverting it:

3a, dowtyr, trow þow ryght wel þat I lofe wyfes also, and
specyal þo wyfys whech woldyn levyn chast, 3if þei mygtyn
haue her wyl, & don her besynes to plesyn me as þow dost,
for, þow þe state of maydenhode be mor parfyte & mor holy
þan þe state of wedewhode, & þe state of wedewhode mor
parfyte þan þe state [of] wedlake, 3et dowtyr I lofe þe as wel as
any mayden in þe world. Þer may no man let me to lofe whom
I wele & as mech as I wyl. . . . (49)

[Yes, daughter, but rest assured that I love wives also, and
specially those wives who would live chaste if they might
have their will, and do all they can to please me as you do. For
though the state of maidenhood be more perfect and more

> holy than the state of widowhood, and the state of widowhood
> more perfect than the state of wedlock, yet I love you,
> daughter, as much as any maiden in the world. No man may
> prevent me from loving whom I wish and as much as I
> wish. . . .] (84–85)

"Christ's reassurance," says Lochrie, "is a radical one, for it overturns
the accepted tradition usually identified with Paul and Jerome by
rendering God's love non-hierarchical, and all women, as recipients of
his love, equal" (48). Kempe's response to this reassurance and new
awareness is the weeping that so sets her off from others: "Than þis
creatur lay stylle all in wepyng & sobbyng as hir hert xuld a brostyn
for þe swetnesse of spech þat owyr Lord spak on-to hir sowle" (50)
[Then this creature lay still, weeping and sobbing as if her heart would
burst for the sweetness of speech that our Lord spoke to her soul (85)].

Jesus again affirms Kempe's spiritual virginity and marital
identification with him:

> for-as-mech as þu art a mayden in þi sowle, I xal take þe be þe
> on hand in Hevyn & my Modyr be þe oþer hand, & so xalt þu
> dawnsyn in Hevyn with oþer holy maydens & virgynes, for I
> may clepyn þe dere a-bowte & myn owyn derworthy derlyng. I
> xal sey to þe, myn owyn blyssed spowse, "Welcome to me
> wyth al maner of joye and gladnes. . . ." (52–53)

> [Because you are a maiden in your soul, I shall take you by the
> one hand in heaven, and my mother by the other, and so you
> shall dance in heaven with other holy maidens and virgins,
> for I may call you dearly bought and my own beloved darling.
> I shall say to you, my own beloved spouse, "Welcome to me,
> with every kind of joy and gladness. . . ."] (88)

Not only does Kempe receive approbation for her awakening insights
about her identity as a sexual woman but in this instance she is
initiated into the intimacy of potential marriage with Christ himself,
imagery usually reserved to celibate religious. What is unmistakable is
the centrality that sexuality has for this woman. She was, affirms
Partner, "a highly sexual woman."

> Her sexuality was central to her sense of identity, central to
> her experience of longing, gratification, fulfillment, and to
> her conceptions of deprivation and loss. Her sexuality was
> the compelling force which governed her imagination and
> passions, and it was a lifelong force. ("Reading the Book"
> 54)

Kempe's awakening spirituality enables her to integrate her sexual
identity into her deepest awareness of herself not merely as a physical
person but also as a spiritual person.

This initial identification of Kempe as bride of Christ is further
confirmed in a later vision where "hir affeccyon was al drawyn in-to þe
manhod of Crist & in-to þe mynde of hys Passyon" (208) [her affection
was entirely drawn into the manhood of Christ and into the memory of
his passion (249)]. Thus in a kind of sleep she sees "wyth hir gostly
eye owr Lordys body lying be-forn hir, & hys heuyd, as hir thowt, fast
be hir wyth his blissyd face vpward, þe semeliest man þat euyr myth be
seen er thowt" (208) [with her spiritual eye, our Lord's body lying
before her, and his head, as she thought, close by her, with his blessed
face turned upwards, the handsomest man that ever might be seen or
imagined (249)]. The physicality of Christ reflects and projects
Kempe's own need to integrate her physicality into an acceptable praxis
of spirituality. Projected onto the holy figures, she, as it were,
legitimates her own identity and sexuality. Not only is the absolute
domesticated (Beckwith 46) but the domestic is also reinscribed with
value. Nevertheless, the extreme tension between the awareness to
which she is awakening and what she had previously interiorized of
rejection of female selfhood gives vent to streams of tears and
moanings. Subjective knowing, we are reminded, is "subject to an
extraordinary range of emotional pushes and pulls" (Belenky 76). Split
in her identification of self, Kempe must not only integrate a new sense
of herself but also struggle with her own resistance to this new
awareness. Furthermore, this resistance will find plentiful expression
within the social and religious world.

The strongest argument for Kempe's awakened awareness is
found in her self-assertion which rejects patriarchal interpretations of her
experience. Though torn and fearful that what she is experiencing is
from the devil, when faced by opposition, she firmly stands her ground.
Uncharacteristically confident, she astonishes the clerks because she
answers their many hard questions "so redyly & pregnawntly" (35) [so

readily and pregnantly]. Furthermore, it is precisely because she is subverting the traditional models of behavior for laywomen that the forces of patriarchal authority are polarized against her. The mayor of Leicester rebukes her and repeats indecent words the force of which her response suggests are sexually insulting; she says,

> Sir, . . . I take witnesse of my Lord Ihesu Crist, whos body is her present in þe Sacrament of þe Awter, þat I neuyr had part of mannys body in þis worlde in actual dede be way of synne, but of myn husbondys body, whom I am bowndyn to be þe lawe of matrimony, & be whom I haue born xiiij childeryn. For I do ȝow to wetyn, ser, þat þer is no man in þis worlde þat I love so meche as God, for I lofe hym a-bouyn al thynge, &, ser, I telle ȝow trewely I love al men in God & for God. (115)

> [Sir, . . . I take witness of my Lord Jesus Christ, whose body is here present in the sacrament of the altar, that I never had part of any man's body in this world in actual deed by way of sin, except my husband's body, to whom I am bound by the law of matrimony, and by whom I have borne fourteen children. For I would have you know, sir, that there is no man in this world that I love so much as God, for I love him above all things, and, sir, I tell you truly, I love all men in God and for God.] (153)

But the mayor's agenda is quite clear when he insists, "I wil wetyn why þow gost in white clothys, for I trowe þow art comyn hedyr to han a-wey owr wyuys fro us & ledyn hem with þe" (116) [I want to know why you go about in white clothes, for I believe you have come here to lure away our wives from us, and lead them off with you (153)]. The archbishop of York implies a similar concern when he asks: "Why gost þu in white? Art þu a mayden?" (124) "Why do you go about in white clothes? Are you a virgin? (162)]. Their concern is not unfounded. Other women are interested in her insights, her strength of purpose, and her determination to live a spiritual life consistent with her embodied values. Kempe is indeed subverting the established order; she asserts that the legitimacy of her spiritual identity is in no way contradicted by her sexual identity. Her third trial centers precisely on this issue of female behavior. The men of the Beverly district say to her, "Damsel, forsake þis lyfe þat þu hast, & go spynne & carde as oþer women don, & suffyr not so meche schame & so meche wo" (129) [Woman, give up this life that you lead, and go and spin, and card wool, as other women do, and do not suffer so much shame and so much unhappiness (168)]. Kempe, however, rejects this summary of her life; her shame and unhappiness come not from being true to her new insights but from the marginalized spinning and carding and childbearing that keep her from realizing other possibilities.

Clearly intending to trip her up a cleric asks her to interpret the words, "Crescite et multiplicamini" [increase and multiply]. She again responds out of the new awareness that she has gained:

> Ser þes wordys ben not vndirstondyn only of begetyng of chyldren bodily, but also be purchasyng of vertu, whech is frute gostly, as be heryng of þe wordys of God, be good exampyl ʒeuyng, be mekenes & paciens, charite & chastite, & swech oþer, for pacyens is more worthy þan myraclys werkyng. (121)

> [Sir, these words are not only to be understood as applying to the begetting of children physically, but also to the gaining of virtue, which is spiritual fruit, such as by hearing the words of God, by giving a good example, by meekness and patience, charity and chastity, and other such things—for patience is more worthy than miracle working.] (159)

Rejecting the marginal definitions of what a woman's role can be, Kempe claims her new insight and asserts new definitions of previous traditional behavior. In effect, Kempe "clears away the social and biological restrictions which deny the 'wey of hy perfeccyon' to women" (Lochrie 50).

Having awakened to new possibilities, and asserted her voice against various authorities, Kempe continues to speak and name her own experience, marking the third element in her spiritual quest. From her experience she constructs new knowledge. Although female roles are traditionally relegated to those of wife and mother, Kempe transforms these marginal roles by claiming them in a wider context. Rejecting the limited dualistic representations permitted her by her sexual and cultural reality, she enters into the contradictions of identity accessible through spiritual reality. Moving beyond the constrictions of either/or thought, she represents the possibilities of "not only/but also" thinking.[7] She both renames and reidentifies herself, first in the clothing episodes and second in her identification as bride, mother, and sister of Christ. Her spiritual identity is informed by her sexuality but not circumscribed by her sexual reality. She can be at one and the same time a wife, mother, and sexually experienced woman and a spiritual virgin, bride, lover, even mother, of her mystic lover. She is his devoted daughter. Out of these relational roles she gains the ability to articulate, to voice, to claim power.

Kempe expresses the ideal of spiritual virginity externally by wearing white clothes.[8] Clothing provides a metaphor for Kempe's self-expression even before her spiritual awakening. Early in her journey to wholeness, we are told

> sche wold not leeuyn hir pride ne hir pompows aray þat sche had vsyd be-for-tym, neiþyr for hyr husbond ne for noon oþer mannys cownsel. And ȝet sche wyst ful wel þat men seyden hir ful mech velany, for sche weryd gold pypys on hir hevyd & hir hodys wyth þe typettys were daggyd. Hir clokys also wer daggyd & leyd wyth dyuers colowrs be-twen þe daggys þat it schuld be þe mor staryng to mannys syght and hi-self þe mor ben worshepd. (9)

> [she would not leave her pride or her showy manner of dressing, which she had previously been used to, either for her husband, or for any other person's advice. And yet she knew full well that people made many adverse comments about her, because she wore gold pipes on her head, and her hoods with the tippets were fashionably slashed. Her cloaks were also modishly slashed and underlaid with various colours between the slashes, so that she would be all the more stared at, and all the more esteemed.] (43)

Clothing is an extension of herself (Mueller 61) as well as a symbolic code "governing social class and gender" (Partner, "Reading the Book" 40). Her ability to represent the new spiritual ideal, however, is neither abrupt nor capricious. Two years before her journey to the Holy Land, Kempe is commanded by Christ to dress according to his will, that is, to wear white clothes. She initially objects, but after arriving in Rome, "sche went & ordeynd hir white clothys & was clad al in white liche as sche was comawndyd for to do ȝerys be-forn in hir sowle be reuelacyon, & now it was fulfilt in effect" (80) [she went and got her white clothes and was clad all in white, just as she was commanded to do years before in her soul by revelation, and now it was fulfilled in effect (116)]. This

wearing of white clothes is in stark contrast to the hair shirt she wears
early in her spiritual journey, a hair shirt of repentance representing the
rejection of her body which Christ too commands her to put off:
"Dowtyr, þu hast an hayr vp-on þi bakke. I wyl þu do it a-way, & I
schal ȝiue þe an hayr in þin hert þat schal lyke me mych bettyr þan alle
þe hayres in þe world" (17) [Daughter, you have a hair shirt on your
back. I want you to leave off wearing it, and I shall give you a hair
shirt in your heart which shall please me more than all the hair shirts in
the world (51)]. Thus, from early on, clothing signals interior reality.

It is out of this restoring and nurturing relationship with Christ
that Kempe's identity is transformed. And she is not changed into
something other than what she is; rather, her identity as wife and
mother is translated into the spiritual realm. Christ says to her:

> I preue þat þow art a very dowtyr to me & a modyr also, a
> syster, a wyfe, and a spowse. . . . Whan þu stodyst to plese
> me, þan art þu a very dowtyr; whan þu wepyst & mornyst for
> my peyn & for my Passyon, þan art þow a very modyr to haue
> compassyon of hyr chyld; whan þow wepyst for oþer mennys
> synnes and for aduersytes, þan art þow a very syster; and whan
> thow sorwyst for þow art so long fro þe blysse of Heuyn, þan
> art þu a very spowse & a wyfe, for it longyth to þe wyfe to be
> wyth hir husbond & no very joy to han tyl sche come to his
> presens. (31)

> [I prove that you are a daughter indeed to me, and a mother
> also, a sister, a wife and spouse. . . . When you strive to
> please me, then you are a true daughter; when you weep and
> mourn for my pain and my Passion, then you are a true
> mother, having compassion on her child; when you weep for
> other people's sins and adversities, then you are a true sister;
> and when you sorrow because you are kept so long from the
> bliss of heaven, then you are a true spouse and wife, for it is
> the wife's part to be with her husband and to have no true joy
> until she has his company.] (66–67)

Renamed as daughter, mother, sister, and wife by Christ, Kempe
presents her relationships with others as likewise transformed. The
German priest at St. John Lateran in Rome receives her "ful mekely &
reuerently as for hys modyr & for hys syster" (83) [very meekly and
reverently, as if she were his mother and his sister (119)]. Another
priest addresses her as "mother" (139) as does Thomas Marchale in

Newcastle (145). Indeed, we are told that "þe processe of tyme hir mende & hir thowt was so ioynyd to God þat sche neuyr forȝate hym but contynualy had mende of hym & behelde hym in alle creaturys" (172) [by process of time her mind and her thoughts were so joined to God that she never forgot him, but had him in mind continually and beheld him in all creatures (212)]. She becomes the mother, sister, wife of all God's creatures. "þe sayd creatur was desiryd of mech pepil to be wyth hem at her deying & to prey for hem" (172) [The said creature was also so desired by many people to be with them at their dying and to pray for them (212–13)]. Further, her relationship with her husband is likewise transformed; whereas he initially resents her imposed celibate relationship, in his final illness she serves him as a loving sister and mother, cleaning him, feeding him, assisting him. Christ makes explicit the connection between serving him and caring for her husband.

> And þu hast seyd many tymys þat þu woldist fawyn kepyn me.
> I prey þe now kepe hym for þe lofe of me, for he hast sumtyme
> fulfillyd þi wil & my wil boþe . . . and þerfor I wil þat þu be fre
> to helpyn hym at hys nede in my name. (180)

> [And you have said many times that you would gladly look
> after me. I pray you now, look after him for love of me, for he
> has sometime fulfilled both your will and my will . . . and
> therefore I wish you to be available to help him in his need,
> in my name.] (220)

Transformed in her identity, Kempe is herself a new creature, the term she uses for herself throughout her book. In union with the divine creator, she is created, re-created, creature, awakened to her essential creatureliness, not as an oppressive reality but as full of life and potential.

Out of this new sense of her identity, Kempe gains authority to assert herself in the face of opposition and heresy accusation. She speaks out, refusing to be silent. Uneducated as she is, she speaks with wit and wisdom (128); she resists the fabrication that the source of her tears is due to illness (151). Confident and increasingly certain of the powers in her own being, Kempe remains true to the new vision of herself and being.

This objectively articulated creature, a transformed unlettered housewife who would never have conceived the notion of writing a book, does precisely that. However, although the Bishop of Lincoln had advised her to write down her feelings (34), it is only after twenty years of silence, and as a result of her newfound identity, that she undertakes the task. Responding to her initial concern that the time taken to dictate is distracting her from her usual prayer and devotions, Christ reassures her: "þi stody þat þu stodiist for to do writyn þe grace þat I haue schewyd to þe plesith me ryght meche" (216) [Your concentration on getting written down the grace that I have given you pleases me greatly (257)]. As a result she develops a narrative sense of her own past. While unable to read her own text, she translates herself as it were into text for the benefit of others. Awakened again, she renames herself and her experience again by dictating her story. Once translated into text, her voice cannot be silenced.

Interpreting Margery Kempe's spiritual journey by means of a template using spiritual and psychological theory leads to several cogent considerations: first, it articulates a paradigm that encompasses Kempe's actual experience, not what according to some other model she was supposed to feel, do, or be. Feminist psychology thus informs our understanding of women's spirituality in general and of the mystic path in particular. They are not two paths, but one. Looking at them together only advances the discourse about women's interior struggle and journey. Second, Kempe provides lively evidence that awakened female spirituality embraces rather than rejects the full range of female roles and expands them "to encompass all the souls of Christendom in a homely love" (Mueller 67). Finally, reading Kempe by means of this paradigm suggests that this pattern may be useful in evaluating other women's spiritual journeys and thus lead to a better sense of what may truly constitute feminine spirituality. Indeed, as the psychologists suggest, this experience is common to all woman but intensified for female mystics. At the very least, this kind of reading may help to sensitize the reader to the struggle of a single woman who transformed the classic dualisms of the spiritual quest even as she moved into wholeness.

Rhodes College

NOTES

1. My own previous work places Kempe firmly within the tradition of affective piety known as the gift of tears. See especially *The Doctrine of Compunction* 151–61.

2. A useful summary of the scholarship to date on Kempe's spirituality can be found in Fries, especially 227–30. Partner's *Exemplaria* essay also provides a sympathetic consideration of Kempe's use of the metaphors of love. See also Sarah Beckwith's analysis of Kempe in the light of Irigaray's speculum model.

3. See especially Riehle.

4. The list is extensive but represented by Underhill, Thurston, Chambers, Knowles, Weissman, and Stargardt.

5. Sidonie Smith in discussing the narratological aspect of the book also cites this moment as the locus of Kempe's internal conflict. "The moment that marks the origin of Kempe's narrative thus locates the origin of her struggle as a sexually contaminated woman who has sacrificed the integrity of her body to the fruits of lust. In this context, her postpartum madness reveals a logical subtext. Through physical excesses she enacts a ritual of self-punishment that suggests her understanding, however unconscious, that her body is the source of cultural insignificance. Motherhood, tying her to Eve's curse, threatens to imprison her in cultural fictions limiting female possibilities for selfhood" (70).

6. "Margery's story would probably not have been so dramatically conflicted had she not had to live it out in a world which so incessantly taught fearful lessons about female sexuality. Margery was emphatically . . . a married woman, a woman whose virgin purity was irretrievably lost and whose sexuality, released on herself and others, degraded her and made her an occasion of sin as long as she lived. It did not matter that she was illiterate and had not read the relevant works of Jerome or Augustine on sexuality; the steady, pervasive flow of misogynist ideas through medieval culture could not fail to reach her and every woman" (Partner, "Reading the Book" 47).

7. "Society at large, however, clings to either/or thinking with respect to Margery, especially in England where, if anywhere, she has her place" (Mueller 61).

8. See Partner, "Reading the Book," and Mueller for more complete discussions of Kempe's clothing.

Her Work

FROM WOE TO WEAL AND WEAL TO WOE: NOTES ON THE STRUCTURE OF *THE BOOK OF MARGERY KEMPE*

Timea K. Szell

In *A Room of One's Own*, Virginia Woolf advises the fictional writer, Mary Carmichael, to ignore as much as possible the disapproving, jeering crowd assessing her efforts in order to succeed at her vocation:

> And as I watched [Mary Carmichael] lengthening out for the test, I saw, but hoped that she did not see, the bishops and the deans, the doctors and the professors, the patriarchs and the pedagogues all at her shouting and warning advice. You can't do this and you shan't do that! Fellows and scholars only allowed on the grass! Ladies not admitted without a letter of introduction! . . . So they kept at her like the crowd at a fence on the race-course, and it was her trial to take her fence without looking to right or left. If you stop to curse you are lost, I said to her; equally, if you stop to laugh. Hesitate or fumble and you are done for. Think only of the jump, I implored her, as if I had put the whole of my money on her back; and she went over it like a bird. (97)

Margery Kempe, one of the most remarkable and controversial holy women of the late Middle Ages, repeatedly "went over" that metaphorical fence like Woolf's bird, a feat all the more admirable for the fact that she accomplished it while indeed paying constant attention to the commenting and challenging voices of the bishops, preachers, and sundry other spectating "Fathers" along her way. Comments such as the one repeatedly directed at Kempe by several men in the duchy of Bedford, "Damsel, forsake þis lyfe þat þu hast, & go spynne & carde as oþer women don, . . ." (129) [Woman, give up this life that you lead, and go and spin, and card wool, as other women do, . . . (168)] occur frequently in *The Book of Margery Kempe*. Although, to quote Woolf again, Kempe neither got "lost" nor became "done for" as a result of heeding, and occasionally even enabling and provoking, these voices, she negotiated the fences all but comfortably. In fact, one of the most salient qualities of *The Book of Margery Kempe* is a pervasive sense of anxiety and unease on the part of the author, her priestly scribes, and many in her environment.

Physically and spiritually restless even as an elderly woman, Kempe lacked a conventionally sanctioned place in the English spiritual tradition. Accordingly, one of the central thematic concerns of the *Book* is the problematics of self-validation, in part engendered by the extent to which Kempe herself was implicated, perhaps inevitably so, in internalizing the social and cultural censure directed at her behavior which was considered eccentric at best by many of her contemporaries.

Throughout her *Book*, Margery Kempe, both vigorously assertive and insecure, is preoccupied with self-validation and a struggle against public mistrust.[1] Paradoxically and importantly, her struggle for public legitimacy frequently coexists with her efforts to maintain the very tensions against which she ostensibly fights.[2] These tensions are the sharpest when her public experiences difficulty in categorizing and thus in comfortably appropriating her. Kempe does indeed defy facile appropriation. Deeply uncomfortable with the traditionally inscribed status of wife and mother and unwilling to respect conventionally sanctioned and practically confining restrictions on her sphere of action as a woman, she also remains outside the official ecclesiastical hierarchy as she was neither a monastic nor sedentary as were the majority of medieval female mystics and visionaries. Concerning Margery Kempe's status as saintly or mad, authentic or hypocritical, public opinion, as reported in her *Book*, is more divided and fragile than it is of any other English or continental woman saint or mystic.

In many episodes recounted in her *Book*, Kempe behaves as a persistent social and moral gadfly and courageous foe of corrupt churchmen. Her autobiography represents her as the notorious undesired element in company, particularly at times, such as dangerous travel abroad, when company would be most desperately needed by her. A simultaneous narrative concern involves the imaging and re-creation of Kempe as spiritually perfect following the problematic and elusive models offered for such perfection to women by late medieval culture. In the double process of negotiating her social relations *and* striving for perfection, she constantly exposes herself to the ridicule and violence of those about her, an exposure represented in the text as a species of martyrdom.[3] I argue that the narrative structure of her *Book* (especially and most consistently the structure of external episodes) mirrors and embodies the ultimate impossibility of reconciling and synthesizing Kempe's diametrically opposed desires: to be socially accepted either by persuading the public (and herself) of her authenticity or by succumbing fully to the "superego" (i.e., the dictates of her patriarchal cultural context), on the one hand, *and*, on the other, to be publicly humiliated or punished for her own perceived inability to meet society's (and her own superego's) expectations.

Narrative and structural tension frequently arises in the text as a result of these contradictory impulses in Kempe. These moments of tension appear both in relatively minor incidents and in more significant ones. In a passing episode, she rejects the perceptions of a cleric, who, when substituting for her regular confessor, expresses serious doubt concerning the spiritual validity of Kempe's "felyngs" (44) [feelings]; yet she is still compelled to double-check her rejection with her returning confessor. In the process she elicits the reassuring words, "It is no wondyr, dowtyr, yf he kan nowt beleuyn in ȝour felynges so sone" (44) [It is no wonder, daughter, that he can't believe in your feelings so soon (80)].

Conversely, the tension may be apparent in more important incidents, as when Kempe experiences a conflict between dictating her *Book* and saying her rosary and carrying out other devotional exercises. In the latter case, Christ reassures her in a lengthy speech that her work on her *Book* is even more important than protracted prayer because "be þis boke many a man xal be turnyd to me & beleuyn þerin" (216) [by this book many a man shall be turned to me and believe (257)].

A strikingly large number of episodes in the *Book* are devoted to formulaic and repetitious accounts of Kempe suffering public mistrust and attacks, which she endures with considerable courage and dignity.[4] During a visit to Canterbury, for example, she is threatened with the stake as a Lollard—a threat which is to come her way repeatedly— momentarily abandoned even by her husband, who walks away from her as if he did not know her, and menaced by a throng of monks who question her sharply and with more than just an edge of hostility (27ff.). On another occasion, the clerks of York, even after ascertaining the orthodoxy of Kempe's faith, declare that they "wil not suffyr hir to dwellyn a-mong [them], for þe pepil hath gret feyth in hir dalyawnce, and perauentur sche myth peruertyn summe of hem" (125) [will not allow her to dwell among [them], because the people have great faith in her talk, and perhaps she might lead some of them astray (163)]. Often Kempe actively exposes herself to what she knows to be a potentially humiliating or explosive encounter with her environment as, for example, when she visits York and overstays her welcome in an apparently gratuitous way (Ch. 51).[5]

Her compulsion to seek outside institutional validation of her spirituality, despite her refusal to submit to a socially sanctioned spiritual gender role, is described in general terms early in the text:

> Than had þis creatur mech drede for illusyons & deceytys of hyr gostly enmys. Þan went sche . . . to many worshepful clerkys, bothe archebysshopys & bysshoppys, doctowrs of dyuynyte & bachelers also. Sche spak also wyth many ankrys and schewed hem hyr maner of leuyng. . . . (3)

> [Then this creature had great dread of the delusions and deceptions of her spiritual enemies. She went . . . to many worthy clerks, both archbishops and bishops, doctors of divinity, and bachelors as well. She also spoke with many anchorites, and told them of her manner of life. . . .] (34–35)

Among several other ecclesiastical and spiritual authorities, she seeks out Archbishop Arundel to see "ȝyf he fond any defawte eyþyr in hyre contemplacyon er in her wepying" (36) [if he found any fault with either her contemplation or her weeping (72)], and visits Julian of Norwich with the expressed purpose of allowing Julian to test her for any "deceyte" (42) [deception]. A German priest, Wenslawe, who—in an episode with Pentecostal echoes—speedily receives the gift of understanding Kempe's English and thus can hear her confession, declares her revelations authentic, and she approaches the "worschepful doctowr" (165) [worthy doctor (205)], Master Custawns, while he is attending the General Chapter of the Friar Preachers in Lynn, specifically to "schew" him "why sche cryed & wept so sor, to wetyn ȝyf he myth fyndyn any defawte in her crying er in hir wepyng" (165) [show him why she cried and wept so bitterly, in order to learn if he could find any fault in her crying or in her weeping (205)].

Each instance of such reassurance, however, bears but short-lived comfort for Kempe and even appears to excite her desire both for more punishment and reassurance. Her visions of and encounters with the quintessential authority figure, Christ, serve as particularly revealing sources of her psychological conflicts and misgivings and frequently lead to public attacks on her.[6] Not only does Christ repeatedly reassure her in extravagant terms, as, for example, when he says, "dowtyr, þu art as sekyr of þe lofe of God as God is God . . ." (89) [daughter, you are as sure of the love of God, as God is God . . . (125)], but his potentially provocative and inconsistent directives regarding Kempe's garb and diet further confound the public's "reading" of her and exacerbate her precarious social status. When Christ orders her to wear white on her pilgrimage to Jerusalem, Kempe tries to change his mind, precisely because she anticipates public outrage: "A, der Lord, yf I go arayd on oþer maner þan oþer chast women don, I drede þat þe pepyl wyl slaw[n]dyr me. Þei wyl sey I am an ypocrat & wondryn vp-on me" (32) [Ah, dear Lord, if I go around dressed differently from how other chaste women dress, I fear people will slander me. They will say I am a hypocrite and ridicule me (67–68)]. Christ, however, persists in his commandment, pointing out that the more shame Kempe incurs on his behalf, the better he will love her. Later, nevertheless, he changes his mind and orders her to resume wearing her black clothes, much to the consternation of her public (89), only to reverse his orders once more to have her don white garb again (91–92).[7] Similarly, on another occasion, Christ abruptly takes away Kempe's ubiquitous ability to weep and cry loudly, so that her sudden silence again arouses the suspicion of those around her (Ch. 63).[8]

Again, Christ's commands keep changing regarding Kempe's diet, another instance of a publicly scrutinized aspect of her life. When Christ directs her to abandon her meatless diet, she begs him not to do so in terms very similar to the ones cited above: "A, blisful Lord, þe pepil, þat hath knowyn of myn abstinens so many ȝeres & seeth me now retornyn & etyn flesch mete, þei wil . . . despisyn me & scornyn me þerfor" (161–62) [Ah, blessed Lord, the people who have known of my abstinence over so many years and who now see me returning to eating meat, will . . . despise me and scorn me because of this (201)].

These incidents typify Kempe's portrayal of a fairly complex network of psychological projections and internalizations. On the one hand, Christ in a certain sense embodies her inclination to provoke and goad her public both in general and in specific by creating a troublingly nebulous public image of herself. This image is unpredictable because it keeps shifting and at times is grotesque because when, for example, she wears white, it represents the middle-aged, sexually experienced Kempe as a youthful virgin. The willfully manipulated public outrage, on the other hand, objectifies Kempe's own censure of the seemingly exhibitionistic tendency to call attention to herself, to offend, amuse, and outrage, and even of her desire to *be* difficult to "read" and to *be* the youthful virgin.

How then are these public attacks on Margery Kempe, her meetings with authority figures for the purpose of personal validation, and Christ's directives shaped and ordered within the narrative?

The most important structural and thematic principle of Kempe's "autohagiography," as Richard Kieckhefer calls it (6), is neither chronological nor thematic in the sense of being predicated upon a clearly discernible line of spiritual progress. Achronological jumps occur frequently; references to long stretches of time, pocketed within the mere semblance of a chronological narrative, fragment linear time. As one of the scribes explicitly asserts: "Thys boke is not wretyn in ordyr, euery thyng aftyr oþer as it wer don, but lych as þe mater cam to þe creatur in mend . . ." (5) [This book is not written in order, every thing after another as it was done, but just as the matter came to this creature's mind . . . (36)].

Thus the narrative structure is in a sense established by Kempe's free-associating. This order can best be described as a pattern consisting of cumulative incidents of partial or near loss and defeat or disempowerment (e.g., loss of Kempe's credibility, safety, dignity, serenity, or threats to her chastity, freedom, etc.) followed by a partial and temporally circumscribed restoration or recovery—indeed, a reaffirmation (e.g., her vindication by reputable ecclesiastical figures, reassurances from Christ, gratuitous human kindness), followed, yet again, by endangerment of Kempe's sense of self or physical safety, never attaining even illusory narrative closure.

Consciousness of self and literal physical safety are often synonymous for Kempe in a psychological sense. When she seeks out Archbishop Arundel, for example, she confronts the gathering of venerable clerks and churchmen and reprimands them for their moral shortcomings. This moment of courageous triumph is immediately followed by the sudden appearance of a woman who declares Kempe a Lollard fit to be burnt. The accuser intervenes at a moment when the men Kempe has just chastised would be most inclined to listen. This tense moment is dissolved by the Archbishop's summons of Kempe, clearly a turn for the better. Kempe, however, endangers his subsequent acceptance of her as a holy woman—the next discernible narrative unit—by accusing the Archbishop of mismanaging his money. Arundel's humble acceptance of her criticism, in turn, reestablishes her position of strength (Ch. 16).

This pattern of repeated loss followed by gain can be discerned in even the homeliest and most trivial incidents narrated in the *Book*. In one such incident, the creature loses a ring she has made following Christ's command, but then finds it under her bed. A similarly pragmatic incident during a pilgrimage involves Kempe's difficulties in climbing to the top of Mount Quarentyne. In strikingly close narrative proximity, first her companions refuse to help the creature up; then a "Saracen," for nominal payment, carries her to her desired destination; whereupon her fellow pilgrims once again refuse to help her in her thirst, until finally some Grey Friars come to Kempe's aid.

At times Kempe falls in and out of favor with stunning rapidity. In her sojourn in Leicester, for example, the following events take place in quick succession: she is ignominiously jailed as a troublemaker and potential heretic and thrown into a cell full of male prisoners; she is rescued by a merciful jail keeper who takes her to his home, treats her as a visiting dignitary, and houses her in a fair chamber; she is summoned by a lascivious steward; she is then saved, just in the nick of time, by the jail keeper's wife, who refuses to deliver her to the steward; and, finally, before her ultimate escape, she is threatened by the jail keeper himself who, afraid of his superior, delivers her up to the steward (Chs. 46–47).[9]

Most pervasive in the narrative of external incidents, this pattern at times becomes discernible in episodes pertaining to Kempe's revelations as well. While Christ's see-sawing directives concerning her attire and diet have been noted above, several other exchanges between Christ and Kempe are also structured in this manner. In a typical example, one of Christ's grandest revelations, concerning who would be saved and who damned, is immediately followed by the mystic's doubts about the soundness of the revelations and by a return of her dreaded unclean thoughts.[10]

Furthermore, the few instances where Kempe's (and her text's) relationship with her priestly scribes figures in the narrative, the interpersonal and textual dynamic tends to be patterned in this manner.

One such example occurs in the Proem (incidentally, largely devoted to recounting Kempe's tribulations in finding willing or appropriate scribes, getting the text finished, etc.) when the priestly scribe, finally located after much fruitless searching, refrains from writing because he becomes unduly influenced by negative public opinion of Kempe:

> Than was þer so euel spekyng of þis creatur & of hir wepyng þat þe prest durst not for cowardyse speke wyth her but seldom, ne not wold wryten as he had be-hestyd vn-to þe forseyd creatur. & so he voyded & deferryd þe wrytyng of þis boke wel on-to a iiij ʒer or ellys mor. . . (4)

> [Then there was such evil talk about this creature and her weeping that the priest out of cowardice dared not speak with her but seldom, nor would write as he had promised the said creature. And so he avoided and deferred the writing of this book for nearly four years or more. . . .] (36)

Hope Phyllis Weissman argues that "the narrative technique is used by Margery to articulate a complex new relationship to authority—one which mediates between her desire for formal validation and her awareness that such validation might finally be withheld" ("Margery Kempe in Jerusalem" 208). Weissman's point may be carried further by including under the concept of "authority" Kempe's *internal* dividedness, in which sense external confrontations can also be understood as the would-be holy woman's confrontations with herself. As Nancy Partner notes, a certain "kind of formal repetition with a reversed key element signalling a reversal of meaning" characterizes "Kempe's associational memory" ("And Most of All" 257–58).

I propose that this structure plays a significant role both in implicitly acknowledging and assuaging anxiety—Kempe's, the scribes', the fictional public's, and, arguably, that of the contemporary fifteenth-century audience as well. This anxiety primarily centers on slipperiness and loss of meaning, and the difficulty of arriving upon and retaining spiritual, epistemological, and psychological clarity and fixity concerning Kempe. The structure of near constant wavering between weal and woe, imposed on the *Book* by Kempe's particular mode of recollection,[11] thus both expresses and compensates for the precariousness of the would-be holy woman's identity, the beleaguered and wavering nature of Kempe's sense of self (and others' perception of it), and her need for the unceasing interpretation and testing of perceptions.[12]

From the very beginning of her text, Kempe implicitly acknowledges articulation, interpretation, and proper expression of the hermeneutic outcome, as difficult but constantly necessary endeavors. In the beginning she is openly at a loss as to how to interpret her own experience of spiritual turmoil: "Ne hyr-self cowd neuyr telle þe grace þat sche felt, . . . so hy a-bouen hyr reson & hyr bodyly wyttys, and hyr body so febyl in tym of þe presens of grace þat sche myth neuyr expressyn it wyth her word lych as sche felt it in hyr sowle" (3) [Nor could she herself ever tell of the grace that she felt, . . . so high above her reason and her bodily wits; and her body so feeble at the time of the presence of grace that she could never express it with her words as she felt it in her soul (34)]. In her vision of an angel showing her the "Book of Life," where her own name appears immediately following that of the Trinity, Kempe seeks out the quintessential Book of all books, the worthiest antecedent of her own, to establish her supreme importance in creation (206). Significantly, at this crucial moment, most likely illiterate and thus dependent upon someone else to *read* the text, she desperately needs the angel's interpretive skills to get at her wish-fulfilling truth.

The very draft of her *Book*, namely, the first part written by the earlier scribe, literally has to be deciphered (i.e., interpreted) by the priest who takes over the task of recording her dictation (4). The task is finally accomplished by nothing short of a minor miracle. Given her likely illiteracy and consequent diminished control over her own text, Kempe's "authority as author" is at best "delicate and tenuous" (Lochrie 34).

Public perceptions of her can be sharply divided, as a young monk who hears her discoursing on the Scripture aptly summarizes: "Eyþyr þow hast þe Holy Gost or ellys þow hast a devyl wyth-in þe" (28) [Either you have the Holy Ghost or else you have a devil within you (63)]. Designated by Christ, significantly, as a mirror to the people, Margery Kempe constantly prompts and teases her public to carry out interpretive acts regarding her: "summe seyd it was a wikkyd spiryt vexid hir; sum seyd it was a sekenes; sum seyd sche had dronkyn to mech wyn; sum bannyd hir; sum wisshed sche had ben in þe hauyn; sum wolde sche had ben in þe se in a bottumles boyt; and so ich man as hym thowte" (69) [some said it was a wicked spirit tormented her; some

said it was an illness; some said she had drunk too much wine; some
cursed her; some wished she was in the harbour; some wished she was
on the sea in a bottomless boat; and so each man as he thought (105)].
Indeed no single instance of interpretive opinion regarding Kempe is
allowed to stand by itself in the text; whether damning or affirming, it
is usually balanced by the opposite sentiment as the following
sentence, chilling in its rhetorical balance implying the equation of
"Jew" and "bad woman," underscores: "Sum of þe pepil askyd whedyr
sche wer a Cristen woman or a Iewe; sum seyd sche was a good
woman, & sum seyd nay" (124) [Some of the people asked whether she
were a Christian woman or a Jew; some said she was a good woman,
and some said not (163)].

The division can at times be found within individuals as well.
An initially well-meaning London widow promises to allow Kempe in
her company yet, at the last minute, flees from Aachen without the
troublesome holy woman (II, Ch. 7). A member of the retinue of the
Duke of Bedford, while in the process of arresting Kempe, laments the
way in which encountering her person has confounded his initial
"reading" of her: "Me ouyrthynkyth þat I met wyth þe, for me semyth
þat þu seyst ryth good wordys." (130) [I rather regret that I met with
you, for it seems to me that you speak very good words (168)].

Another incident in which an individual finds it impossible to
sustain a judgment of Kempe occurs when, as an elderly woman and
once again on pilgrimage, she attracts the attention of an initially
benevolent man who volunteers to guide and protect her (II, Ch. 5). Her
insistent weeping, however, irritates him so much that, meaning to
lose his charge, he purposely walks too fast for the aging woman to
follow. Her pitiful predicament moves the compassion of some women
in the countryside who witness the scene. Here, in quick alternating
succession again, the narrative juxtaposes two opposing responses
toward Kempe.

To some degree characteristic of saints' lives, romances, and fairy
tales,[13] this see-sawing structure, moving from woe to weal, is
psychologically soothing. Through it the narrators, Kempe and her
scribes, can, on the one hand, purge their persistent fears of being
discredited or inadequately inscribed as holy. On the other hand, they
may also enjoy the repeated resolution—on some level deeply atavistic,
yet on another satisfyingly predictable—attendant upon the turn from
travail to happiness.

One of the earliest and most powerful similes used to describe Kempe suggests this monotonous yet soothing flexibility inherent in the see-sawing back-and-forth, or swaying structure:

> And euyr sche was turnyd a-ȝen a-bak in tym of temptacyon, lech vn-to þe reedspyr whech boweth wyth euery wynd & neuyr is stable les þan no wynd bloweth, vn-to þe time þat . . . Cryst . . . tyrnyd helth in-to sekenesse, prosperyte in-to aduersyte, worshep in-to repref, & love in-to hatered. Thus alle þis thyngys [were] tyrnyng vp-so-down. . . . (1)

> [And she was always turned back in time of temptation—like the reed which bows with every wind and is never still unless no wind blows—until . . . Christ . . . turned health into sickness, prosperity into adversity, respectability into reproof, and love into hatred. Thus all these things [were] turning upside down. . . .] (33)

The alternating structure, epitomized by the image of the swaying reed, enables the audience, in turn, to diminish its own anxieties attendant upon Kempe's elusiveness and refusal (or inability) to fit any of the categories conventionally allotted to holy women, categories which are comforting because they are familiar and hagiographically validated.

To a certain degree, Margery Kempe fits all four conventional hagiographic categories of female saints: those of the chaste married or widowed woman (for she ceases to have sexual relations with her husband); the virgin martyr (in that her "virginal" status is established by her white garb and by Christ's reassurances of his love for her equalling that for virgin saints and by the metaphorical martyrdom she suffers repeatedly at the hands of her public); the reformed prostitute (in the sense that, before Kempe's repentance, she enjoys her sexuality and, even subsequent to her repenting, is haunted by temptations which take the shape of extravagant sexual fantasies at times involving several men); and, finally, the "transvestite" saint who dresses as a man and passes her life in a monastery of monks (in the sense that, following Christ's directives, Kempe uses clothing in a potentially misleading way). Richard Kieckhefer sees in her the embodiment of several tendencies characterizing fourteenth-century sainthood: her cultivation of the virtue of patience, her raptures and revelations, and her spirit of intensity that distinguish her as a remarkable woman and a troublesome gadfly, depending upon the beholder's point of view (185).[14] Indeed, one may argue that the text, specifically Kempe's construction of herself, reflects many of the psychological and spiritual concerns of the lives of women saints: her deep need for validation, her continuing attempts to establish her own worth, her attempts to escape and evade confines of gender, her fear of illusion and madness, her desire to be identified with Mary and to be chosen as a bride of Christ, and the extremely public nature of her career all align her with the hagiographic tradition.

Throughout her life as a religious convert, Kempe seemed bent on living and reenacting saintly characteristics, some of which do pose an uncomfortable challenge to the public. While many of the combative and aggressive women saints in the *vitae* still popular in Kempe's day were legendary figures and, at the very least, historically remote, Margery Kempe lived and moved in fifteenth-century England. The stylized, conventional attacks of the universal saints upon legendary or historically remote pagan judges and emperors cannot be glibly equated with Kempe's provoking her contemporaries, among them renowned preachers and high ecclesiastical leaders. While the hagiographically appropriated saints' challenges to worldly authority and their public were still imaginatively potent in the late Middle Ages, those challenges were, nevertheless, to a significant degree contained and metaphorized by the *vitae*. Even after fully ascertaining the orthodoxy of Kempe's faith, for example, Archbishop Arundel remains clearly uneasy about his visitor and eager to facilitate her speedy departure from York. He addresses a member of his household as follows: "Se, her is v s., & lede hir fast owt of þis cuntre." (128) [See, here is five schillings, and now escort her fast out of this area (166)]. And when the troublesome holy woman is carried to him again some time later, he cries out in exasperation, "What, woman art þu come a-ȝen? I wolde fayn be delyveryd of þe" (131) [What, woman, have you come back again? I would gladly be rid of you (170)].

The fact that Kempe has some characteristics of all, but ultimately does not fit any, of the above categories points to her attraction to several images of holy womanhood, her wavering sense of self, and, most important, her intense aversion to her given social status and culturally constructed identity.[15] Arguably and tellingly, even before she repents and embarks upon her life as a pilgrim and holy woman, Kempe behaves in somewhat exhibitionistic and unusual ways,[16] and while one way of reading the narrative of her life prior to conversion is to see it as determined by the exigencies of a familiar hagiographic convention, one could also argue that Kempe, in a certain sense, simply switches the means whereby she attracts attention and creates herself as different from ordinary women.

While winningly courageous and genuinely warm with her supporters, Kempe, to put it mildly, is a difficult and contentious person to deal with for almost everyone whose life she touches. The resistance put up by Kempe to comfortable categorization also manifests itself in the see-sawing structure of her text as she moves from one category of holy womanhood to the next, practically from one episode to another. Kempe proudly and stubbornly cultivates her identity as marginal outsider (both to the traditionally ascribed roles of motherhood and wifehood *and*, strictly speaking, to the ecclesiastical establishment because that identity gives her mobility and a certain spiritual distinctiveness). This identity, however, is also untenable for Kempe without a lingering sense of anxiety, an anxiety and unease which persist until the end of the *Book*, despite Christ's repeated (and wish-fulfilling) reassurances that he loves her as much as any maiden in the world.

Kieckhefer notes that while saintly criticism of members of the church hierarchy is not uncommon, most fourteenth-century saints voice these criticisms "from a safe and well-defined position within the Church" (189). Although respected and endorsed by many, Kempe evidently proved too complicated for the Church to categorize according to the highest terms of sanctity. A self-made and headstrong woman, a somewhat grotesque virgin-martyr wearing white on her aging, sexually used body, fostering what today we would call a "public relations" problem, Kempe railed at churchmen and, by her inarticulate screams, competed for attention with distinguished preachers, albeit from no safe enclave within the establishment.[17]

The narrative structure of an overwhelming number of episodes and sections of the *Book* thus mirrors Kempe's experience of loss or lack (of meaning, certainty, and a spiritual position securely validated by the patriarchy) and repeats the same over and over again. Even as Kempe's hermeneutic grasp of her own experience slips away repeatedly, the structure (or the structural expression of that loss) momentarily assuages the anxiety over that same loss.[18]

The alternating loss and gain, so pervasive in *The Book of Margery Kempe* as a structural principle, and the element of her attempted mastery over her life and text (with the accompanying elusiveness of that mastery) in fact recall Freud's concept of the repetition compulsion according to which one unconsciously "repeats" some version of a negative experience with the (unconscious) hope of mastering and appropriating it.[19]

The structure of the event which led Freud to articulate the notion that certain repeated human gestures, even if negative or unpleasurable, functions to assuage anxiety and master an earlier experience of passivity, loss, pain, etc., strikingly resembles the structure of several episodes in the *Book*. Freud recounts observing his grandchild at play:

> The child had a wooden reel with a piece of string tied round it. It never occurred to him to pull it along the floor behind him, for instance, and play at its being a carriage. What he did was to hold the reel by the string and very skillfully throw it over the edge of his curtained cot, so that it disappeared into it, at the same time uttering his expressive "O-O-O-O-" [the childish approximation of the German word "fort" or "gone"]. He then pulled the reel out of the cot again by the string and hailed its reappearance with a joyful "da" ["there"]. This then was the complete game—disappearance and return. (9)

Freud explains the function of the boy's behavior as that of mastering the painful and potentially alarming experience of the occasional departure of his mother. Clearly the "fort/da" structure of the child's game resembles episodes, such as that of Kempe's lost-and-found ring, very closely.

In fact, several critics have suggested that Kempe is reenacting and attempting to master the initial trauma of revealing herself to one who found her severely lacking, i.e., an early confession referred to in her *Book*, during which a harsh cleric refuses her absolution. I would agree, however, that while the repetition compulsion is a useful model for the understanding of the literal and textual drama in the *Book*, Kempe's problem is more endemic than having to master a single painful event. Instead of stemming from a single experience, however traumatic, the "creature's" unease can be related to her precarious fit into the very fabric of her society. Her cultural context, no matter how relatively heterogeneous, ultimately failed to accommodate a woman like Kempe who, as discussed above, is never appropriated by an ecclesiastical institution. In turn, Kempe herself appears unable fully to dismiss or disregard this failure of her human environment.

Hope Weissman explains the "recurring tests of faith to which [Kempe] is subjected" as "metaphors for a still more fundamental interrogation—Margery Kempe . . . is being summoned to justify her very nature before the Church whose ideology continues to dominate her world" ("Margery Kempe in Jerusalem" 202). One might add that Kempe is also "being summoned to justify her very nature before" *herself*, in the sense that, as Sheila Delany argues, she has all too successfully internalized the critical, chastising, punishing aspects of her society and religious context ("Sexual Economics" 109).

Unlike the structure of saints' lives and fairy tales, which end with the resounding validation and triumph of their protagonists (but perhaps similar to that of the open-endedness of contemporary late medieval romances), the structure of *The Book of Margery Kempe*, from woe to weal and back to woe, does not resolve itself even at the end. As pointed out above, the very structure of loss *versus* gain is often made possible and enabled by Kempe's own controversial behavior and emotionality. That is, the structural and psychological see-sawing between momentary triumph and loss is as self-generated and unresolvable as her anxieties which she endlessly attempts to master.

She carries within her both the formidably strong impulse to become someone she is not and cannot, by definition, be—in secular terms, a human being free from certain paralyzing gender-based constraints, accepted for herself, and, in spiritual terms, the virgin-martyr saint (an impulse which pushes her into the realm of momentary gain and at times more than ephemeral triumph)—and an equally powerful sense of self-censure toward her own inappropriateness. This self-censure and apprehension of inappropriateness are, though frequently objectified in her enemies, indelible parts of her psyche, consciousness, and text. One of the last summary comments of the *Book* points to her persistent sense of estrangement from her very self: ". . . þe drede þat sche had of hir felyngys was þe grettest scorge þat sche had in erde . . ." (220) [. . . the fear that she had of her feelings was the greatest scourge that she had on earth (261)].

Karma Lochrie locates the main reason for Kempe's wavering sense of identity in the very act of her authoring the text:

> In the transformation of her own life from experience to
> authority—that notorious medieval antithesis so manipulated
> by the Wife of Bath—Kempe as author becomes a cypher to
> herself. . . . This, more than all the scorn, spite, and reproof
> of the world, must have caused her suffering and self-doubt.
> For Kempe to become author, her life to become book, she
> had to undergo an alienation of self which constituted the
> painful final stage along the way to high perfection—a stage
> which an illiterate woman on the margins of society must
> finally travel alone. (55)

The persuasiveness of Lochrie's argument notwithstanding, it is
possible to argue that Kempe's alienation from herself is both more
chronic and more profound a dilemma than that posed by the particular
(and in itself symptomatic) problematics of her status as author. In fact,
the creation of the text (like her life and visions in general) serves
simultaneously to master her deep sense of uncertainty *and*,
paradoxically, to deepen it, uncertainty being practically the sole
certainty she knows. This perennial anxiety then marks the text much
as the ever-visible scar, created by her own bite, marks her hand.

Kempe's is a truly "double-voiced" discourse containing a
"dominant" and a "muted" story (Showalter 266). While the rebellious
stance of the legendary saints written about in the fourteenth century
was an ultimately safe, stylized, and acceptable one, Kempe must have
struck a bit too close to home and been too idiosyncratic for full
appropriation and approval. Nevertheless, she lived a passionate and
uncompromising life of action and rapturous compassion for Christ,
coming close to refashioning herself in the image of the ideal saintly
woman as she understood it. Despite her rebelliousness, however,
Kempe herself has completely accepted and internalized the inherently
contradictory and punishing notions of the good woman her time held,
and thus she was bound to remain forever tense and doubtful of her own
worth and of the worth of her experience. If, as David Aers argues, she
"catalyzes specifically masculine anxieties about potential female
autonomy, the potential freedom of will to select life-projects in which
servicing males is not on the agenda" (100–01) (and, surely, the
traveling virgin-martyr saint quintessentially personifies such a drive for
female autonomy), she also fully internalizes the same anxieties. The
subjunctive is telling in Kempe's following words to Christ: "Þu art
as gracyows to me *as þei* I wer as clene a mayden as any in þis

worlde . . ." (141) [You are as gracious to me *as though* I were as pure a maiden as any is in this world . . . (180) emphasis added]. Kempe and her story thus remain poised on the borderline between saintly "arrivedness" and creaturely, even mad, defeat: the failure to become her cherished model. Appropriately enough, the narrative and thematic structures of her story, too, finally, remain open-ended.

Barnard College

NOTES

1. In *Mystic and Pilgrim* Clarissa W. Atkinson points to the widespread and intense anxiety over related questions of discernment of spirits, religious fervor, spiritual direction, and female visionaries in general in Kempe's lifetime (127). See also Karma Lochrie for an argument that "Kempe's chief concern is to legitimize both her life and her *Book*, that is, to establish her authority both as writer and as mystic" (34).

2. David Aers speaks of Kempe's "drive" as "potentially both effect and cause of a compulsive discontent, a haunting anxiety which seeks alleviation from the very processes that stimulate it" (79).

3. Discussing Kempe's sufferings, Aers writes, "These torments are not presented simply as external impositions on an integrated, homogeneous self but the guilty product of her own struggles for an identity which would enable a relative autonomy in relation to priest, husband, and others. The cost of this individual struggle is a terrifying isolation combined with immense aggression against her husband, her community, and the self formed by conflicting tendencies within it" (85).

4. Lochrie observes the same in the following light: "To the degree that she is rejected and slandered by the townspeople of Lynn and the clerks and friars of the Church, she is assured as an author and as a mystic of God's grace. As Kempe is well aware, an identity based on social and institutional rejection is a tenuous and dangerous one" (38).

5. In her "Margery Kempe and the English Devotional Tradition" Susan Dickman shows how Kempe's equation of sound spirituality and social humiliation becomes obsessive after her pilgrimage to Jerusalem (170).

6. When reading Christ's reversals as projections of Kempe, I do not mean to imply that Margery Kempe is "imagining" or fabricating her visions; nor do I mean to discount or undermine the possibility of reading

these passages "straight." It seems to me inescapable, however, even from the theoretical standpoint of an orthodox Christian reader, that to a large extent, the "Christ" of the visionary *is* indeed the narrative/psychological construction of the mystic herself—the embodiment of the mystic's desire.

7. As Nancy Partner argues, clothing "was not a trivial concern, and not an especially feminine concern, in the Middle Ages. One's dress was a display of rank and wealth and a *symbolic demand for whatever deference and privileges belong to one's status.*" See "And Most of All for Inordinate Love," especially 256.

8. Spells of spiritual dryness, as it were (which might be another model to interpret Kempe's loss of tears), of course, occur frequently in mystical literature. The focus here, however, appears to be explicitly on how the "creature's" sudden change and unusual silence will affect her public's understanding of her.

9. One way of interpreting Kempe's recurring tribulations centering on the endangerment of her chastity, in particular, is to see them as poignant reminders of the female body reasserting itself as a burden and a liability (insofar that it has to be defended), despite Kempe's fervent desire to redefine, or at least bend, the conventionally sanctioned limitations of her gender.

10. In addition to Christ's revelations being patterned in this manner, the ebb and flow of money and food, two crucially significant entities in enabling Kempe's travels and very existence, emerge as important structural *loci* of expressing the constant movement from woe to weal, a subject indeed meriting further future study. Kempe's connection with food (diet, availability thereof, companions with whom to share it, etc.) is richly problematic; it is by no means incidental that her odd diet gives rise to a proverbial utterance her contemporaries repeat with contempt, "fals flesch, þu xalt ete non heryng" (244) [false flesh, you shall eat no herring (288)].

11. As Estelle C. Jelinek argues, an "apparent[ly] disjointed or fragmented style" in general characterizes early autobiographical and visionary writing by women (15). So the style of *The Book of Margery Kempe* is not atypical as far as its lack of chronological or coherently synthesized presentation is concerned. I would argue, however, that the specific structural shape this fragmented style takes is indeed a unique feature of Kempe's text, or, at the very least, it characterizes her autobiography more pervasively than it does the writing of other women visionaries.

12. Nancy Partner points to the *Book* as having a "sense of struggling near-chaos" and argues that "two stories, one sequential, one linear, and progressive in time and spiritual perfection, the other timeless, static, regressive in its replaying scenes of desire and shame, *both* demand a hearing in Margery's narrative" ("And Most of All" 255).

13. For structural analyses of these genres, see Alison Goddard Elliott, *Roads to Paradise: Reading the Lives of the Early Saints*; Erich Auerbach, *Mimesis: The Representation of Reality in Western Literature*; and Vladimir Propp, *Morphology of the Folktale*.

14. Incidentally, the fact that Kempe may have been construed as potentially saintly by her contemporaries literally and repeatedly comes across in the text. One man, for example, implores her, "Damsel, yf euyr þu be seynt in Heuyn, prey for me" (130) [If ever you're a saint in heaven, lady, pray for me (168)].

15. Aers sees Kempe's "reinfantilization of Jesus" as a gesture which "enabled [her] to identify with the 'good' mother in a way that her experience in the earthly family had denied. This identification made reparation possible for her objections to traditional female roles and tasks while it offered an idealized object for her 'maternal' care . . ." (105).

16. Jelinek puts it, "A pious woman, [Kempe] was nonetheless a maverick for her time and circumstances; she loved clothes and fine jewelry, and tried her hand at various business ventures. Such vanity and industriousness were considered unfitting in a virtuous woman and earned her society's criticism, even before she chose her religious vocation" (16). See also Mary G. Mason, "The Other Voice: Autobiographies of Women Writers," who sees Kempe engaged in an "attempt . . . to discover herself in worlds usually opposed but here joined by the being of the autobiographer" (42).

17. See Atkinson and Aers for detailed analyses of Margery Kempe's historical, religious, and economic contexts.

18. It is also true, of course, that one of the most salient features of mysticism, in general, is the propensity for paradox and the loss or blurring of distinctions between subject and object. Perhaps Kempe can be viewed as one who literally lives out these "features" of the mystic rather than, as her more sophisticated and intellectually complex contemporaries (e.g., Julian of Norwich) who had expressed them in their writings in a less direct, more metaphorized, manner.

19. For a discussion of the concept of the repetition compulsion, see Sigmund Freud, *Beyond the Pleasure Principle*, in particular 6–11.

VOICE, AUTHORITY, AND BLASPHEMY IN *THE BOOK OF MARGERY KEMPE*

David Lawton

For it is conuenyent þe wyf to be homly wyth hir husbond. Be
he neuyr so gret a lorde & sche so powr a woman whan he
weddyth hir, ȝet þei must ly to-gedir & rest to-gedir in joy &
pes. Ryght so mot it be twyx þe & me, for I take non hed what
þu hast be but what þu woldist be. And oftyn-tymes haue I
telde þe þat I haue clene forȝoue þe alle thy synnes. Þerfore
most I nedys be homly wyth þe & lyn in þi bed wyth þe.
Dowtyr, thow desyrest gretly to se me, & þu mayst boldly,
whan þu art in þi bed, take me to þe as for þi weddyd husbond,
as thy derworthy derlyng, & as for thy swete sone, for I wyl
be louyd as a sone schuld be louyd wyth þe modyr & wil þat þu
loue me, dowtyr, as a good <wife> owyth to loue hir husbond.
& þerfor þu mayst boldly take me in þe armys of þi sowle &
kyssen my mowth, myn hed, & my fete as swetly as thow
wylt. (90)

[For it is appropriate for the wife to be on homely terms with
her husband. Be he ever so great a lord and she ever so poor a
woman when he weds her, yet they must lie together and rest
together in joy and peace. Just so must it be between you and
me, for I take no heed of what you have been but what you
would be, and I have often told you that I have clean forgiven
you all your sins.

Therefore I must be intimate with you and lie in your bed
with you. Daughter, you greatly desire to see me, and you may
boldly, when you are in bed, take me to you as your wedded
husband, as your dear darling, and as your sweet son, for I
want to be loved as a son should be loved by the mother, and I
want you to love me, daughter, as a good wife ought to love

93

her husband. Therefore you can boldly take me in the arms of
your soul and kiss my mouth, my head, and my feet as sweetly
as you want.] (126–27)

The addressee is Kempe; the speaker is of course Jesus. The
passage has been much quoted since the discovery of the Butler-Bowden
manuscript in 1934, and has determined many responses to *The Book of
Margery Kempe* in its full form. I assume here—on plausible but not
invulnerable grounds—that the full form was largely unknown in the
fifteenth century, at least outside Mount Grace, the important
Carthusian house in Yorkshire where the manuscript (now British
Library Additional manuscript 61823) was preserved. Certainly, the
collection of pious sayings published by Wynkyn de Worde in 1501
gives no sense of Kempe as the overwhelming personality to be met in
The Book. There is no direct historical evidence to support most of the
detail of her book, beyond her existence, and no local cult pushing for
canonization after her death. This essay treats with twentieth-century
views of Kempe and twentieth-century guesses about why her book
seems to have failed to endure in the fifteenth century: guesses, that is,
about why Kempe failed, as a saint or as a writer, and about why she
was excluded from both the literary and the ecclesiastical canons.

I leave until the end the question of whether she was in fact so
excluded: what matters for now is the overwhelming sense in the
criticism that she was, the agreement among critics who agree about
nothing else that she failed, and their sense that the failure and the
exclusion require explaining. The explanations have fluctuated between
eccentricity—on a sliding scale of hysteria, unreliability, religious
megalomania, even paranoid schizophrenia—and, on the other hand,
heterodoxy, or blasphemy, of the type that canon law calls indirect: that
is, not that Kempe sets out to defame Jesus but in her text he
nonetheless is defamed, by association with Kempe, and so she does
take his name in vain. The first kind of explanation was common
among male critics, especially in holy orders, well into the 1970's;[1] the
second kind, emphasizing Kempe's independence and creativity, was
first offered as a tentative reorientation in the work of Clarissa Atkinson
and Susan Dickman, and has been strongly historicized and theorized in
the study of the *via positiva* of laywomen and men in fourteenth- and
fifteenth-century Europe.[2] Sometimes the two types of judgment
converge, as in Barry Windeatt's gratuitous value judgment: "we cannot
claim Margery's *Book* to be the autobiography of a great mystic—the

quality of her mystical experience prevents this—but it remains one of the most immediate 'Lives' of the period" (23).[3] The text is at once demoted out of religious writing and promoted into literature, into the critic's field of expertise.

Underlying both approaches is the premise that on the face of it Kempe is an unlikely vessel of divine revelation: a woman, uneducated (by her own account illiterate), long married and having given birth to no fewer than fourteen children, an entrepreneur, an inveterate pilgrim and talker. She has taken on an almost exclusively fictional force, a character midway between the Wife of Bath and Moll Flanders; and where she is seen as insisting upon the literal reading of her experience, she invites judgment—favorable or, more commonly, hostile. Here is Wolfgang Riehle's response to the passage I first quoted: "in Margery there is frequently a crude realism which intrudes in a very embarrassing manner" (38). Riehle's remark resembles Ute Stargardt's complaint, equating the concretization of metaphors with "distortions":

> Like the Beguines and the Dominican nuns, Margery channeled her suppressed sexual needs into her adoration of the heavenly bridegroom and, as was the case with these women who preceded her, it is in this aspect of her religious utterances and experiences where the most serious perversions of mystical concepts occur. Her consistent inability to differentiate between metaphor and actual experience appears with most embarrassing clarity in her descriptions of her soul's marriage to the Godhead. (299–300)

If Riehle and Stargardt are right, Kempe stands convicted of heresy and blasphemy—not against some ecclesiastically or critically sanctioned model of what mysticism should be like, but against the doctrine of the Trinity and the Person of Jesus. Yet this step is never taken: instead, the suspicion is left hanging over Kempe's head without being pressed, making a bizarre counterpart in modern critical practice to the continual male slanders and innuendo from within the fifteenth-century Church, as described in *The Book of Margery Kempe*. Riehle and Stargardt are not appalled or horrified; they are, they write, "embarrassed." There is surely no need to spare critics from embarrassments they have worked hard for; but I shall advance a very different reading of the textual reception of *The Book of Margery Kempe*, and its scope for interpretation.

The notion of Margery Kempe as eccentric actually rests mainly on the premise of blasphemy even where that premise is not overt. If her book is not blasphemous, it may not be particularly eccentric either—or rather, its distinctive characteristics will be cultural or subcultural rather than personal. This essay yields a new reading of the place of Kempe's book in fifteenth-century English culture. But it has a bearing beyond this, on the types of authority in that culture, and on the cultural importance of blasphemy to the production of literary and other texts. I shall argue that the issue of potential blasphemy has misled practitioners of criticism who have approached Kempe with tools more suited to Langland and Chaucer, to a literary canon. I shall develop this contrast with extended reference to Langland and Chaucer in order to gauge the extent of the difference. Admittedly, the division this implies between literary and non-literary is vulnerable, but we need something like it to make sense of fifteenth-century writing and editorial practices of scribes: the fifteenth century marks the inception of the self-consciously constructed English literary manuscript. The aim is not to give an account of why Kempe, having failed, was excluded. It is rather to give a full explanation of why *The Book of Margery Kempe* was ever preserved. So the remainder of this paper deals partly with *The Book of Margery Kempe* and partly with the prisms through which modern readers try to read it, which include other sorts of writing.

It is all too easy to cast Kempe in the role of a great English primitive, someone Stanley Spencer could have painted stepping heavily out of a grave in Cookham churchyard. In fact, the Kempe presented in *The Book of Margery Kempe* is first and foremost a knowledgeable laywoman—so knowledgeable that overtly at issue throughout the text is the question of her Latinity.

"Eyþyr þow hast þe Holy Gost er ellys þow hast a devyl wythin þe," says a young monk of Lincoln, "for þat þu spekyst her to vs it is Holy Writte"—that is, Latin (28) [Either you have the Holy Ghost or else you have a devil within you because what you speak here to us is of Holy Writ]. The problem is not Margery's orthodoxy, but orthodoxy from a channel to which it would normally be rationed. What Kempe has to prove is not erudition but inspiration: to the men of law in Lincoln, who profess themselves amazed at her knowledge, Kempe asserts no book learning but the linguistic power of the Holy Ghost:

"We han gon to scole many ȝerys, & ȝet arn we not sufficient
to answeryn as þu dost. Of whom hast þu þis cunnyng?" &
sche seyd, "Of þe Holy Gost." Þan askyd þei, "Hast þu þe Holy
Gost?" "Ȝa, serys," seyd sche, "þer may no man sey a good
word wyth-owtyn þe ȝyft of þe Holy Gost, for owr lord Jhesu
Crist seyd to his disciplys, 'Stody not what ȝe schal sey, for
it schal not be ȝowr spiryt þat schal spekyn in ȝow, but it
schal be þe spiryt of þe Holy Gost.'" And thus owr Lord ȝaf
her grace to answer hem, worschepyd mote he be. (135)

[There were men of law who said to her, "We have gone to
school many years, and yet we are not sufficient to answer as
you do. From whom do you get this knowledge?"
    And she said, "From the Holy Ghost."
    Then they said, "Do you have the Holy Ghost?"
    "Yes, sirs," said she, "no one may say a good word
without the gift of the Holy Ghost, for our Lord Jesus Christ
said to his disciples, 'Do not study what you shall say, for it
shall not be your spirit that shall speak in you, but it shall be
the spirit of the Holy Ghost.'"
    And thus our Lord gave her grace to answer them,
worshiped may he be.] (174)

It is the Holy Ghost, then, not Kempe, who knows to quote Matthew
10:19–20. Oddly, however, it is her claim to inspiration that is
highlighted, not the more obvious question of derivation, by the priest
who tells her, "Now wote I wel þat þu hast a deuyl wyth-inne þe, for I
her hym spekyn in þe to me" (85) [Now I well know that you have a
devil inside you, for I hear him speak in you to me], and from the
steward of Leicester who offers as a rationale for his attempted rape: "Þu
xalt telle me wheþyr þu hast þis speche of God or of þe Devyl" (113)
[You shall tell me whether you get this talk from God or from the
Devil]. What that steward offers her before his "fowyll rebawdy wordys"
is a test in Latin: as soon as he sets eyes on her, he begins to speak
Latin. When Kempe responds: "Spekyth Englysch, yf ȝow lyketh, for I
vndyrstonde not what ȝe say" [Speak English, please, since I do not
understand what you are saying], the steward counters: "Þu lyest falsly
in pleyn Englysch" (113) [You lie falsely in plain English]. When the
Abbot of Leicester examines her on the articles of the faith, Kempe
goes well beyond the range of a vernacular penitential manual: the
orthodoxy of her answer on the sacrament is in every sense a studied
performance. Chapter 51 is even more suggestive: a great cleric

examines Kempe on her understanding of a passage of Scripture (Genesis 1:22), and Kempe correctly underscores the spiritual sense as well as the literal. What is of particular interest here, in a text that so often works as if by reported dialogue, is that the words, *Crescite et multiplicamini*, "Go forth and multiply," are quoted only in Latin and nowhere translated into English. If the lay reader of the *Book* is confused, Kempe is not: she glosses words that she, like the reader, is supposed not to understand.

Before this is discounted as a simple scribal slip, it is worth recalling the extraordinary communication between Kempe and her German confessor on pilgrimage. The German is asked to dinner by the English in Kempe's party, among them an English priest and "satt al stille in a maner of heuynes for cawse he vndirstod not what þei seyden in Englysch les þan þei spokyn Latyn. & þei dede it in purpose, hys vnwetyng, to preuyn ȝyf he vndirstod Englysch or not" (97) [sat quietly in a sort of swoon, because he did not understand what they said in English, but only when they spoke Latin. And they did it on purpose, unbeknown to him, to prove whether he understood English or not]. It transpires that he does not, except when Kempe speaks to him and "telde in hyr owyn langage in Englysch a story of Holy Writte whech sche had lernyd of clerkys whil sche was at home in Inglond" [told a story in her own English language which she had learned from the clerks while she was at home in England] and this he is able to repeat *in Latin*—"for he cowde neyþyr speke Englysch ne vndirstondyn Englisch saue only aftyr hir tunge" (98) [for he neither spoke English nor understood it except from her tongue]. There is a minor miracle here, of course, and a suppressed apostolic claim, but what I find most suggestive in this bizarre and self-conscious passage is the inference that English from the tongue of Kempe is the equivalent of Latin to a clerk. Divine grace bestows upon Kempe's English an honorary Latinity.

Then, one might ask, are there signs of such Latinity in the production of *The Book of Margery Kempe*? There are, I think: provisionally, because it will take a lot of work to establish beyond doubt quotations in this text from texts available both in Latin and English. We have rarely been looking for such quotation, because we have mostly taken the text's word for it that it cannot be there. Twice, of course, the text lists its own close relations, such as Hilton and Rolle, and provides a plausible context: these were the texts read (and sometimes translated?) to Kempe by her confessor/amanuensis. One text, the *Liber Celestis* of St. Bridget, is so important that it receives editorial endorsement from Jesus himself, who makes Kempe the second authorizer of Bridget's authority, characteristically, by aligning Kempe's voice with Bridget's book: "For I telle þe forsoþe ryght as I spak to Seynt Bryde ryte so I speke to þe, dowtyr, & I telle þe trewly it is trewe euery word þat is wretyn in Brides boke, & be þe it xal be knowyn for very trewth" (47) [For in truth I tell you, just as I spoke to St. Bridget, just so I speak to you, daughter, and I tell you truly that every word that is written in Bridget's book is true, and through you shall be recognized as truth indeed].[4] There is also, however, a degree of detail that may imply a source open at a page rather than a memorial reconstruction or a general indebtedness, like the use in Chapter 28 of the dove-cote conceit derived from Rolle's *Meditations on the Passion*. There are many such biblical references. There may well be references to Rolle's Latin as well as his English works, especially the *Incendium Amoris*. Above all is the debt to the text that is least acknowledged, that (as it were) plays Boccaccio to Kempe's *Troilus*, the *Meditationes Vitae Christi* (*MVC*) of the pseudo-Bonaventura. Kempe's most extensive meditation on the Passion, in Chapters 79–81, probably needs re-annotating on the premise that it might actually be a crafted collage of quotations from major sources. It is plausibly an ingenious and densely textured combination of the *MVC* and Bridget.

All credit to Barry Windeatt who recognizes the similarities between Kempe's account and the *MVC*, twice referring to the *MVC* in his notes on Chapter 81, the references, detailed though they are, headed with a bare "cf." because their status was unresolved. Once one starts looking at the sections of the *MVC* toward which Windeatt directs attention, it becomes apparent that Kempe's account is modeled closely on it but with significant differences, particularly in the deposition of Jesus from the cross. Here (Ch. 80) there is a departure from the *MVC* in order to introduce the marble stone of deposition, a stone that Windeatt comments, "Margery had seen . . . for herself in Jerusalem" (326 n. 7). Kempe's own eyes, however, are at best, if at all, a secondary witness. The reference to the stone is imitated from St. Bridget and echoes her account. Of interest too is the stress upon the manner in which the body of Jesus is cherished on deposition, the Virgin Mary embracing his head and shoulders and Mary Magdalen his feet. This is a motif never particularly common in England but found in Italian art from the thirteenth century on.[5] Kempe's development of it goes beyond the scope of Nicholas Love's translation of the *MVC*.[6] Indeed, it is vital for Kempe to assume the role both of the Virgin and the Magdalen. The whole Passion sequence is distinguished by two frame-breaking interventions on Kempe's part. One occurs when, not content with speaking to the Virgin and being her handmaiden like St. Bridget, Kempe rushes in to comfort her: where St. Bridget converses, Kempe makes a hot drink. The other is when Kempe takes over the grieving with Jesus immediately before the Crucifixion, and falls to the ground weeping and embracing his feet, thereby taking upon herself the role of Mary Magdalen. The combination of roles covers the spectrum of wife, mother, daughter, and lover, and is a typology familiar from other European mystics such as Bridget herself, Catherine of Siena, and Dorothy of Montau. Evidently, Kempe understands very well the significance of Jesus's feet and her own relation to them in the role of a Magdalen: she is, in a limited sense, learned.

Scholars have not explored the extent of Kempe's learning—that is, Latinity—for they have mostly taken at face value the disclaimers of the text (disclaimers most would expect to be rhetorical if the writer were a male). At least two critics, however, have acknowledged it and allowed for it in their discussion of *The Book of Margery Kempe*. Anthony Goodman looks at Kempe's scriptural quotations and the readings derived from mystical treatises and concludes that here we have the hallmark of activity by the compilers mentioned in the text itself. John C. Hirsh concludes an interesting discussion on a note that raises as many questions as it begs: "it may be confidently stated that the second scribe, no less than Kempe, should be regarded as the author of *The Book of Margery Kempe*" ("Author and Scribe" 150). In other words, the qualities emphasized here are present in the text, but they are there because, as the text itself witnesses, authorized male clerics, knowledgeable if not learned, put them there. Here is a final impediment to a textual view of Margery Kempe: clerical mediation, the masculine construction of the feminine.

Readers must allow for such mediation on several levels, but I cannot accept that the explanation comes close to being the last word on Kempe. It is conventional, admittedly, for the works of women mystics to be mediated in some way by their confessors. Even St. Teresa wrote for hers. The numerous books of St. Bridget are the compilations of Archbishop Gregersson, and it is Bridget's confessors who are credited with translating into Latin what was originally written in Swedish. *The Flowing Light of the Godhead*, by Mechthild of Magdeburg, is a text made problematic by the activity of its editor, Heinrich Halle. The *Life* of Dorothy of Montau was written by her confessor, and that of Mary of Oignies by Jacques de Vitry. But there is simply no account of textual mediation as complex and as circumstantial, almost wantonly obscure, as that provided in *The Book of Margery Kempe*. Its outlines are almost too familiar to require recapitulation. If it had been designed by Vladimir Nabokov, it could no better serve the end of depriving the mediator of any authority whatever: it emasculates the pen. The second scribe reports that he could make neither head nor tail of the first scribe's ill-written book, for it was neither good English nor German. It was only at length, when he began to trust in Kempe's prayers, that he was able to understand it at all. Then his eyes failed, and spectacles were no help: again, only Kempe's intercession makes the task even possible. Even during the writing, his only role is that of backslider (dramatized in Chapter 62 as a drama of other texts), notwithstanding that the writing of the book is a clerical project, repeatedly pressed upon a reluctant Kempe throughout the work. The last chapter of Book I represents the activity of writing as an act of charitable labor on Kempe's part, one which interfered with her prayers, but proved recuperative for the scribe—who himself starts weeping in response to the fire of love. He is there as a part of Kempe's story, proof in himself of her efficacy as intercessor. His other major role is to make an inordinate to-do about the sequence of the book and the fact that it falls short of some notion of order. The point is only to underscore the dependence of the writing on Kempe's dictation and memory—literally, on her voice.

Other than this, the use of the editorial first-person pronoun in the text could hardly be more tentative. Take the opening of Chapter 4: "Ower mercyful Lord Crist Ihesu, seyng this creaturys presumpcyon, sent hir, as is wrete befor, iij ʒer of greet temptacyon, of þe whech on of þe hardest I purpos to wrytyn for exampyl of hem þat com aftyr . . ." (14) [Our merciful Lord Christ Jesus, seeing this creature's presumption, sent her—as is written before—three years of great temptations, of one of the hardest of which I intend to write as an example to those who come after]. Who is "I" here? Is the judgment that of the scribe, and if so, the first or the second, or merely a translation of Kempe's words substituting words for writing in the place of words for speech? No reconstruction is possible: for practical purposes "I purpos" is as unmarked as "as is wrete befor." The personal pronoun is hardly the imprint of a firm editor.

I suggest that we reverse the notion of editorial control. Here, the text constructs its editor, and it places him in the role of reader. At least, it does so if we apply to *The Book of Margery Kempe* Domna C. Stanton's lucid generalization in her essay in *The Female Autograph*, "the speaking 'I' constitute[s] the reading 'you' as the representation of society's view of women and thus is the personification of the writing interdiction" ("Autogynography" 13).[7] This text is a perfect literal example: its first reader is its scribe and fulfills a generic "writing interdiction." It is conventionally acceptable for a woman mystic not to write. Positively, it is a helpful generic attribute of a woman mystic to dictate. But there is a radical dislocation here between writing and speech. In the medieval vocabulary made newly familiar by Alastair Minnis, the most that the second scribe claims to be is *compiler*, and that leaves Kempe—the illiterate of the book—in the role of author. Generically, the editor is there as part of Kempe's story, the male cleric subordinate to the laywoman. Authority thus passes from what is written to what is spoken: to voice.

I do not use "voice" here as some might be tempted to use it of *The Canterbury Tales*. Nothing would be gained by going through *The Book of Margery Kempe* attempting to isolate Kempe's voice or that of any other character. Nor do I intend "voices" in the polyphonic sense used in a fine discussion of Kempe by Sidonie Smith: "[t]he voices that haunt her text from beginning to end—inside its pages and outside—are the voices of male church authorities" (79). By voice I mean simply the sense of speech, a series of speech-acts that commentators pick up on again and again. For Smith herself, "there is the voice of Kempe's narrative, intimate, close to the surface of the text, self-effusive rather than self-effacing[, a]lways in the foreground, never in the background" (82). Windeatt writes constantly of Kempe's "voice" and "accent," and talks much of the relation between that and the structure of her work: "In these dictated recollections of a woman who could not read or write it is human speech itself which continually catches and sharpens the attention" (22).

Windeatt catches the frequency of his verbs for speech from *The Book of Margery Kempe*, from the "ful many holy spechys & dalyawns þat owyr Lord spak to hir sowle" (42), the "holy dalyawns þat owyr Lord Ihesu Crist dalyed to hir sowle" (72), the "wonderful spechys &

dalyawns whech owr Lord spak and dalyid to hyr sowle" (2). To the great cleric who produces a book against her from which he quotes St. Paul, forbidding women to preach, Kempe replies: "I preche not, ser . . . I vse but comownycacyon & good wordys" (126) [I do not preach, sir . . . I use only conversation and good words]. It is fitting that St. Paul is sent to comfort her because she had "suffyrd mech tribulacyon for cawse of hys wrytyng" (160) [suffered much tribulation because of his writing]—writing which is here subject to continual verbal update. Writing in this book is seen as something provisional, always on the verge of being overthrown by speech; and all the fuss that the compiler makes about the blemishes of the book—"For, þow þe mater be wretyn be-forn þis, neuyr-þe-lesse it fel aftyr þis" (165) [for, although that matter is written before this, nevertheless it happened after this]— confirms and enacts this provisionality. Chapter 25 opens by noting a breach of temporal order on grounds of "felyng" and, as we would say, relevance ("conuenyens"), but it also imitates a spoken interruption. At length the book simply ends, and Kempe is still going: voice again is superior to the edited text, actively outlasting it. As Windeatt writes: "She has simply ceased to speak" (15). It is Kempe's gift of speech that amazes clerics—"Damsel, I her seyn God spekyth onto þe," says a Monk (26) [I hear it said that God speaks to you]; and it is a clerical interference with Kempe's speaking (of her secret) that induces madness at the beginning of the book. Even where she cannot speak her grief, she voices it—in crying, weeping, mourning, roaring, and so on.

There is the corrective note at the end of Book I: "sumtyme þat sche vndirstod bodily it was to ben vndirstondyn gostly" (220) [For sometimes, what she understood physically was to be understood spiritually]. In fact, the emphasis on actual bodily contact, on direct access to Jesus through the five senses, is strong but guarded. *The Book of Margery Kempe* goes to some pains to remind its readers that the conversations with Jesus take place in Kempe's soul; it is more careful and less radical in this than the Middle English translation of St. Catherine of Siena's *Dialogus, The Orchard of Syon*, the *Incipit* of which speaks of visions "3ouen . . . to þe intellecte of þe glorioys virgyn . . . when sche was in contemplacioun inrapt of spirit, & she *herynge actueli* and in þe same tyme tellynge tofore meny what oure Lord God spoke in her" (18) [given . . . to the intellect of the glorious virgin . . . when she was rapt in spiritual contemplations, and she *hearing actually* and at the same time telling before many what our Lord

God spoke in her] (emphasis added). Kempe mainly avoids the unforced
doctrinal error of "herynge actueli," but retains the link with bodily
senses by a metonymy between vision and locution, in the specks of
light which "sche sey wyth hir bodily eyne" [she saw with her bodily
eyes] and of which Jesus tells her: "Be þis tokyn, dowtyr, beleue it is
God þat spekyth in þe" (88) [By this token, daughter, believe it is God
who speaks in you]. Vision here is secondary to locution.

This is not some eccentricity or spiritual failing of Kempe's.
The importance of the locution is primary in St. Teresa's
autobiography, Chapter 25 of which deals with true and false locutions
after a digression on several types of prayer and their efficacy. A true
locution, writes St. Teresa, confers a new order of eloquence; and divine
locutions "fall upon the inner ear with the authenticity of actual speech"
(13).[8] *The Book of Margery Kempe* puts forward a similar rationale,
also with colloquial eloquence:

> And I telle þe trewly, dowtyr, euery good thowt & euery good
> desyr þat þu hast in þi sowle is þe speche of God, al yf it be so
> þat þu her me not spekyn to þe sumtyme as I do sumtyme to þi
> cler vndirstondyng. And þerfor, dowtyr, I am as an hyd God in
> þi sowle. (204–05)
>
> [And I tell you truly, daughter, every good thought and every
> good desire that you have in your soul is the speech of God,
> even if you do not hear me speaking to you sometimes, as I
> sometimes do to your clear understanding. And therefore,
> daughter, I am like a hidden God in your soul.]

For Kempe's understanding of locutions one need look no further than
The Scale of Perfection. Hilton's treatment of the fire of love in
Chapter 26 is followed by his defense of vocalized prayer in Chapters
28 and 29: the next stage of the fire of love (Ch. 31) leads into "the
third degree of prayer, which is only in the heart and without words"
(Ch. 32), and this itself leads quickly into meditations on the Passion
and, by inference, the power so to meditate. Kempe makes all but the
self-same distinctions, and is granted an exemption from the need to
cease vocalization:

> And I haue oftyn-tymes, dowtyr, teld þe þat thynkyng,
> wepyng, & hy contemplacyon is þe best lyfe in erthe. And þu
> xalt haue mor meryte in Heuyn for o ȝer of thynkyng in þi

mende þan for an hundryd ȝer of preyng wyth þi mowth, & ȝet
þu wylt not leuyn me, for þu wilt byddyn many bedys whedyr I
wil or not. And ȝet, dowtyr, I wyl not be displesyd wyth þe
whedir þu thynke, sey, or speke, for I am alwey plesyd with
þe. (89–90)

[And I have often told you, daughter, that thinking, weeping,
and high contemplation is the best life on earth. You shall
have more merit in heaven for one year of thinking in your
mind than for a hundred years of praying with your mouth; and
yet you will not believe me, for you will pray many beads
whether I wish it or not. And yet, daughter, I will not be
displeased with you whether you think, say, or speak, for I am
always pleased with you.] (126)

The need for speech binds both parties: the Second Person of the Trinity
is forced to speak the words of the marriage ceremony in order for
Kempe to consent to marriage. Again, Hilton furnishes a sufficient
gloss. The secret voice of Jesus represents the movements of grace in
the human soul. If God is both Love and Word, Jesus is always speaker
and lover. For a male cleric, this may lend itself to trans-gender
metaphor. For a woman mystic, especially a lay one in the world, it
may be neither stably literal nor stably metaphorical.

Whatever else it may be at a given time, locution is never
merely a capricious exercise of speech; rather, it calculatedly claims a
privilege. The issue in *The Book of Margery Kempe* is therefore not
voice but authority. Authority is taken away from writing and given to
voice in a manner that rests not on individual foible but a doctrine of
locution found not only in later medieval women mystics but also, for
example, in Walter Hilton. I have tried to show that this is nevertheless
a more complex textual performance than is usually represented, and I
have sought to trace some levels of connection between "voice" and
"book." Surely it is important to insist that the textual strategies of
The Book of Margery Kempe rest on subtle theological foundations.
Equally, however, I am reminded of Hélène Cixous's proposition that
femininity in writing can be discerned above all in a privileging of
voice: "Writing and voice . . . are woven together."[9] If anything,
Margery Kempe as historical subject recedes further from view, split
between the writing and the voice, neither the writing nor the voice
being stably or consistently "hers."

If Kempe's voice is unstable, the voice of Jesus in this work is not. It invariably expresses spiritual relationship, however provocative its metaphors. Such a discourse is arguably quite constant in its metaphoricity or otherwise. Is it more or less metaphorical to have Jesus talking to you than it is to have him touching you? (Kempe uses the words "speche" and "dalliance" interchangeably.) However one categorizes this transplanting of *The Song of Songs* to an East Anglian bedchamber, it does not seem at all volatile, or produce any developed doubleness of meaning: readers do not have to beware of fluctuating or variable levels of metaphoricity as we read. Arguably too the notorious passage quoted near the beginning of this essay communicates a false sense of difficulty through its sole gesture of caution, the inclusion of the reference to the soul—"take me in the arms of your soul"—which actually incorporates a gloss on what the passage would have to be taken to mean anyway. It is already quite over-determined.

That may help explain why, according to the *Book* itself, Kempe's religious betters—apart from those who simply objected to being cried over and shouted at—were untroubled by the exact nature of her intimacy with Jesus. Their worry was that she might be a Lollard, and the points she had to satisfy them on were her view of the sacraments and the Church's mediation of Scripture. Against ecclesiastical charges of heresy and accusations of being Oldcastle's daughter, Kempe and the text counterattack with the accusation of blasphemy. The allegation that she is a heretic is always conveniently "sworn with great oaths," and the laywoman is therefore able to rebuke the clergy. But the discourse of heresy and blasphemy in and around the text is actually unrelated to the language of lovelonging; it points rather, like the Latinity of the text, to lay challenge against ecclesiastical authority.

In that challenge lies a general resemblance between *The Book of Margery Kempe* and *Piers Plowman*. What both texts do is to present in an English religious work consideration of materials normally dealt with in Latin, within the clergy, in the Church and (for Langland) the universities. Kempe was (necessarily) a layperson; Langland was not. But that may not be the distinction that counts. Wendy Scase's book, *Piers Plowman and the New Anticlericalism*, does a fine job of demonstrating how *Piers Plowman* takes various kinds of anticlerical discourse—parish priests against friars, friars against monks, monks against parish priests—and compounds them into a general anticlerical position from what (since it is the only one left) can only be a lay viewpoint. Criticism of the Church as institution no longer operates horizontally, across the hierarchy, but vertically from the bottom, denying the validity of hierarchy. In such an analysis, the project of the poem begins to look like a program of subversion; and the very form of the poem, as an extended gloss on Latin quotations, now looks like an act of defiance, of illicit copying, violation of the clergy's confidentiality in order to make public their concerns: taking power in English.

Such strategic subversion is related not to heresy but to sacrilege and, especially, blasphemy. Interest in both sacrilege and blasphemy burgeons, not accidentally, in the outgrowth of serious vernacular texts of the fourteenth century, such as *Handlyng Synne, Cleanness, Piers Plowman*; and it is in the space made by such precursors that *The Book of Margery Kempe* is able to function as the work of a layperson using English, not Latin. The general resemblance between *The Book of Margery Kempe* and *Piers Plowman* extends further. For underlying the unease in Kempe's version of Jesus as her husband/son is her greater discomfort with the doctrine of the Trinity, a discomfort that comes to a head in Chapter 35, where the Father of Heaven proposes marriage to His Godhead. Kempe is reluctant: "for al hir lofe & al hir affeccyon was set in þe manhode of Crist & þerof cowde sche good skylle & sche wolde for no-thing a partyd þerfro" (86) [for all her love and affection were fixed on the manhood of Christ, and of that she did have knowledge and would not be parted from that for anything]. There follows a passage in which Kempe's stress on the corporeality of Christ is vividly realized, as the text recounts how she tried to snatch Italian children from their mothers' arms because they reminded her of the child Jesus, and how

> ȝyf sche sey a semly man, sche had gret peyn to lokyn on hym les þan sche myth a seyn hym þat was boþe God & man. & þerfor sche cryed many tymes & oftyn whan sche met a semly man & wept & sobbyd ful sor in þe manhod of Crist as sche went in þe stretys at Rome. . . . & þerfor it was no wondyr ȝyf sche wer stille & answeryd not þe Fadyr of Hevyn whan he teld hir þat sche xuld be weddyd to hys Godhed. (86–87)

[If she saw a handsome man, she had great pain to look at
him, lest she might see him who was both God and man. And
therefore she cried many times and often when she met a
handsome man, and wept and sobbed bitterly for the manhood
of Christ as she went about the streets of Rome. . . . Therefore
it was not surprising if she was still and did not answer the
Father of Heaven when he told her that she should be wedded
to His Godhead.]

Jesus is forced to intervene in order to inspire an appropriate level of
enthusiasm. If this is orthodox—as Kempe gropes to express the nature
of the Trinity in an opposition of Godhead and manhood that it would
be unduly charitable to describe as dialectic—it is so almost by default.

The doctrine of the Trinity is a particular stumbling block for
serious vernacular writers of the fourteenth and fifteenth centuries. This
may have more to do with the language used and the audience at which
it is aimed than with a desire necessarily to challenge orthodoxy. It is as
if the complex doctrine exists safely in complex Latin, but, for both
writer and reader, is acutely vulnerable to translation. Like the
invocation of the Trinity in the final stanza of Chaucer's *Troilus*, drawn
from Bernard's hymn in the final canto of the *Paradiso*, the exposition
of the Trinity as fist and as taper late in *Piers Plowman* B and C seems
hard-won, a tour-de-force or vernacular watershed. Before it occurs, the
most spectacular blasphemy in A and C texts concerns the Trinity, in a
famous passage in which Dame Study laments the decline of modern
minstrelsy and its falling away from religious themes into bawdy, and
goes on to imagine a learned feast after the minstrels are silent, though
the poor and distressed cry at the gate:

> Ac if thei carpen of Crist, thise clerkes and thise lewed,
> At mete in hir murthe whan mynstrals beth stille,
> Thanne telleth thei of the Trinite [how two slowe the thridde],
> And bryngen forth a balled reson, and taken Bernard to witnesse,
> And puten forth a presumpcion to preve the sothe.
> Thus thei dryvele at hir deys the deitee to knowe,
> And gnawen God with the gorge whanne hir guttes fullen.
>
> (B X 51–57: Schmidt 101)

[If they speak of Christ, these clerks and these laity, in their
cups at dinner when minstrels are quiet, then they speak about
the Trinity, how two slew the third, and adduce a threadbare
reason, and take Bernard as witness, and set up a presumption

> to establish the truth. Thus they drivel at high table about
> knowing deity, and chew on God when their guts are full.]
> (Kane-Donaldson 409)

Though the subject of both is the Trinity, Dame Study's use of blatant blasphemy could hardly differ more from the presumed blasphemy of *The Book of Margery Kempe.* Dame Study sets out to shock and disturb: so successfully that all B-text manuscripts substitute an anodyne reading, "a tale other two," for line 53b. It also reflects a very artful use of blasphemy in an orthodox cause: its target is a heresy such as Arianism, and it uses blasphemy as a classic ecclesiastical substitution for the *idea* of the heresy—as an emotive means of avoiding the need to engage with heretics on a cognitive level. It naturalizes doctrine as dogma: that is, by offering a blasphemous parody of the Trinity it encourages a sense that the righteous beholder, who recognizes the distortion, also thereby understands the doctrine that is being distorted, though this does not follow.

Readers must then add several extra layers of complexity. There is uncertainty about the reliability of the speaker and also the rhetorical direction of the text here; and there is a wider anxiety throughout the surrounding passages. Dame Study's challenge is to the very possibility of a morally valid vernacular writing as embodied in the dreamer's poetic aspirations. How can one make vernacular poems that are not in themselves blasphemous betrayals of Christ, the devil's work, and which corrupt neither oneself nor others? It is as if blasphemy—what *The Catholic Encyclopaedia* calls secularism or modernism—is inherent in the very project of vernacular composition. Hence J.A.W. Bennett stressed that "goliard" meant both versifier and "any clerk who had abandoned or dishonoured his vocation" (99)—and in Langland's case the institutionally sanctioned language of clerkship/clergy, Latin.[10] Dame Study's example hints at a powerful connection between vernacular writing and (Baudelaire's phrase, embellished by Bataille) "the desire to sin."[11] There is no trace of any such attitude or anxiety in Kempe. The difference is the sombre dialogism of the *Piers Plowman* passage.

There is a more decisive contrast still: Chaucer's "Pardoner's Tale," which, on one persistent reading, is a longer version of the same blasphemy as Dame Study's and, symbolically or subliminally, tells "of the Trinity, how two slew the third." This is one tale where allegorical readings thrive. It is told against blasphemy as the rhetorical

culmination of the "cursed synne of alle cursednesse" (PardT 895). The
swearing of the rioters of the Tale wounds the body of Christ, so that
they take on the role of His torturers. The three are a parody Trinity:
"We thre been al ones," they swear (696). The two older ones send the
youngest one to town—Rodney Delasanta reads this as a parody of the
Incarnation; and certainly the actions of all three then parody the
Eucharist and the Crucifixion. The youngest returns with poisoned
bread and wine, and he officiates over their final meal. Before it is over,
he himself as victim lies dead under a tree, riven through the side by
slayers who proclaim their sacrifice by a meal of bread and wine;
murderers who, when they had "acorded . . . to sleen the thridde"
promised to play at dice (835–36). The tale is told against blasphemy
by a self-confessed blasphemer, the sexually anomalous lay Pardoner,
who boasts of his skill in preaching and of taking the divine name in
vain for his own profit—and who tells his tale toying with cakes and
ale that are sometimes interpreted as being proleptic of the eucharistic
parody of his Tale.

The Tale condemns blasphemy, produces blasphemy, and is
blasphemy. And if Chaucer's purpose in this is to condemn blasphemy
by showing two versions of it, then in order to condemn it he must
first speak it. In this respect, the poet is inescapably like the Pardoner,
which is why the Pardoner's artistic performance strikes so many
critics, in diverse ways, as a parodic mirror of the construction of *The
Canterbury Tales*. In this performance we see why another great
vernacular poet put blasphemy, sodomy, and usury together in the
seventh circle of hell as sins against the Holy Ghost, sins of exchange
and of language: blasphemy perverts Scripture into common currency.
Robert Payne sees in "The Pardoner's Tale" Chaucer's return to the
issues of classical rhetoric, can an evil man persuade an audience to do
good? The fifteenth century thought not: beside the vastly effective
peroration of the Tale, an appeal to mankind to cease being untrue to
Christ, the scribe of the Ellesmere manuscript wrote "*Auctor*,"
presumably because he could not bear the thought of being moved by
the ostensible speaker. But "The Pardoner's Tale" induces a chronic
instability, a crisis of voice and of reference, in the interplay between
literal and metaphorical, truth and falsehood; and it seems to occlude the
possibility that any language can escape the circle of paradox it
establishes. Metaphoricity, like blasphemy, is here an infinite

regression. It marks a willed collapse of linguistic and scriptural authority.

The Tale works this collapse of authority in terms of the rhetoric, and the theology, of the lie. Chaucer's interest in the lie occurs because he lacked what we too often forget he lacked: a neutral term, and an easy distinction and defense, for "fiction." He must take authority over his readers and over language itself, in order to make room for his fiction—in order in "The Pardoner's Tale" to turn the substance of Latinate theology into the accident of vernacular fiction. The room is that of literary tradition in English, the room that Salman Rushdie assumed was still available when he wrote *The Satanic Verses*; and Chaucer and Langland actively helped construct it. Margery Kempe did not.

In fact, this is just the ground on which Kempe would have stood in solidarity with the ayatollahs. She does not seek the space of fiction, or the reflexivity of language: we are mistaken to thrust either upon her book. She does not cultivate instability of voice or metaphor, nor does she wish to acknowledge it. Her only challenge to authority is in her desire for recognition by it. She does not set out to write or dictate a literary text; and *The Book of Margery Kempe* has no place in English literary tradition as it was self-consciously constructed (and circumscribed) for and by the fifteenth century. It may be worth speculating that *The Book of Margery Kempe* was never excluded from a literary canon because it never sought to be part of one.

The annotations in the manuscript demonstrate that her book in fact won an unusual form of religious authority. The marginalia in the Mount Grace manuscript respond to Kempe's weeping, or falling down in the fields and roaring, her twisting her head and her neck, her behavior on Holy Thursday which was to do all these things at once and more; and, far from sounding a note of caution or disapproval, they note examples of similar behavior by well-known and respected Carthusians of Mount Grace. Richard Metheley "was wont to say"; "father M was wont so to doo"; "so dyd prior Norton in hys excesse"; "so father RM and father Norton and of the Wakenes of the passyon." I do not see why this should be read as the use of male evidence to support Kempe. It looks more like a recognition of a saintly pattern of behavior, a discovery of an authority that further justifies the clerics. Just as we should reverse the notion of editorial control, so should we reverse the direction of the authority we have tended to see in these comments. The evidence for this is highly persuasive.

The manuscript is either the original described in the text or a very near copy. It is inscribed "Liber Montis Gracie, This boke is of Mountegrace." Mount Grace is the priory from which the English translation of the pseudo-Bonaventure's *Meditations on the Life of Christ* proceeded; and there is evidence that many of its members practiced an extreme form of devotion to the body of Christ and the affective cult of the Passion[12]—none more so than the Richard Metheley cited in the marginalia as one who cried and swooned like Kempe. Metheley translated *The Mirror for Simple Souls*, that difficult and intense book of French *Minnemystik*, the author of which, Marguerite Porete, was put to death by burning for heresy and blasphemy. Metheley did not know that Marguerite Porete was its author, but he saw her text as one for adepts, not for general readers: he translated it not into English but into Latin. The Mount Grace reading of Kempe is, I think, similar. "I wold þou were closyd in an hows of ston" (27) [I wish you were closed up in a house of stone], says a monk of Canterbury to Kempe. This is intended as an insult; yet in this text it serves to confer on Kempe the sought-after status of anchoress and further authorizes her as a role model for Carthusian hermits in their houses of stone.[13] Whether or not Kempe herself ever achieved such privileged enclosure, by being incorporated in a charterhouse, her text did.

Why would male hermits of Mount Grace have regarded Kempe as a spiritually significant expert in crying and roaring? First, for the general reason sketched by Caroline Walker Bynum, which can serve as a final gloss on the passage I first cited:

> If religious women spoke less frequently in gender terms than did religious men, it is because they understood that "man . . . signifies the divinity of the Son of God and woman his humanity" (Mechthild of Magdeburg). And they understood that both equations were metaphorical. But, given the ultimate dichotomy of God and creation, the first was only metaphorical. Man was not divinity. The second ("and woman his humanity") was in some sense, however, literally true. (*Fragmentation* 179)

Second, however, it is because the crying and roaring of Margery Kempe are associated, in the book and in the annotations, with Christ's Passion; and it is clear from the annotations that the men of Mount Grace understood the word "*passio*" as still encompassing the important primary meaning, childbirth. The association is apparent in the work of a Carthusian woman, Marguerite of Oingt:

> Ah, my sweet and lovely Lord, with what love you laboured for me and bore me through your whole life. But when the time approached for you to be delivered, your labour pains were so great that your holy sweat was like great drops of blood that came out from your body and fell on the earth. . . . Ah! Sweet Lord Jesus Christ, who ever saw a mother suffer such a birth! For when the hour of your delivery came, you were placed on the hard bed of the cross . . . and your nerves and all your veins were broken. And truly it is no surprise that your veins burst when in one day you gave birth to the whole world. (qtd. Bynum, *Fragmentation* 162–63)

Bynum points out that it is also used by Richard Rolle and the monk of Farne. It appears too in *The Mirror for Simple Souls*, and in the work of Julian of Norwich. The crying and the roaring are the sounds of labor. And when it comes to labor, Kempe is the expert, not Father Metheley, Prior Norton, and the Carthusians of Mount Grace. Her having borne fourteen children acts as the guarantor of her spiritual authority.

If this is so, then the issue of blasphemy probably did not arise at Mount Grace. The entire history of blasphemy suggests the dangers in unduly emphasizing that Jesus (or, if you are Rushdie, Mahomet) had a body; but these are dangers to which Kempe and her readers at Mount Grace were equally impervious. In its uniquely homely and outspoken use of the Song of Songs, *The Book of Margery Kempe* authoritatively expresses the esoteric spiritual impulses of those distinguished fifteenth-century Carthusians. I do not wish to elide in this another version of Kempe, the woman tormented by her dream of men's genitals in explicit contrast to God's manhood; yet this is a conflict that might itself have struck chords of empathy among male recluses.[14] The reading produces, in sum, a rehistoricizing of *The Book of Margery Kempe*—one that separates it generically and spatially from the texts of a fifteenth-century literary tradition.

In short, if I return to my first question: Was Kempe a blasphemer? No. Chaucer was—it is implicit in the ambition of his writing. Langland worried that he might be. But Kempe's destiny in the fifteenth century, though hardly at all in the twentieth, was to be read more or less justly—if not literally, then univocally. Had Kempe been a blasphemer, she would have had some greater chance of literary currency in spite of being a woman. As it was, her text survived *because* she was a woman—with a woman's voice, and the authority of a woman's body.

University of Sydney

NOTES

1. See, for example, Eric Colledge, "Margery Kempe" and R.M. Wilson, "Three Middle English Mystics."

2. Particularly helpful is David Wallace, "Mystics and Followers in Siena and East Anglia: A Study in Taxonomy, Class, and Cultural Mediation."

3. I should add that Windeatt's introduction is very useful.

4. There are several versions of St. Bridget. See *The Liber Celestis of St. Bridget of Sweden*, ed. Roger Ellis.

5. Gertrud Schiller, *Iconography of Christian Art* 2:167–68.

6. *The Mirrour of the Blessed Lyf of Jesu Crist*, translated by Nicholas Love. For the Latin source I have consulted the translation by Ragusa and Greene, and *Opera Omnia Bonaventurae*.

7. See also Alastair J. Minnis, *Medieval Theory of Authorship*.

8. Cited from Cohen's introduction.

9. Hélène Cixous, *La Jeune Née* 170: translation in Toril Moi, *Sexual/Textual Politics: Feminist Literary Theory* 114. Cf. Shulamith Shahar, *The Fourth Estate: A History of Women in the Middle Ages*: "It seems to us that a comprehensive study of the writings of female mystics, & their comparison with the works of male mystics, could substantiate the claim that much that was attributed to the foibles of their sex could in fact be related to the tenets of the Christian faith" (64).

10. See David Lawton, "The Unity of Middle English Alliterative Poetry" 78.

11. Georges Bataille, *Eroticism* 127–28.

12. See James Hogg, "Mount Grace Charterhouse and Late Medieval English Spirituality."

13. I am indebted through private correspondence to Gina Bloom Fitzmaurice for this point.

14. Richard Kieckhefer, *Unquiet Souls*: "Integral to the notion of sainthood in Christianity is a tension between the imitability and the 'otherness' of the holy personage" (190). Another version of Kempe I should wish to read as simultaneous with mine is that by David Aers, "The Making of Margery Kempe: Individual and Community" in *Community, Gender, and Individual Identity*.

MARGERY KEMPE AND THE CRITICS: DISEMPOWERMENT AND DECONSTRUCTION

Eluned Bremner

> How can we speak to escape their enclosures, patterns, distinctions and oppositions: virginal/deflowered, pure/impure, innocent/knowing? . . . How can we shake off the chains of these terms, free ourselves from their categories, divest ourselves of their names? Disengage ourselves, *alive*, from their concepts?
>
> Don't weep. One day we will learn to say ourselves. And what we say will be far more beautiful than our tears. (Luce Irigaray, "When Our Lips Speak Together" 75, 77)

In her deconstruction of patriarchal discourse, in particular the discourse of Lacanian psychoanalysis, French feminist theorist Luce Irigaray primarily investigates possible sites of female self-representation within these prevailing systems. As a revisionist psychoanalyst, Irigaray seeks simultaneously to reveal the way in which female subjectivity is structured by social representations of the female body as castrated or fundamentally lacking and to provide the means for women to express their desires in autonomous terms. While there are critics who take a sympathetic approach to Margery Kempe's life as reflected in her *Book*,[1] many have made efforts to deny and suppress signs of female autonomy, efforts which Kempe also encountered frequently during her radical life.

The following essay presents an analysis of the writings of some twentieth-century literary critics of *The Book of Margery Kempe* and of episodes from the *Book* itself in which Kempe comes under criticism from various figures of authority. Several continuing critical charges against Kempe reproduce the anxieties of medieval clerics and other

authority figures in the *Book*, and the charges reveal specific areas
where Kempe was seen to challenge female suppression, where she
attempts to act or speak out her desire for autonomy and power. The
essay focuses on the two aspects of Kempe's lifestyle which most
disarm her critics: her public role as a "wandering wife" and her
remarkable gift of tears.

My aim in presenting this analysis is, in Catherine Belsey's
words, to begin "to release the possible positions of [the text's]
intelligibility" (109), and to suggest more radical readings of the *Book*
for feminists. Such readings might focus on the sites of repression of
Kempe's subjectivity within the text, especially where her voice
threatens most to destabilize and call its unity and sameness into
question. My approach is thus "deconstructive" in the sense in which
Irigaray presents her project: signaling a strategic focus on the repressed
terms within dominant discourses. In Margery Kempe's case, it is her
successful efforts to achieve an albeit limited autonomy which
discomfits her critics and which they most commonly seek to eliminate
from their versions of her gifts and life. From Irigaray's psychoanalytic
perspective the difficulty of achieving female autonomy is inseparably
linked to the way in which female sexuality is circumscribed by the
phallocentric order. This does not necessarily constitute an ahistorical
approach, as Elizabeth Grosz explains:

> French feminists, among them . . . Irigaray . . . wish to
> reclaim a notion of the body which refuses traditional binary
> oppositions and places it firmly within a sociohistorical
> context. Following psychoanalytic precepts, they see the
> structure of subjectivity as an effect of the ways in which the
> subject represents and understands its own body. (xv)[2]

Irigaray locates potential sites of textual subversion and the
expression of a feminine specificity in the vestigial aspects of female
experience to be found in phallogocentric texts, those which the texts
most commonly marginalize or try to exclude. As she sees it these are,
most often, issues concerning female sexuality. Her strategy is thus to
uncover and investigate what patriarchal discourse tries to ignore,
divining that what is marginalized, that is, female "eroticism and
corporeality" (Grosz 109–10), is potentially threatening to the stability
and closure of the literary text.

The marginalization of female sexuality is central to *The Book of Margery Kempe* because Kempe's monumental task, in the *Book* as in her life, is to prove that she is able to escape the contaminations of her sex. Medieval women, continually characterized as daughters of Eve, were made constantly aware of the evil inherent in their bodies and sexual desires (Elizabeth Robertson, "The Rule of the Body" 132). A woman's reproductive system was seen by medieval thinkers to weaken her mind and make her unfit for public life and leadership.[3] The woman who "reveals her desire for an empowered life" by seeking to have her life story sanctioned and preserved as autobiography may achieve it only through the denial of her sexuality: "To the extent that she establishes her chastity within the text, to the extent that she reaffirms through the text, as well as in the text, her subordination to all fathers, she is allowed the voice of authority" (Smith 55). Thus phallogocentric discourse appropriates the feminine as fundamentally lacking in order to preserve its presence to itself and its own power. Female sexuality is central to the two components of Kempe's life and vocation which I will examine and which her denigrators seem most concerned to repress and deny.

Kempe's crossing of traditional role boundaries set up by Church and society for women frequently causes clerics and civil authorities alarm. As Sidonie Smith shows, the suppression of women in patriarchy, in the Middle Ages as now, depends upon a strict channeling of female speech and sexuality. In Kempe's time this was clearly enacted in the lives of most professional female religious:

> The profession of virginity—the espousal of the nun to Christ—and retirement to the cloister enabled the medieval woman to transcend the malediction of Eve: The closed womb, the closed mouth, and enclosure ensured woman spiritual legitimacy and authority within the paternal legacy of the medieval church. In the womb-like space made for her by the Father, the fathers (patristic writers), and the priestly fathers who advised her, she could escape the contamination of the maternal origin and, with the integrity of her material body intact, silence the threat of her womb and her words. (68)

Thus a woman was forced to deny her sexuality in order to achieve a sanctioned role within the Church, or her sexuality effectively denied her holiness. In contrast Margery Kempe creates for herself a role which sidesteps both of these requirements: she consents to be neither shut away nor speechless. As a wife and mother of fourteen children she is marked as a sexually active woman yet she resists the cloister as a means of redemption from her fleshly past. Her vocation consists of wandering the world alone, speaking and prophesying publicly, and influencing many people with her words.[4]

Kempe chooses as a distinctive symbol for this vocation the "white clothys" which she wears. Traditionally they represent purity and she uses them to signify that her life is dedicated to the service of God. Kempe's white clothes, like her tears, are seen by her critics as disruptive in that they are a sign of strategic movement between sexual categories into which patriarchal society classifies women. As with her tears, Kempe persistently claims divine authority for her singular dress and public-speaking role. Her prophetic role grows out of her daily communings with Christ and other members of the Holy Family and extends to include counseling, chastising, and mediating between Christ and other laypeople. She continually defends this activity by means of reference to the Gospel.

In Chapter 48 of the *Book*, attention is drawn to Kempe's white clothes by the Mayor of Leicester, who says: "I wil wetyn why þow gost in white clothys, for I trowe þow art comyn hedyr to han a-wey owr wyuys fro us & ledyn hem wyth þe" (116) [I want to know why you go about in white clothes, for I believe you have come here to lure away our wives from us, and lead them off with you (153)]. While this may reflect concern about the popular sect known as Flagellants, who also wore white clothes, it more directly reflects the way in which Kempe refuses the fixed categories associated with these garments, enclosed religious orders such as the Carthusians, for example. Kempe's clothes thus carry symbolic protest value at the circumscribed roles available to medieval women, and the fact that the male authorities find her self-definition threatening and fear her influence on other women may reflect the unhappy position of medieval wives, particularly those of Kempe's social group. In regard to this David Aers notes that in the Middle Ages merchant wives may well have been in a "far more passivized and domestically powerless position than those of lower-class urban and rural families" because in Kempe's class "wives' work, and the relative increase in autonomy and domestic power this could bring, was *not* an economic necessity" (87).

The repressed term or material reality which is both central to and absent from the encounter between Kempe and the Mayor of Leicester is the unstated conditions in which most medieval women lived as wives. As an unrepresented group in medieval Christianity many wives might well have desired more freedom than they were granted. Kempe is, in fact, assured of this by Christ, who says: "Dowtyr, ȝyf þu knew how many wifys þer arn in þis worlde þat wolde louyn me & seruyn me ryth wel & dewly, ȝyf þei myght be as frely fro her husbondys as þu art fro thyn" (212) [Daughter, if you knew how many wives there are in this world, who would love me and serve me well and duly, if they might be as free from their husbands as you are from yours (253)], but in sections of the text where men of authority interrogate Kempe, female desire is hidden from view.

Kempe's attempt at self-definition through her assumption of an unconventional public role arouses another aggressive response from an old monk at Canterbury (Ch. 13) who says: "I wold þow wer closyd in an hows of ston þat þer schuld no man speke wyth þe" (27) [I wish you were enclosed in a house of stone, so that no one should speak with you (63)] and when she visits Beverley (Ch. 53) she and her companions "mettyn many tymes wyth men of þe cuntre, whech seyd vn-to hir, 'Damsel, forsake þis lyfe þat þu hast, & go spynne & carde as oþer womyn don, & suffyr not so meche schame & so meche wo'" (129) [many times met with men of that district who said to her, "Woman, give up this life that you lead, and go and spin, and card wool, as other women do, and do not suffer so much shame and so much unhappiness" (168)]. Both responses enact the negation of Kempe's desire by relegating her to the circumscribed spaces of acceptable role-divisions for women in medieval society: the cloister or the nuclear family.

In Chapter 52 of Part I of the *Book*, the Archbishop of York also questions Kempe about her white clothes: "At þe last þe seyd Erchebischop cam in-to þe Chapel wyth hys clerkys, & scharply he seyde to hir, 'Why gost þu in white? Art þu a mayden?' Sche, knelyng on hir knes be-for hym, seyd, 'Nay, ser, I am no mayden; I am a wife'" (124) [At last the said Archbishop came into the chapel with his clerics, and he said to her abruptly, "Why do you go about in white clothes? Are you a virgin?" She, kneeling before him, said, "No, sir, I am no virgin; I am a married woman" (162)]. The Archbishop finds Kempe's independent action and speech in wearing white clothes while claiming to be a wife threatening and has her fettered, calling her a heretic. In the chapter house at Beverley she is again brought before the Archbishop and many other powerful clerics and authorities by a priest who declares:

> Serys, I had þis woman before me at Cowode, & þer I wyth my clerkys examynd hir in hir feyth & fond no defawte in hir. Forþermor, serys, I haue sithyn þat tyme spokyn wyth good men whech holdyn hir a parfyte woman & a good woman. Notwythstandyng al þis I ȝaf on of my men v s. to ledyn hir owt of þis cuntre for qwietyng of þe pepil. And, as þei wer goyng in her jurne, they wer takyn & arestyd, my man put in preson for hir, also hir gold & hir syluer was takyn a-wey fro hir wyth hir bedys & hir ryng, and sche is browt her a-ȝen befor me. Is her any man can sey any-thyng aȝen hir? (131–32)

> [Sirs, I had this woman before me at Cawood, and there I with my clerics examined her in her faith and found no fault in her. Furthermore, sirs, I have since that time spoken with good men who hold her to be a perfect woman and a good woman. Notwithstanding all this, I gave one of my men five shillings to lead her out of this part of the country, in order to quieten the people down. And as they were going on their journey they were taken and arrested, my man put in prison because of her; also her gold and her silver was taken away from her, together with her beads and her ring, and she is brought before me again here. Is there any man here who can say anything against her?] (170)

In the above account and in the discussion which follows, the central focus of the text is clearly upon men of influence, and the effect is to objectify Kempe and deny her autonomy. Despite "good men" having declared Kempe a "good woman," the Archbishop has paid a man to take her from his diocese, a gesture which negates her often evidenced mobility and independence. When the Archbishop finds Kempe in his presence again, he objectifies her by inquiring if any of the men have new charges to bring against her. In response a friar claims that Kempe "disprauyd alle men of Holy Chirche" (132) [disparaged all men of Holy Church (170)] and two more men, who had previously arrested Kempe, accuse her of Lollardy with the phrase "Combomis dowtyr" so that even the charge of heresy focuses on a man. The charge is a reference to John Oldcastle, Lord Cobham, who was accused of heresy in 1413 and hanged and burnt in 1417 before the Duke of Bedford (Windeatt 320, n. 3).

In the interchange which follows, Kempe's subjectivity continues to remain absent while those of the men concerned is central: how Kempe is perceived as a threat to men by men forms the gist of the dialogue. Unable to convict her of heresy, the friar passes authority over her to another man, saying "my Lord of Bedforthe is wroth wyth hir, & he wyl han hir" (132) [my lord of Bedford is angry with her, and he will have her (171)]. The friar, however, refuses the Archbishop's command to escort Kempe to the Duke, stating that it is not a friar's job to escort a woman, and the Archbishop in turn declares that he will not have the Duke angry with him on her behalf.

Kempe's autonomy and her efforts at self-definition are likewise the repressed but central term in several twentieth-century critics' anxiety over her rejection of sexual categories. These critics simultaneously negate the desires and the material reality of the experiences of medieval women, of which there are traces in the *Book* and which feminist critics might explore. John Hirsh, in a recent book which claims to place Kempe in her cultural context, completely represses her possible intentions, strategies, and desires in his discussion of her *Book*, denying her self-determination and presenting her as an object, a mere reflection or phenomenon of medieval popular culture. Once again, Kempe's desire is the repressed term which allows the critic to make statements which assume knowledge of her situation as a marginalized laywoman mystic, statements which effectively silence her voice and critically disempower her (*Revelations* 85).

Hirsh makes statements about Kempe's position without offering the kind of multifaceted information which, for example, David Aers provides in his book with regard to Kempe, indicating previously neglected factors which help to reveal the kind of experience she may have had.[5] Thus Hirsh's statements often depend on what appear to be blatant misreadings of the *Book*. His persistent use of the conditional tense reinforces the wishful quality of a historically unsupported reading. Discussing the burning of Oldcastle in 1417, the year in which Kempe was herself suspected of heresy and labeled "Cobham's daughter," he maintains:

> It seems to me easy to overstate the degree of peril which Margery faced. . . . Never recalcitrant in the face of ecclesiastical authority, a brief conversation would have

> assured any competent authority of her essential orthodoxy,
> and certain of her mannerisms—her unconventional clothing,
> her tenor of address—would have had the effect of showing
> her without harm, or at least dispelled the idea that she was a
> subversive. . . . There is no shortage of conflict in *The Book
> of Margery Kempe*, but . . . very little real danger. (6–7)

However, like several other critics, Hirsh blames Kempe for the
"stressful" life she led. He applies to her a definition of "psychosomatic
disorder" by John Pollitt which holds that:

> stress itself is not the cause of the illness, for healthy life
> consists of surmounting, adjusting to, or avoiding difficulties
> in one's path. In psychosomatic disorder . . . the patient's
> handicap . . . lies in the possession of a combination of
> personality traits usually found in obsessional and hysterical
> personality types. (qtd. Hirsh 85)

Hirsh further remarks that Kempe often "seems to have created her own
stressful situation, either by reprimanding another, particularly a social
superior, or by her dress, or by her outbursts—her loud cries and
boistrous weeping." The critic thus excludes Kempe's subjectivity from
his discussion, and makes her into an object of speculation as do the
Archbishop and his men in Chapter 54 of the *Book*.

In thus wishing away the elements in Kempe's text which signal
her desire for self-determination and the strategic means by which she
went about achieving it, Hirsh reveals his desire to banish the woman
from her text and to silence the emergent possibilities of the female
voice, as the monk at Canterbury would do in having her enclosed in
stone so that no one may hear her speak. In an earlier essay on Kempe's
Book, Hirsh actualizes this desire through a constant focus on Kempe's
male scribes, along with a complete disregard for the politics of her
situation and the way in which her life and *Book* depend upon gaining
the favor of male authorities:

> She shows a tendency to attach herself to—perhaps even to
> batten on—her spiritual confessors. . . . [H]er attachment to
> her confessor-priests played a marked role in her spiritual
> life, and the relationship should qualify the degree of
> independence with which, in spite of her travels, she is to be
> credited. . . . [T]he saintly aspirations that Margery

> undoubtedly entertained did not prevent her from injecting her own extraordinary narrative into the pattern the scribe set down. (*Middle English Prose* 112)

Elsewhere he asserts:

> The second scribe . . . took a part in forming the basic structure of the *Book* if only by putting Margery's random thoughts into a larger context, and by giving them direction. Because of him, the reader is not overwhelmed by detail, and is shown the spiritual growth of a temperamentally static human being. ("Author and Scribe" 149)

In the first extract, Hirsh portrays Kempe's "attachment to her confessor-priests" as an unusual phenomenon in the life of a medieval laywoman mystic, and in both extracts he clearly regards Kempe's life as the mere material basis for the work of her scribes.

In his early review of the *Book* Herbert Thurston paraphrases the old monk at Canterbury in an implicit comparison of Kempe with Julian of Norwich which occurs in later critical writings. He contends, as though assuming Kempe's thwarted desire to live an enclosed life: "If she had really been an ancress, living secluded in her cell, these peculiarities would not have mattered. But she insisted on going everywhere, following, as she believed, the special call of God" (in Atkinson 201). The repression of self-generated desire by Kempe (and by implication all medieval women) results in the prevalent and pejorative comparisons with Julian of Norwich by critics who insist that a medieval woman's desire could lead her to only one of two patriarchally constructed categories for its expression and containment.

R.W. Chambers provides another example of this attitude, implicitly blaming Kempe for the difficulties she encountered during her courageous life, in observing that "things might have been better for Margery if she had been a recluse. . . . But that she should wander about, rehearsing tales of scripture, was felt to be irregular" (7). David Knowles, in *The English Mystical Tradition*, also compares Kempe unfavorably with Julian of Norwich and reinforces fifteenth-century clerical attitudes toward women who define themselves outside of traditional gender roles, in applauding the renunciation of her contemplative vocation to return to her role as a wife:

> The readiness with which she abandoned for the time her life
> of retirement to nurse and serve her ageing husband, after he
> had been disabled by a serious fall and had been reduced in his
> last years to helplessness, must weigh heavily in her favour
> in the final reckoning. (149–50)[6]

The appropriation of god-language in the final clause of this summary
of Knowles's judgment of the *Book* affects the denial of Kempe's desire
for an autonomous life by calling in her own highest authority to
foreclose, once again, her text on possibilities for the empowerment of
medieval women.

　　Few critics have denied that Margery Kempe is at the center of
her *Book*, though reactions to this have certainly been mixed. In the
preceding essay of this volume David Lawton notes that the pervasive
sense of Kempe's personality in her *Book* is largely due to its
privileging of her voice, to the way in which "authority . . . passes
from what is written to what is spoken" (102) in the *Book*:

> Writing in this book is seen as something provisional,
> always on the verge of being overthrown by speech. . . . At
> length the book simply ends, and Kempe is still going: voice
> . . . is superior to the edited text, actively outlasting it. . . . It
> is Kempe's gift of speech that amazes clerics. . . . [And] it is a
> clerical interference with Kempe's speaking (of her secret)
> that induces madness at the beginning of the book. *Even
> where she cannot speak her grief, she voices it—in crying,
> weeping, mourning, roaring, and so on.* (103; emphasis
> added)

　　In response to this vocal presence, literary criticism of *The Book
of Margery Kempe* has most notably taken up the task of
disempowerment begun by Kempe's original detractors in its continued
concern with Kempe's tears, her alleged "hysteria." The frequency with
which the charge of "hysteria" recurs in the writings of (mostly male)
critics who objectify and thus seek to disempower Kempe signals to
feminist critics that Kempe's tears may be a potential site of textual
subversion, one of what Irigaray calls "blindspots" in patriarchal
discourse.[7] These blindspots are expressions of female sexuality for
which the phallic libidinal economy has no place. As Elizabeth Grosz
explains it, they "indicate points of 'repression' and sites of

symptomatic eruption of femininity which can be exploited in critical feminist analyses of . . . texts" (109–10).

Following the insights of Irigaray, it seems that the vestiges of female sexuality which form blind spots in *The Book of Margery Kempe* are most evident in the traditionally "feminine" sounds which form sites of reported disruption in the text: Kempe's outbursts of loud, public wailing, her phenomenal "gift of tears." While strangely present in the varied and often violent responses they arouse in her critics, the tears themselves are by their nature absent from the text. They thus function as a symbol of Kempe's marginalization: while her inarticulate cries and their conceivable meanings are absent from the written version of her life, they are constantly presented within the text, always filtered through at least one male consciousness: people's responses to the tears are recorded by the final authority to whom she must prove herself (and her story) orthodox, Kempe's scribe.

In Chapter 61 of the *Book*'s first part a well-known friar visits Lynn to preach. Before the sermon the local parish priest goes to warn the visiting preacher that Kempe may disrupt his speech with her tears; he thereby takes over the task of defending Kempe which she herself is certainly capable of, but in the circumstances is apparently unauthorized to do. The friar preaches on the Passion and Kempe cries "amazingly bitterly" which the friar bears patiently as requested. When, however, he preaches at the church again and Kempe once more falls into "violent weeping" he objectifies her: instead of speaking to her directly he declares to the congregation: "I wolde þis woman wer owte of þe chirche; sche noyith þe pepil" (149) [I wish this woman were out of the church; she is annoying people (188)].

Some of Kempe's friends try to excuse her to the friar on the grounds that she herself persistently claims: that she cannot control her tears as they are a gift from God. This claim from a woman, however, makes the tears threatening to male clerical authority. The friar is angry that Kempe disrupts *his* speech with her own and thereby distracts the attention of his listeners. He sees her as a rival and a battle begins between the two. The friar refuses access to the Word of God (which is Christ, Kempe's very means of empowerment) unless she takes up the traditional Christian female position and listens in submissive silence to his words. Following this many people turn against Kempe and side with the friar, and strengthened by his influence former charges of demon-possession are repeated against her.

In the face of the friar's threat Kempe depends upon the intervention of four *more* priests for her defense. She is excluded from her own defense—only men can counter the authority of men on her behalf. The *Book* goes on:

> Þer was þan a good preyste whech had red to hir mech good Scriptur & knew þe cawse of hir crying. He spak to an-oþer good preyste, þe whech had knowyn hir many ȝerys, & telde hym hys conseyt, how he was purposyd to gon to þe good frer & assayn ȝyf he myth mekyn hys hert. Þe oþer good preyste seyd he wolde wyth good wyl gon wyth hym to getyn grace ȝyf he myth. So þei went, boþe preystys to-gedyr, & preyid þe good frer as enterly as þei cowde þat he wold suffyr þe sayd creatur quyetly to comyn to hys sermown & suffyr hir paciently ȝyf sche happyd to sobbyn er cryen as oþer good men had suffyrd hir be-fore. (150)

> [There was then a good priest who had read to her much good Scripture and knew the cause of her crying. He spoke to another good priest, who had known her many years, and told him his idea: how he proposed to go to the good friar, and try if he could humble his heart.
>   The other good priest said he would willingly go with him, to obtain grace, if he might. So they went, both priests together, and begged the good friar with all their hearts that he would allow the said creature to come quietly to his sermon, and bear with her patiently if she happened to sob or cry, as other good men had borne with her before.] (188–89)

In response to this the friar repeats his condition that Kempe must remain silent: "he wolde not suffyrn hir to crye in no wyse" [he would not allow her to cry in any way].

In the above extract the credentials of the clerics concerned are prominently displayed. The first "good preyste" to whom we are introduced is invested with considerable power as a man close to God by means of his knowledge of the unspoken cause of Kempe's tears. The friar is imbued with godlike qualities as the two men go "wyth good wyl" to "getyn grace" from him if he will choose to grant it. Finally, the priests appeal to "good men" like themselves and the friar.

The presentation of credentials escalates with the next attempt on the part of Kempe's male supporters. This time:

a worshepful doctowr of diuinite, a White Frer, a solem clerk
& elde doctowr, & a wel a-preuyd, whech had knowyn þe sayd
creatur many ȝerys of hir lyfe & beleuyd þe grace þat God
wrowt in hir, toke wyth hym a worthy man, a bacheler of
lawe, a wel growndyd man in scriptur & long exercisyd,
whech was confessowr to þe sayd creatur, & wentyn to þe sayd
frer as þe good preystys dedyn beforn & sentyn for wyne to
cheryn hym wyth, preyng hym of hys charite to fauyr þe
werkys of owr Lord in þe sayd creatur & grawntyn hir hys
beneuolens in supportyng of hir ȝyf it happyd hir to cryen er
sobbyn whyl he wer in hys sermown. & þes worthy clerkys
telde hym þat it was a ȝyft of God & þat sche cowde not haue it
but whan God wolde ȝeue it, ne sche myth not wythstande it
whan God wolde send it, & God xulde wythdrawe it whan he
wilde, for þat had sche be reuelacyon, & þat was vnknowyn to
þe frer. (150–51)

[a worthy doctor of divinity, a White Friar—a very serious-
minded cleric and elderly doctor, and very well thought-of—
who had known the said creature many years of her life, and
believed the grace that God worked in her, took with him
another worthy man, a bachelor of law, a man well grounded
and long practised in scripture, who was confessor to the said
creature, and went to this friar as the good priests did before,
and sent for wine to cheer him with, praying him of his
charity to look favourably on the works of our Lord in the
said creature, and grant her his benevolence in supporting
her, if she happened to cry or sob while he was in the middle
of his sermon. And these worthy clerics told him that it was a
gift of God, and that she could not have it but when God would
give it, nor could she withstand it when god would send it, and
God would withdraw it when he willed—for that she had
through revelation, and that was unknown to the friar.] (189)

The credentials of these men are stronger than those of the first two and
are listed at greater length. They are likewise invested with power as
men close to God; one is, in fact, as Kempe's confessor the Church's
official mediator between Kempe and God himself. These men also
appeal to godlike qualities of charity and benevolence in the friar and
they stress, like the previous supporters, that Kempe cannot control her
tears which depend wholly upon the will of God. They thus set up an
implicit alliance between themselves, the friar, and God, excluding
Kempe's claim to authority in taking it up for her.

The people, mainly men, who represent Kempe to the friar all claim special knowledge (of varying degrees) of the source of her tears and of her relationship to God. In authorizing her tears they reinforce their own power by revealing themselves to be close to God and able to recognize a God-given gift. What is conspicuous by its absence in all of these discussions, however, is the same voice which so often defends Kempe before civil and clerical authorities and which precipitates the diplomatic assays described here: her own. Kempe's version and voice in defense of her gift is the repressed term in this portion of the text.

In response to these efforts on Kempe's behalf the friar de-authorizes her tears by insisting on calling them an illness. He requires that she take back her claim to spiritual authority and call her tears a mere sickness (with connotations of the gift being an affliction from the devil) in order to gain his support. In thus trying to bargain with Kempe he offers her the traditional female escape from the rigors of combat with patriarchy: anachronistically speaking, the infirmary or the madhouse. Kempe refuses this bargain and as a result she is refused access to the Word of God in the form of preaching and thereby to Christ, the divine Logos, in the Eucharist. This causes her immense grief and her cries increase in violence when she hears snatches of the Word from outside the church. Her cries signify the anguish of the marginalized laywoman, separated from her community in its central meeting place and from her only means of personal empowerment, Christ the Incarnate Word.

Twentieth-century critics of Kempe's *Book*, apparently troubled by the pervasive presence of her voice, undertake to rename her gift of tears as the medieval authorities do. Like the friar, modern critics are quick to provide explanations for her "deviant" behavior. In the 1930's Herbert Thurston used the phrase "terrible hysteria" of Kempe and said he found it "impossible to forget the hysterical temperament revealed in every page of the narrative portions" of the *Book* (Atkinson 201). Edmund Colledge, in 1965, classified her as "a hysteric, if not an epileptic" ("Margery Kempe" 222). Even in 1980, Kempe was described as "quite mad—an incurable hysteric with a large paranoid trend" (Howard 34–35). More recently, critical speculations about Kempe's "psychosomatic" disturbances have been similarly used to avoid further investigation of the process of her empowerment through her gift of tears (Hirsh, *Revelations* 85).

David Knowles continues the objectification of Margery Kempe along with the focus on the credentials of others—implicitly and explicitly men—which occurs in Chapter 61 of the *Book*. He lists views of Kempe held by "writers of repute" and then notes that "in her favour it must be noted that editors and most readers agree that her story gives an impression of basic sincerity," that she "never abuses her opponents and even suppresses their names" (in other words she is kind to men), and that "she had among her advisers and supporters many whom we know from other sources to have been theologians and preachers of repute." As an example of extreme objectification, he states that "when she can be checked, she is found accurate and truthful" (*The English Tradition* 143).

In discussing Kempe's tears Knowles further notes that "a majority, which included some of the most influential friars, were only too ready to accept her at her own valuation." He continues: "Even the various prelates into whose presence she came treated her with considerable respect, particularly two who are not usually represented as spiritual men: Philip Repingdon of Lincoln and William Courtenay of Canterbury" (148). While this may be read as a backhanded half-compliment to Kempe for attracting the attention of some worthy men, the focus is disempowering because it depends upon the repression of her own desires. Conversely, Kempe's vocational ambitions might be explored in terms of the motivations behind and the strategic uses of her tears, with regard to her claiming the authority to disrupt the officially endorsed sermon of a powerful cleric.

Knowles, like many other critics, uses the charge of "hysteria" to foreclose Kempe's text and diminish its importance for the student of mystical literature. In this way "hysteria" operates as the unexamined, repressed term in his summary:

> There existed quite clearly from the beginning of her adult life, a large hysterical element in Margery's personality. . . . In general, we may perhaps say that there is nothing in the words themselves that suggest any other origin than the vivid imagination and retentive memory of a sincere and devout, but very hysterical woman. (146–47)

In contrast to critics who attempt to foreclose the text of Kempe's *Book* on the destabilizing effect of her tears, feminist critics may examine more closely a gift which, by virtue of its position at the margins of logocentric discourse, has the potential to disrupt logocentric representational systems (as Kempe's tears break into the friar's sermon) and thereby create a possible space for women's self-representation.

Irigaray's discussion of the potential of tears for female self-definition helps illuminate the politics of Kempe's disallowed speech in the previous extract. Irigaray describes hysteria as a means for women to reopen a path into the logocentric system which "connotes [them] as castrated of words" in order to interrogate that system. In describing this subversive endeavor Irigaray also describes the effect of the tears with which Kempe interrupts the friar's sermon. She challenges women:

> Turn everything upside down, inside out, back to front. *Rack it with convulsions*, carry back, reimport, those crises that her "body" suffers in her impotence to say what disturbs her . . . *overthrow syntax* by suspending its eternally teleological order, by snipping the wires, cutting the current, breaking the circuits, switching the connections, by modifying continuity, alternation, frequency, intensity. (*Speculum* 142)

Margery Kempe's tears thus open up possibilities for self-referential female speech within her text which the clerics and critics who speak for and classify her seek to close. While Kempe chooses to authorize her tears by claiming them as a gift from God, the power focus shifts when the male clerics make this claim. What feminist critics might productively focus on is not the claims or credentials of the clerics but the potential of Kempe's voice to destabilize the masculine-inscribed text of her *Book*.

Irigaray claims that hysteria can be seen as a means of rebellion against patriarchal constructions of femininity which are based on female lack and passivity, as "the symptomatic acting out of a proposition the hysteric cannot articulate" because she may only speak within this order. The hysteric, frustrated at her inability to figure autonomously in discourse (because of the way patriarchy inscribes female sexuality), "refuses heterosexual passivity and the sexual compliance with social norms by transferring sexual intensity and meaning onto her symptoms." Thus "the hysteric 'articulates' a corporeal discourse" (Grosz 134–35). A focus on the tears may thus also be used to challenge critical charges against Kempe's violation of patriarchal strictures on female speech and sexuality:

> The hysteric's symptom is a response to her annihilation as active subject, a resistance or refusal to confirm what is expected of her. Not able to take up an active position by will alone . . . she lives out and uses her passivity in an active defiance of her social position. She (psychically) mutilates herself in order to prevent her brutalisation at the hands of others. (Grosz 138)

More investigation into how, why, and where Kempe "acts out and uses her passivity" in this way needs to be attempted if we are to understand more of her problematic position and her troubled life.

Kempe's attempted articulation of a corporeal discourse may also be instructive for our own efforts to find a place from which to speak as women. As Irigaray tells us, a self-referential female speech involves new ways of inscribing female sexuality or speaking the body, ways that go beyond Kempe's radical but reactive attempts, while simultaneously taking up her position on the margins of the system which inscribes us as inactive subjects:

> Let's leave definitiveness to the undecided; we don't need it. Our body, right here, right now, gives us a very different certainty. Truth is necessary for those who are so distanced from their body that they have forgotten it. But their "truth" immobilizes us, turns us into statues, if we can't loose its hold on us. If we can't defuse its power by trying to say, right here and now, how we are moved. (*This Sex* 214)

> And if I were claiming that what I am trying to articulate, in speech or writing, starts from the *certainty* that I am a woman, then I should be caught up once again within "phallocratic" discourse. I might well attempt to overturn it, but I should remain included within it.
>
> Instead, I am going to make an effort—for one cannot simply leap outside that discourse—to situate myself at its borders and to move continuously from the inside to the outside. (*This Sex* 122)

If we recognize that "strategies of writing *and* of reading are forms of cultural resistance" (de Lauretis 7), then in exploring Kempe's processes of empowerment by examining the blind spots in her patriarchally inscribed text we will be both validating her radical endeavor and following in her footsteps. In attempting this our inquiry will be on the way to becoming "that political, theoretical, self-analyzing practice by which the relations of the subject in social reality can be rearticulated from the historical experience of women" (de Lauretis 186), and the historical experience of women can then teach us a great deal. We as yet have much to learn from the courageous life of Margery Kempe, and much to recognize and to reclaim.

University of Otago

NOTES

1. For example, David Aers, *Community, Gender, and Individual Identity: English Writing 1360–1430*; Sarah Beckwith, "A Very Material Mysticism: The Medieval Mysticism of Margery Kempe"; and Sidonie Smith, *A Poetics of Women's Autobiography: Marginality and the Fictions of Self-Representation* which includes a provocative and insightful chapter on the *Book*.

2. Grosz continues: "For Irigaray, not only is subjectivity structured with reference to the (symbolic) meaning of the body, but the body itself is the product and effect of symbolic inscriptions which produce it as a particular, socially appropriate type of body. . . . The body is thus the site of the intersection of psychical projections, and of social inscriptions. Understood in this way, it can no longer be considered pre- or acultural. Common feminist objections to theories utilising notions of the body—the charges of essentialism, naturalism and biologism—are not appropriate in this case." Diana Fuss, in *Essentially Speaking: Feminism, Nature and Difference*, also presents an illuminating exploration of what she describes as "Irigaray's strategic use of essentialism" (55).

3. See Prudence Allen, *The Concept of Woman*, especially 103–11, and Ian Maclean, *The Renaissance Notion of Woman* 42.

4. While Kempe's self-proclaimed vocation as a laywoman mystic was unusual in fifteenth-century England, she had several models for this way of life on the continent, for example, Dorothea of Montau in Prussia, Catherine of Siena in Italy, and Mary of Oignies in France.

5. Aers critiques the masculine consciousness through which most historical knowledge of women has been filtered, and includes socioeconomic, political, and legal considerations in his treatment of the *Book*.

6. Another critic, T.W. Coleman, in *English Mystics of the Fourteenth Century*, similarly applauds Kempe's decision to nurse her infantilized husband, calling it a "splendid act of self-sacrifice" (158).

7. Luce Irigaray, "Part One: The Blind Spot of an Old Dream of Symmetry," *Speculum of the Other Woman*.

Her World

MARGERY KEMPE AND KING'S LYNN

Deborah S. Ellis

Margery Kempe is best known for her rather exceptional originality: an illiterate bourgeois mystic whose participation in the tradition of affective piety ranges from the mundane to the hysterical, and whose *Book* is an increasingly valuable source for students of medieval history, religion, and, especially, the experiences and feelings of medieval women. But in focusing on her uniqueness, we tend to lose sight of the roots from which she emerged, and which influenced her all her life. As Atkinson says, Kempe "remained an English woman, formed in a specific time and place and by a particular family, church, and society" (67). It is my purpose in this essay to explore King's Lynn, Kempe's hometown in East Anglia, as the community that shaped her self-image (both holy and mundane), and to investigate some of the ways in which her town and she influenced each other's understanding of what home is for a pilgrim.[1] In King's Lynn, we see Kempe flourishing on the tensions between her two goals of inclusion (acceptance by the townspeople) and exclusion (their repelled recognition of her special status). This double perspective gives her a way to resolve the tension between her secluded married life and her intense public interests.

The author of the fourteenth-century *Cloud of Unknowing* advised his readers to remain passive against the force of divinity: ". . . lat that thing do with thee and lede thee wherso it list. . . . Be thou bot the tree and lat it be the wright: be thou bot the house, and lat it be the hosbonde wonyng therin" [let that force act on you and lead you wherever it wants. . . . You be only the wood and let it be the carpenter; you be only the house and let it be the husband dwelling within] (qtd. Medcalf, "Medieval Psychology" 145). But Kempe thought otherwise. Her assertion that the home defines the woman, and not just the "hosbonde wonyng therin," marks her work from beginning to end, providing a metaphor for both the instability and the integrity that limn the experiences of medieval women. She defines that home not just as a house, but emphatically as the town that she grew up in, the town in which her father, who "arguably played a more important part in the government of Lynn than any other individual in the later fourteenth century" (Goodman 351), was mayor five times, and the town in which she herself, as an old woman, probably achieved the final acceptance of guild membership. The implications of Kempe's identification with her hometown have been largely ignored by critics, who focus instead on the nature of her affective piety or the peculiarly domestic expression of her mysticism (esp. Dickman; also Ellis, Fienberg, and Atkinson). Such expressions, however, can be best understood in the larger context of Kempe within King's Lynn.

For Kempe's society the idea of home acted "as a unifying concept in social, family and cultural life" (Ladurie 25).[2] In Margery Kempe's image of the home, its dynamics include interaction with the larger community. It is not surprising that she so often expresses her struggle, as a sort of meta-townswoman, through house imagery. The role of the medieval house, by its very nature—annexing as it did semi-independent chamber units, that offered some scope for privacy, to a central, public hall—was to provide an uneasy alliance between the central and peripheral experiences of life (esp. Wood; and Faulkner, Pantin, and J.H. Parker and Turner).[3] For medieval women the home acted as a consistent symbol, defining both their personal integrity derived from their power or alienation within the home, and their social identity, the effect of the "domus" within the community. This tension between center and periphery, inclusion and exclusion, and power and dispossession, so conveniently encapsulated in the structure of the house, dominates *The Book of Margery Kempe* and provides a key for understanding the relationship between Kempe and her town. For just as Kempe's image of the home, however fragmentary and transcendent, is firmly rooted in the actual medieval house of her period (Deborah Ellis, "The Image of the Home" Ch. 1), so her idea of "hometown" is rooted in her community of King's Lynn.

Kempe's deep identification with her town appears to have been established at an early age. She never stops identifying herself as John de Brunham's daughter, from a family in which both father and daughter represent King's Lynn.

Þan þe Meyr askyd hir of what cuntre sche was & whos dowtyr sche was. "Syr," sche seyd, "I am of Lynne in Norfolke, a good mannys dowtyr of þe same Lynne, whech hath ben meyr fyve tymes of þat worshepful burwgh and aldyrman also many ȝerys. . . ." (111)

[Then the mayor asked her what country she was from and whose daughter she was. "Sir," she said, "I am from Lynn in Norfolk, a daughter of a good man from Lynn who has been mayor of that worshipful town five times, and also alderman many years. . . ."]

Kempe's father, John de Brunham, was not only mayor five times but also served as alderman and MP, and held several other public offices, including those of justice of the peace and coroner (*Book* App. III 359–60). With her marriage, however, Kempe became part of a larger network of interrelationships, and her in-laws' involvement in the community would also have become vitally important to her status and identity. Probably shortly after 1393, when she would have been around twenty, Kempe married John Kempe, the younger son of a skinner (*Book* App. III and 259, n. 6/25). Kempe's father-in-law (also named John Kempe) eventually became a prosperous merchant, who "seems to have had a larger part in the economic life of Lynn than Margery's husband" (*Book* 364). It has been suggested that Kempe was unable "to bear that as Kempe's wife she was less 'worshipful' than as Brunham's daughter: she reproached Kempe with his lower status and his failure to provide for her in the style she desired" (Goodman 352), but this suggested dissatisfaction seems alien to the tenor of life in King's Lynn, with its close network of associations among the leading merchant families. Leading Lynn families such as the Belyeteres, Brekeropps, Drewes, Ffeltwelles, Ryghtwys, and Secchefords were linked by business, social, and residential connections. Lists of executors and testatees in wills in the *Red Register*, a fourteenth-century miscellany from Lynn, support the evidence of close connections suggested by, for instance, patterns of enfranchisement (Ingleby, hereafter *RR*, and appendices below). The Kempes and the Brunhams were united not only by Kempe's marriage—which would in all likelihood never have occurred had it not been in the two families' best interests—but also by mutual interests and associations. There are many instances in the *Red Register* of the John de Brunhams (father and son) and the John Kempes (father and son) serving on the same councils, or their relatives doing so, as when Simon Kempe (Margery's brother-in-law) and Robert de Brunham (Margery's cousin?) were city chamberlains together in 1395 (e.g., *RR* 120; *Book* App. III 359–68). John Kempe, Sr., though never mayor himself, held several important city positions around the time of John de Brunham's mayoralties, including those of chamberlain and royal tax collector (*Book* App. III 363).

The constant repetition in the *Red Register* of the same people acting as each other's pledges, executors, agents, and the like forms a strong picture of the interlocking fabric of the lives of the merchant class in Lynn. Yet, despite this, there are very few names that can be positively associated with Margery Kempe. Even her fourteen children, her daughter-in-law, and her granddaughter are only mentioned in her *Book*, not named. Of her family, we know of or suspect the existence of only her father, her mother (again unnamed), her brother John, and her grandfather Radulfus de Brunham, as well as the uncertainly connected Robert, Reginald, and Edmund de Brunham; her husband, her father-in-law, presumably her mother-in-law, and her husband's brother Simon. There is also Simon's widow, who married John Brekeropp in 1416–17. As for town acquaintances, we know only of John de Wyreham, who asked after Kempe in her *Book*, and John Asheden, who paid her way into the Trinity Guild in 1438–39, two apparently otherwise unremarkable men. Of the large number of servants and apprentices that Kempe must have lived with at various times in her life, we know the name only of Thomas Seccheford, John Kempe's apprentice who was enfranchised in 1390–91 (*Calendar*, Norfolk and Norwich Arch. Society *passim*).

Although it is thus impossible to know what place in Kempe's life specific relatives or friends in Lynn had (except, of course, for her husband and her confessors), it is quite possible to reconstruct some of the values and habits of her society. It has, for instance, been said of this period:

> One point which clearly emerges from all the causes is the closely knit bonds of the family, and the overriding importance of the blood relationship, especially between siblings, or between parents or grandparents and their descendants, but almost equally between uncles and aunts and their nieces and nephews. (Owen 337)

Wills in the *Red Register* repeatedly mention properties adjoining those of other members of the same family and passing from one family member to another.[4] Records of members of the same families living near each other seem infinitely more harmonious than do records of families left in one dwelling, but the ideal of family loyalty is irrepressible, even when expressed through mercantile advantage or reconciled bickering.

> Be it noted that whereas the late William de Pikenham bequeathed his house in Bridgegate in Lynn to his wife Cecily for maintaining the sons and daughters of the said William and Cecily, so that after the death of the said Cecily the house might be sold by the executors of the said Cecily; and afterwards disturbances arose among the said sons and daughters concerning their maintenance from the said house, [so that] finally friends intervened so that a final agreement was reached among them.[5]

In another example, a testator had the larger family in mind:

> . . . if it happens that my said house after the death of my children, the said John and Nicholas, is sold and some ones or someone related to me buys that house jointly or separately for their own, I wish that they have the said house . . . for ten pounds sterling less than someone not related to me would pay.[6]

Lynn's size probably helped foster this concern with protecting the family, since there was a fairly steady influx of newcomers, both English and foreign.[7] It was a prosperous and crowded city, and despite its two large markets (held on Tuesdays and Saturdays) and its many public buildings, its streets were narrow, dirty, and bustling. The "venellas communas" that Kempe would have walked along were full of people, rich and poor, merchants and thieves and prostitutes, and animals wandering around out of control, especially on Saturdays.[8] Householders, including Kempe's husband, were always fouling the streets and waterways; John Kempe was fined because "he fills the common river with dung."[9] There were several main streets in Lynn, but access generally depended on a network of small and probably muddy alleys. Vanessa Parker's diagram (34, figure 7) of Damgate Ward in sixteenth-century Lynn is probably a fair picture of life a century or two earlier. It is noticeable that in this diagram [see Appendix B], Fincham Street—the only place where we can be almost certain that Kempe lived—had nine tenants, a conduit, a muckhill, three coalyards, a sedgeyard, and a town wharf. This seems comparable to the eight or more earlier tenements in the area that can be traced from the *Red Register*.[10]

At the same time as most streets and presumably houses were crowded and public, there were alternative areas where the citizens could enjoy a more separate sense of space. Many of the larger houses had private chapels, for instance, and we can imagine such early pubs as Langland describes: "There was leyhing and louryng and 'lat go the coppe!'/Bargaynes and beuereges bygan tho to awake. . . ." (127) [There was laughing and frowning and cries of "let the cup pass around!"/ There was always some new bargaining and drinking starting up] (VI 394–95).[11] The area in general was, even for medieval England, well endowed with religious centers, producing Julian of Norwich as well as Margery Kempe, and people could resort to these centers for rest and thought. Kempe herself did this on a visit to Julian. In King's Lynn, as in the rest of East Anglia, "there must have been few communities more than a mile or two from one or another of the many religious houses in the district. . . ." (Morey 186). In discussing the pre-1500 public buildings of Lynn, Vanessa Parker draws a detailed picture of the available shelters and gathering places:

> The most important public buildings in the medieval town of
> Lynn were those which functioned as meeting places, either
> for religious worship, or for the social and business functions
> of the numerous gilds and fraternities who played such an
> important part in the organisation of the social, economic
> and political life of medieval communities. In addition, there
> was the early accommodation for trade and traders, and finally
> the first steps towards providing shelter for the poor and the
> sick. . . . The three public halls were all located beside the
> market places, the natural foci for the economic life of the
> town and for much of its social and political life. (140–41)

The pattern of the town, then, recapitulated, to some extent, the pattern of the houses within it: that is, areas for withdrawing, if not into privacy at least into a more highly selected company, bordered on the generally public areas. The guildhalls and halls, in this reading, retreat from the markets in much the same way that chambers retreat from halls. Selectivity of grouping, rather than aloneness, seems a central impulse. In this way we can imagine Kempe at home within her community both in the sense that her local attachments would have formed a sort of extended family, and in the sense that her patterns of mobility within the town would echo those within her own house. Such patterns emerge most clearly in her relationship with her husband; although she presents her marriage almost as an experience uncluttered with domesticity, as in fact a series of confrontations with her husband (all designed to demonstrate Christ's superiority as a marriage partner), we can still deduce some of the chaos that must have surrounded that marriage.

Kempe's household, whatever the names of its members, was always disintegrating—she experiences most kinds of domestic discord, having problems with her husband, her children, and her servants. The latter desert her after her attempts at brewing and milling, and her closest personal servant condemns her. "Hir mayden, seying dysese on euery syde, wex boystows a-3ens hir maystres. Sche wold not obeyn ne folwyn hir cownsel. Sche let hir gon a-lone in many good towyns & wold not gon wyth hir" (33) [Her maid, seeing trouble on every side, became rebellious against her mistress. She would not obey her or follow her advice. She let her mistress go alone into many good towns and would not go with her]. This discord would have been the more horrendous because Kempe's household must have been a large one, perhaps as large as that of a substantial gentry family such as the Pastons, but in a much more limited space. It would have included herself, her husband, several of her fourteen children at any one time, her servants, and her husband's apprentice(s). According to Thrupp, in London "the majority of merchants had probably no more than one or two servants" (151–52), and the records in the *Red Register* seem to bear out the assumption that no one had more than two apprentices at a time. On the other hand, in fourteenth-century Lynn, Philip With's will included bequests to two apprentices, two "famulos," several other servants, and perhaps a cook (*Book of Lynn*, f. 10r ff.). In 1365 Thomas Rithgwys, Jr., also of Lynn, left bequests to (besides his family) one male servant, two maidservants, his nurse, one apprentice, one chaplain, presumably one chamberlain ("Waltero Chamberleyn"), and seven other dependents, three women and four men, although they were probably not all living in his household at the same time (*RR*

115). The formulaic nature of medieval wills is not proof against the casual paratactic style that mixes up family and retainers in a manner suggestive of similar familiarity at home:

> Item, I leave to my brother Richard the debts that are owed to me Item I leave to Richard of Thorpe my servant half a mark Item I leave to William of Frenge my servant half a mark Item I leave to my wife Alice our entire chamber [understood: "with all its appurtenances"]. . . . Item I leave to Margaret of Rudham my servant ten pounds. Item I leave to Thomas, William, and John, my sons, all my arms. . . .[12]

Servants in the same household had to get along, occasionally even marrying each other (Owen 335). They could come and go freely, and would accompany their masters and mistresses on errands and visits (Owen 340; Tanner *passim*). Apprentices had less freedom, though more status, than servants did; they were often related to their employers, as the *Red Register* indicates in its records of masters and apprentices with the same surname. John de Brunham's household probably had such an arrangement, for he had an apprentice named Edmund de Brunham who was clearly not his son.[13] The literature of the time—as well as such evidence as lawsuits and guild records—is packed with revelations about the master/apprentice relationship. In one fifteenth-century manuscript, the author hints at the potential behavioral troubles of apprentices in his advice to a young man hopeful of being apprenticed to anyone, a "clerke marchante or artyfycere/Chamberlayne butteler panter or a kern/Ussher sewer ploweman or laborer . . .":

> Love god drede god ther of thou hast skyll
> Be trewe to thy master hys goodys not to spill
> Love hym drede hym be war be not suttyl. . . .
> Jangyll not ne mocke not be not complaynynge. . . .[14]

[a clerk, merchant, or craftsman/chamberlain, butler, pantry official or soldier/usher, server, plowman, or laborer. . . . Love God, fear God, as far as you are able/Be true to thy master and don't destroy his goods/Love him, fear him; beware; don't be subtle/Don't gossip, mock, or complain. . . .]

This somewhat formalized evidence of household conflict complements the more vivid evidence of letters and trials, as appears in, for instance, the Paston letters.[15]

We can assume, then, that Kempe's household shared in two opposite but complementary forces: centrifugal from within, a discordant center of children and adults, employers and employed; and centripetal from without, an attracting periphery of like-minded neighbors and allies. Kempe is drawn to such tension, and her society in Lynn goes far toward explaining the peculiarly public nature of her ideas about marriage, ideas which spill over onto her mystical visions to create an oddly social association with Christ. Kempe expresses her relationship with Christ in domestic terms, visualized in house settings: the wife waiting at home for her husband, leaving the house to accompany the husband on a journey, and lying in bed with her husband. Although Kempe usually hears Christ address her as "my derworthy dow3ter" [my dearly esteemed daughter], her most intense visions rely on marital imagery. But Kempe's vision of Christ as her husband is very sedate; there is no echo of her real life with her husband, "her inordynat lofe & þe gret delectacyon þat þei haddyn eyþer of hem in vsyng of oþer . . ." (12) [their inordinate love and the great delight that each of them had in enjoying the other], when "sche bethowt hir how sche in hir 3ong age had ful many delectabyl thowtys, fleschly lustys, & inordinat louys to hys persone" (181) [she thought to herself how in her young age she had had so many delectable thoughts, fleshly lusts, and inordinate love for his body]. Her intimate religious fantasies have to do only with public approbation. Christ tells her, "I schuld not ben a-schamyd of þe as many oþer men ben, for I schuld take þe be þe hand a-mongs þe peþil & make þe gret cher þat þei schuldyn wel knowyn þat I louyd e ryth wel" (90) [I would not be ashamed of you as many other men are, for I would take you by the hand among the people and treat you very kindly so that they would know very well that I loved you so well]. Her ideal husband, as fantasized by Kempe over and over, is a public figure. He supports her amid public abuse, and the worse the abuse the better the husband. The strongest metaphors she gives Christ express this relationship: "for I far liche a man þat louyth wel hys wife, þe mor enuye þat men han to hir þe bettyr he wyl arayn hir in despite of hir enmys" (81) [for I fare like a man that loves his wife well; the more envious men are of her, the better he will array her in spite of her enemies]. The ideal husband goes to meet her after her journeys and he allows her to travel freely, just as the Wife of Bath wishes her husbands would do: "Thou sholdest seye, 'Wyf, go wher thee liste. . . .'" [You should say, "Wife, go wherever you want to"] (WBP 318). Kempe's ideal husband, moreover, reverses medieval expectations of a husband-wife relationship, in which the wife stays home and waits for her husband to reappear (e.g., Power, esp. Chs. 2 and 3).

The marriage of John and Margery Kempe was clearly a taxing one. Kempe's ethos of the perfect marriage, at least when Christ is envisioned as the partner, is one of wifely loyalty: ". . . it longyth to þe wyfe to be wyth hir husbond & no very joy to han tyl sche come to hys presens" (31–32) [it is a wife's duty to be with her husband and to have no real joy until she comes to his presence]. In real life, however, Kempe leaves John periodically, demands celibacy in their married life, refuses to obey him, and finally gets a formal separation, returning to him only in his final senility. Their sexual life is marked by such behavior as her wearing a hair shirt in bed (and his not noticing this, despite the conceptions of at least fourteen children), and her lusting after another man at the same time that "to comown wyth hir husbond . . . was very peynful & horrybyl vn-to hir" (14) [to have sexual intercourse with her husband . . . was very painful and horrible to her]. John's loyalty in the face of all this in many ways often exceeds hers, as she recognizes:

> And so sche went forth wyth hir husbonde in-to þe cuntre, for he was euyr a good man & an esy man to hir. Þow þat he sumtyme for veyn dred lete hir a-lone for a tyme, ȝet he resortyd euyr-mor a-geyn to hir, & had compassyon of hir, & spak for hir as he durst for dred of þe pepyl. (32)

> [And so she went forth with her husband into the country, for he was always a good and a kind man to her. Even though sometimes for needless fear he would leave her by herself for a time, yet he always returned to her again, and had compassion for her, and spoke for her as much as he dared because of his fear of the people.]

It is interesting to note in this context that Kempe was accused of separating wives from their husbands. She is working within an accepted religious precedent, for St. Bridget, an important model for Kempe, "did help to separate at least one married couple."[16] In this respect Kempe's fellow citizens see her as the worst kind of radical agitator (e.g., 116, 133). Though they disapproved of her ideas about marriage, however, she responded in her own marriage to their ideas.

Whether speaking of her husband or of her spousal link with Christ, Kempe always stresses the public aspect of this relationship, for she judges the quality of a marriage by public opinion. When her husband, long after their separation has been established, falls down and is in danger of death, Kempe mentions public condemnation rather than any private concern or remorse as her main instigation to action. "And þan þe pepil seyd, ȝyf he deyd, hys wyfe was worthy to ben hangyn for hys deth, for-as-meche as sche myth a kept hym & dede not" (179) [And then the people said that if he died, his wife should be hanged for his death, because she could have kept him safe but she did not]. It is characteristic of both herself and her society that she confuses her personal need for contrition with her need for public self-justification. Because once she had felt "inordinay louys to hys persone" [inordinate love for his body], now "sche was glad to be ponischyd wyth þe same persone. . . ." (181) [she was glad to be punished with the same body," but in fact she is cleansing her soul for the community, and even her prayers in this crisis demonstrate the interdependency of these two motives: "þan sche preyid to owr Lord þat hir husbond myth leuyn a ȝer & sche to be deliueryd owt slawndyr ȝyf it wer hys plesawns" (180) [then she prayed to our Lord that her husband might live a year and that she might be delivered from slander if it were his pleasure]. She is responding here to the traditions of Lynn, for disablement was seen, to some extent, as a social responsibility.

In 1388 the king's agent tried to claim the property of Emma de Beston of Lynn, who had been certified as an idiot, and the mayor and townsmen kept Emma from him. The mayor claimed in a subsequent hearing that the question turned on the freedom of Lynn, for

> if any burgess or the wife, son or daughter of a burgess within the town is an idiot from birth or from a certain time or is overwhelmed by disease or old age or is of unsound mind so as to be unable to manage himself, his lands or chattels, the mayor and aldermen for the time being, together with the sufferer's nearest friends and relations, have been wont from time immemorial to provide for his management, guardianship, and maintenance, without intervention of the king. . . .[17]

The fight over Emma illustrates the at least formal interaction between public and private that informs so much of Lynn life and would have been so firmly rooted in the burgess Margery Kempe. Kempe eventually satisfied the town's expectations; we could surmise this from her admission to an important guild, if from nothing else. Yet she presents the need to care for her disabled husband not merely as an act demanded by her society, nor purely as an act of personal contrition, but rather as an aspect of public disapproval that she, with God's grace, will overcome within the privacy of her own home. Public responsibilities are carried out behind closed doors in Lynn. "The doors of the house where [Emma] dwelt were kept firmly closed. . . ."[18] It would be easier to dismiss Emma's case as the rhetorical business proposition it mainly was (the burgesses naturally wanted her property under their control), if we did not know of Kempe's continuing struggle to reconcile the public and the private. A closed door, after all, could only have been a gesture in a house whose ground floor was a public shop and whose other rooms were either freely shared by all or locked against their own inhabitants.[19] Indeed, privacy was so hard to come by that medieval depositions and literature refer to adulteries occurring in the brewhouse, the gatehouse, and even over a latrine, while private conversations are recorded as occurring in the garden, a field, or the corner of a crowded room; and these are all, obviously, ploys that failed.[20] Under these conditions, married life necessarily had a far more pronounced public aspect than it has now.[21]

Such concerns with public life surface over and over in Kempe's life, especially in her interactions with other pilgrims during her several pilgrimages. She demands acceptance, yet at the same time she validates her self-image as Christ's chosen daughter/wife/sister through her rejection by others. Though she dreads being alone, Kempe provokes everyone to desert her.

> Many tymys sche spak as fayr to hym as sche cowde þat he xulde not forsakyn hir in tho strawnge cuntreys & in myddys of hir enmyis. . . . Þe mor sche wept, þe yrkar was hir man of hir cumpany & þe raþar besyd hym to gon fro hir & leeuyn hir a-lone. (233)

> [Many times she spoke as fairly to him as she could so that he would not forsake her in those strange countries and in the middle of her enemies. . . . The more she wept, the more

irritated the man became with her company and the more
eagerly he busied himself to go from her and leave her alone.]

The seyd creatur had a sone, a tal ӡong man . . . &, whan sche
myth metyn wyth hym at leyser, many tymys sche cownselyd
hym to leeuyn þe worlde & folwyn Crist in so meche þat he
fled hyr cumpany & wolde not gladlych metyn wyth hir. (221)

[The said creature had a son, a tall young man . . . and,
whenever she could meet with him at leisure, many times she
advised him to leave the world and follow Christ, to the point
that he fled her company and would not willingly meet with
her.]

Because she is often unable or unwilling to change her own activities to
fit in with the demands of her group, Kempe chooses either to ignore
their desires or to form a new transient group centered around herself.
One result of her repelling those whom she most wants to attract
(pilgrims, bishops, et al.) is that she perpetually draws new people into
her orbit, despite her innate distrust of strangers. Her instincts toward
strangers are a function of her strong identification with Lynn. In Lynn
the known, even when unfriendly, are safer than the unknown, as we
see in her reaction to a stranger whom the local priest had trusted,

in-as-mech as he was an amyabyl persone, fayr feturyd, wel
faueryd in cher & in cuntenawns, sad in hys langage and
dalyawns, prestly in hys gestur & vestur. . . . & [Kempe] seyd
þei haddyn many powyr neybowyrs whech þei knewyn wel a-
now hadyn gret nede to ben holpyn & relevyd, & it was mor
almes to helpyn hem þat þei knewyn wel . . . þan oþer
strawngerys whech þei knew not, for many spekyn &
schewyn ful fayr owtward to þe sygth of þe pepyl, God
knowyth what þei arn in her sowlys. (56)

[inasmuch as he was an amiable person, fair-featured, well-
favored in behavior and in countenance, sober in his language
and his conversation, priestly in his gestures and his vesture.
. . . But she said that they had many poor neighbors whom
they knew well enough needed greatly to be helped and
relieved, and it would be more charitable to help those that
they knew well . . . than other strangers whom they didn't
know, for many speak and appear very fair outwardly in the

sight of the people, but God knows what they are in their
souls.]

It is one of Kempe's more interesting accommodations that she learns
to overcome this conditioned xenophobia in her relationships with the
people of her own, as well as other, towns, for she consistently
challenges and reinterprets civic authority. Mayors and bishops are no
safer than was John Kempe. Significantly enough, however, she
mentions no major quarrels within her own town of Lynn. Despite her
fraught relationship with her town, enough force of protective
coloration was at work to allow her some security. We know enough
about Kempe from her *Book* to know how firmly she was entrenched in
the values of Lynn, even when she was rejecting them. Her pre-
conversion self is haughty, envious, and aggressively stylish: she wore
elaborate clothes "þat it schuld be þe mor staryng to mennys sygth and
hir-self þe more ben worshepd" (9) [so that it would be more striking to
people's sight and so that she herself would be more honored]. She
reproached her husband with her high social status: "sche was comyn of
worthy kinred,—hym semyd neuyr for to a weddyd hir, for hir fadyr was
sum-tyme meyr of þe town" (9) [she had come from a worthy family—
he should not have wedded her, for her father was once mayor of the
town]. Despite her growing eccentricities, she remains one among her
neighbors, going so far as to subdue her public cryings when they
threaten to cause her expulsion from the Church (Ch. 63).

　　Some of the tensions that must have arisen between Kempe and
her town reveal themselves within the attitudes of citizens of other,
attitudinally parallel towns. She often describes these citizens, usually
hostile, and we can clearly glimpse her reviled progress through the
narrow streets of York or Leicester, as she listens righteously to
neighbors' jeers. She is often confronted as a townswoman by other
townswomen and -men who are as much irritated by her flaunting of her
obvious rootedness as they are threatened by her claim to divine
liminality. One striking scene, for instance, shows a town's attempt to
drive her back into her own town where she is to behave as a proper
citizen:

> . . . women cam rennyng owt of her howsys wyth her rokkys,
> crying to þe pepil, "Brennyth þis fals heretyk." So, as sche
> went forth to-Beuerleward . . . þei mettyn many tymes wyth
> men of þe cuntre, whech seyd vn-to hir, "Damsel, forsake þis

lyfe þat þu hast, & go spynne & carde as oþer women do."
(129)[22]

[women came running out their houses with rocks, crying to
the people, "Burn this false heretic." So, as she went toward
Beverley . . . they met many times with men of that country,
who said to her, "Damsel, forsake this life that you live, and
go spin and card as other women do."]

Kempe clearly thrives on such rejection. When "a rekles man, litil
chargyng hys owyn schame" [a reckless man, caring little for his own
shame], threw water on her head in the street, Kempe revels in the
superiority of her reaction: "Sche, no-thyng meuyd þerwyth, seyd, 'God
make ʒow a good man'" (137) [she, not at all disturbed by this, said,
"God make you a good man"]. But the towns' public rejection ends
during crises, when the town or the townspeople are threatened or in a
state of psychic dislocation: for instance, when Lynn is endangered by a
fire at St. Margaret's, or when people are on pilgrimages, or dying.
Often this acceptance is won only at the very moment of crisis: "whan
þe perelys wer sesyd, sum men slawndyrd hir . . ." (164) [when the
perils were over, then certain men slandered her]. Though she incites
threats and irritation in her progress through towns, she is often
welcomed into the homes of strangers, and she is able to soothe the
dying with those very qualities that alienate the secure public at large:

Also þe sayd creatur was desiryd of mech pepil to be wyth hem
at her deying & to prey for hem, for, þow þei louyd not hir
wepyng ne hir crying in her lyfe-tyme, þei desiryd þat sche
xulde bothyn wepyn & cryin whan þei xulde deyin, & so sche
dede. (172–73)[23]

[Also the said creature was desired by many people to be with
them at their dying and to pray for them, for, though they did
not love her weeping and her crying in their lifetimes, they
wanted her to both weep and cry when they died, and so she
did.]

Kempe's powers must always be perceived as operating within a very
small compass. Unlike such holy women as St. Clare or Julian of
Norwich, she has not transformed a cloistered (or sheltered) existence
into an essential source for the town's vitality. Yet her own
contribution to such vitality arises out of comparable tensions. Her

influence increases as its sphere diminishes, for those tensions then force her to reveal all her strengths. Thus her eccentric powers become even starker within the peripheries of a deathbed. It is, perhaps, not surprising that those who mocked her without, welcome her within. And the citizens of Lynn fit into both categories; even as they tried to exclude her (from church services because of her "cryings," for instance), they were unable to distance themselves from her. The identification was too complete.

In exploring the significances of medieval people's outer world, one critic claims that their "external world carried more inherent and given meaning [than does ours]" (Medcalf, "Medieval Psychology" 121).[24] Similarly, he argues that for medieval people, "it was easier to imagine oneself wandering in [their inner world] as a world containing substantial and enduring objects" (121). Margery Kempe's outer world of King's Lynn resonated within her social and religious imagination. The overlap of experiential and imaginative drama is what, finally, makes Lynn so important in understanding her. Just as she overlays her private experiences with a public dimension not merely to aggrandize the former but also to define the reality of both, so she interprets her town as the necessary condition for her to exist at all. She defines herself within a point of friction between both perspectives, as she hears Christ say: "I haue a-sayd þe in pouerte, & I haue chasti3ed þe as I wole my-selfe, boþe wythinne-forth in þi sowle & wyth-owte-forth thorw slawndyr of þe pepil" (157) [I have tested you in poverty, and I have chastised you as I would myself, both within your soul and without, through slander of the people]. We can clearly see here how Kempe conflates public and private, how "þe pepil" are another aspect of "þi sowle." Kempe manages to simultaneously impersonate both mystic and town. Of course, this link raises as many questions about the town as about Kempe, questions that need to be asked in the context of women's history. Rosenthal's warnings about documentary evidence are also true in a larger frame: "To approach the study of medieval women by means of the sources makes us confront a whole range of problems centering around the creation and shaping of texts" (xv). Thus we need to consider the motivations for the people of Lynn who try to integrate Kempe more smoothly into the fabric of the town: how is their "text" shaped? It is, after all, not merely a desire for silence in which to hear the sermon that impels her fellow church members to reject her loud cryings, since, as she says, it is her apparent falsity rather than her noise that irritates them: "& sumtyme sche was al on a watyr wyth þe labowr of þe crying, it was so lowde & so boistows, & mech pepil wondryd on hir & bannyd hir ful fast, supposyng þat sche had feynyd hir-self for to cryin" (185) [And sometimes she was all aflood from the labor of the crying, it was so loud and so boisterous, and many people wondered at her and banned her strongly, supposing that she had feigned that crying]. If they were wrong and she had not "feynyd hir-self," the genuineness of her outbursts would have called into question the entire stability of their lives. We see this process with the people of Leicester, who were perfectly ready to believe that they were suffering from "sweche wederyng of leuenys, thunderys, & reynes contynuyng" (114) [such weather of lightning, thunder, and continuing rains] because they had imprisoned Kempe and two of her fellow pilgrims.

Kempe's involvement in the spiritual aspects of Lynn make her into a kind of church politician—she involves herself in questions about the font, the next prior, etc. (e.g., 170–71)—as well as into a kind of church icon, who not only helps save the church from fire but also manages, in a manner of speaking, to carry the weight of the church on her back and miraculously emerge unscathed, a perfect example of the bonding of town and spirit:

> Sodeynly fel down fro þe heyest party of þe cherch-vowte fro vndyr þe fote of þe sparre on hir hed & on hir bakke a ston whech weyd iij pownd & a schort ende of a tre weyng vj pownd þat hir thowt hir bakke brakke a-sundyr. . . . Soone aftyr sche cryed "Ihesu mercy," & a-noon hir peyn was gon. (21–22)

> [Suddenly there fell down from the highest part of the church-vault, from under the base of the rafter, a stone which weighed three pounds and a short end of a beam weighing six pounds, falling on her head and her back so that she thought her back broke apart. . . . Soon after, she cried "Jesu mercy," and immediately her pain was gone.]

Thus Kempe's own recollections and imaginings depend on her relationship with her town for her sense of her own powers, just as the town seems to have drawn some of its identity through her connections with it. Indeed, in a world in which particular town guilds, full of civic pride, took responsibility for presenting plays that encompassed the religious history of all of creation, it is clear that the relationship between individual and town provides a key for understanding late medieval piety in general and Margery Kempe's version of that piety in particular. Thus studying Margery Kempe in the context of King's Lynn gives us a sense of her options and her sense of self, allowing us another entrance into investigating the kinds of reality we know primarily through literature. We are thus better prepared to consider such questions as

> What . . . was the emotional texture of life for individuals in the past? How did they perceive their world? And their particular social and moral choices? What were the existential consequences of occupying a particular social location? . . . That is, how did social structure shape the emotional reality of individuals? (Rosenberg 2)

And these questions, subtle and far-reaching as they are, are still not adequate for some of the puzzles that Kempe poses, for King's Lynn and Margery Kempe provided "existential consequences" for each other. Only by examining the two together can we approach an understanding of both.

Southwestern University

NOTES

1. It is not my purpose here to provide the architectural, political, or geographical background for King's Lynn. This work has already been amply done, particularly by Vanessa Parker, Helen Clarke, and Alan Carter, G.E. Morey, W.A. Pantin, and (with some need for corrections) Francis Blofield and Charles Parkin.

2. Ladurie is referring to the house, or "domus," of thirteenth-century Montaillou, but his interpretation has resonances for far different expressions of medieval life. See, for example, David Herlihy; also Georges Duby, who says ". . . every [medieval] metaphor that sought to express power relationships . . . in some way made use of the image of the home" (4).

3. For a summary of current architectural theories about the organization and uses of the medieval house, see Deborah Ellis, "The Image of the Home" iii–xxv.

4. E.g., this will of 1349, which presents several such links at once: "In primis lego et assigno Murielle uxori mee ad terminum vite sue totum illud tenementum meum . . . quod mihi jure hereditario accidebat post mortem Ricardi fratris mei et jacet in villa Lenne Episcopi in latitudine inter tenementum Henrici de Betelee ex parte orientali et tenementum quondam Margerie filie mee ex parte occidentale. . . . Et post decessum dicte Murielle . . . lego et assigno predictum tenementum . . . Nicholao filio meo. . . ." (*RR* 90) [In the first place I bequeath and assign to my wife Muriel for the term of her life all my tenement (my entire house) . . . which was left to me by hereditary law after the death of my brother Richard and lies in the town of Bishop's Lynn between the tenement of Henry de Betelee on the east side and on the west side the tenement once belonging to Margery my daughter. . . . And after the death of the said Muriel . . . I bequeath and assign the said tenement . . . to my son Nicholas]. For the historical connection between King's Lynn and Bishop's Lynn, see V. Parker 19–24.

5. "Memorandum quod cum Willelmus de Pikenham nuper legasset tenementus suum in Briggegate in Lenna Cecilie uxori sue ad sustentandum filios et filias eorumdem Willelmi et Cecilia ita quod post mortem dicte Cecilie tenementum venderetur per executores dicte Cecilie Et postea contenciones mote fuissent inter dictos filios et filias pro sustentacione sua de dicto tenemento, tandem amicis intervenientibus sic inter eosdem finaliter concordatum est" (*RR* 47, perhaps c. 1333–35).

6. "Aceciam si contingat predicta tenementa mea post decessum predictorum Johannis et Nicholai filiorum meorum vendi et aliquos vel aliquem de consanguinitate mea illa tenementa vel unum illorum conjunctim seu divisim ad opus suum proprium emere, volo quod habeant seu habeat predictum tenementum . . . decem libris sterlingorum minus quam unus alius qui non fuerit de consanguinitate mea. . . ." (*RR* 90 [1349]).

7. In the late fourteenth century, Lynn had a population of about five thousand. For slightly varying estimates see Clarke and Carter 429, and Morey 38.

8. See, for instance *RR* 185: ". . . Ordinatum est . . . quod nullus decetero dimittet porcos suos ire nec vagare per vicos aliqua die in Septimana nisi in die Sabbati . . ." [It is ordered that no one anymore allows his pigs to go or wander through the alleys any day of the week except Saturday]. For examples of prostitutes on the "venellas communas," see *RR* 35d, 182d.

9. "Ocupet communem fletam cum fimo" (*Book* App. III 364).

10. For Fincham Street: *Book* 367. The *Red Register* shows us several of Margery and John's neighbors: William Amwyke, whose tenement

adjoined the Kempes' in 1391–1402 or longer, and whose property there was taken over by Thomas atte Lathe by 1425; John Mafey, in at least 1391–1402; and, in 1425 or longer, John Ffeltewell, "litster," and Edmund Bonet. The adjoining street, Pursfleet Street or Lane, had another neighbor known to the Kempes, for in 1394–95 John Kempe was one of the pledges for Robert Lystere, described as "morans in Pursflet Lane" (*RR* 119).

11. The translation of line 395 is from Pearsall's note on 127.

12. "Item lego Ricardo fratri meo debita que mihi tenentur Item lego Ricardo de Thorpe famulo meo dimidiam marcam Item lego Willelmo de Frenge famulo meo dimidiam marcam Item lego Alicie uxori mee totam cameram nostram integram. . . . Item lego Margarete de Rudham famule mee, xl. Item lego Thome, Willelmo, et Johanni, filiis meis, omnia armatura mea. . . ." (*RR* 64).

13. Edmund de Brunham secured his franchisement in 1358–59 by apprenticeship rather than birth (*A Calendar of the Freemen of Lynn 1292–1836* 16).

14. BM Sloane Ms. 1315, f. 2d. The rhetoric of the proper goals of the servant to the master, of course, overlap quite precisely with those of the wife toward the husband.

15. A notorious example is the trouble caused in the Paston family by their chaplain, James Gloys. See Norman Davis, e.g., #s 282, 355. The Pastons also, despite their protests, yielded to a marriage between their bailiff, Richard Calle, and Margery Paston. Compare this medieval testator, who expects conflicts between his servants and his children, and takes a clear side: if anyone plans to harass his servants, he asks "that my wyff, with alle the lordeshipe and frendshipe that she may gete, sucour hem, helpe hem, & defende hem, from the malice of myne owne children. . ." (Furnivall 130).

16. *Book* 311, n. 116. For Bridget's importance to Margery, see especially Dickman. In her important introduction to *Medieval Women's Visionary Literature*, Elizabeth Alvilda Petroff puts Margery into context with Bridget's and other women's devotional writings, discussing both themes and style.

17. *Cal. Inq. Misc.* (Chancery), vol. 4, 126–27. For Emma's property and family in Lynn, see *Cal. Inq. P.M.*, vol. 16, 130.

18. *Cal. Inq. Misc.* (Chancery), vol. 4, 125.

19. The sharing is partly a function of the multiple uses to which any room in a medieval house could be put. Bedrooms could serve as dining rooms; people slept in the assembling rooms (i.e., the central hall) or even the kitchen; one room might combine the functions of counting-house or office, warehouse, and parlor. See, for example, Wood 81, 91, 94, and Bennett, *Chaucer at Oxford* esp. 92. For the importance of keys, see *Life of Christina of Markyate* 73, 92; and, closer to home, *Book* 8 (where

Margery's husband deprives her of the keys to the buttery) and 112 (where she is locked into a room in the jailor's house but nonetheless seems able to leave the room at will).

20. For the brewhouse and gatehouse: Owen 335–36. For the latrine: Wunderli 39. For the crowded rooms: Cozens-Hardy no. 2, f. 3. For the garden: Smyser 300–01 (re. *Troilus* ii, 1114–17). For the field: Norman Davis I: 476. Cf. *Book* 180, where Margery and her husband are accused of resorting "to woodys, grouys, er valeys to vsyn þe lust of her bodijs þat þe pepil xuld not aspyin it. . . ."

21. Gillis's history of marriage, relevant in many ways to medieval townspeople (13), emphasizes that the public manifestations of marriage were a positive accommodation to community life, not merely the results of failure to achieve privacy: ". . . people drew a sharp distinction between love and marriage, and took the precaution to strengthen the conjugal bond by enlisting the support of the entire community at the time of marriage" (4).

22. Cf. Thomas Hoccleve, who in his *Address to Sir John Oldcastle* ". . . deplores that even some women of his day argue about Holy Writ (perhaps a reference to Margery Kempe), and he advises them to sit at home at the spinning wheel and 'kakele of sumwhat elles' (v. 148)" (Mitchell 31). It is interesting to note that elsewhere, e.g., 55, Mitchell refers to Hoccleve as a feminist writer.

23. Margery's deathbed role is one entirely suitable for a woman who presents herself through expressions of liminality, one who in this case sees herself as being in contact with both this world and the next. Compare Gurevich's brief discussion of the medieval deathbed scene in art, a scene that combines several planes of perception as devils and angels struggle for the soul of the dying person (186–87).

24. A fuller discussion of these concerns can be found in Stephen Medcalf, "Inner and Outer."

APPENDIX A: CITIZENS OF LYNN

Date	References	Person Admitted to Liberty of Lynn	Pledges	Other Information
16 July 1346	*RR* 181	Ricardus Domynik		finis xl s. Bails out Simon Byteringge who rewards him in will of 1349
29 Jan 1350–51	*RR* 170d	John Kempe I	Ricardus Domynik; Galfridus Hautboys	"skynnere"; finis xl s.
23 March 1352–53	*RR* 172	John de Brunham I	Thomas Ryghtwys sr, Thomas de Bukworth	franchise by birth as Ralph's son
13 March 1363–64	*RR* 143d	Edmund Belyetere	John de Brunham; Thomas Curzon	son of Tho. Belyetere; apprentice of John de Brunham
15 Jan 1370–71	*RR* 150	Thomas de Waterdene	Robt. de Waterdene; Nicholas de Bukworth	apprentice to Robt. de Waterdene
8 July 1384	*RR* 169d	Laurencius de Brunham	Tho. de Couteshalle; Johannes Lokke	finis xl s.
17 Feb 1384–85	*RR* 121d	Ricardus Litell	Thomas Drewe; John Kempe I	
1 Feb 1390–91	*RR* 134	Thomas Seccheford jr.	John Kempe; Thomas Drewe	apprentice of John Kempe
1392–93	*Calendar*	John Kempe II		purchases franchise
1393	*Calendar*	Simon Kempe	Thomas Drewe; Thomas de Waterdene	
14 June 1394	*RR* 118	John de Brunham II		franchise by birth
22 Mar 1394–95	*RR* 119	Robertus Lystere	Ricardus Thorpe; Johannes Kempe	"morans in Pursflet Lane"

APPENDIX B: THE NEIGHBORS OF KING'S LYNN
[see map]

1. tenementum "quondam Galfridi Drewe," 1368–69 (*RR* 149d)
2. two tenements of Robert de Cokesford, 1368–69 (*RR* 149d)
3. tenementum "quondam Thome Ryghtwys jr" (*RR* 149d)
4. tenementum Johannis de Ennemethe, 1369 (*RR* 148d)
5. tenementum Thomas Ryghtwys, at least 1355–65 (*RR* 107, 114d)
6. Thomas Drewe, merchant, 1350
7. Simon Kempe (in this locality): three times
8. tenement with six shops in 1339 (*RR* 75d)
9. ten. Philip Wyth (*Book of Lynn*)
10. ten. quondam William de Hautboys 1348–49 (*RR* 92d)
11. ten. Hugonis de Betele 1348–49 (*RR* 92d)
12. two shops 1368–69, formerly Philip Wyth's (*RR* 110)
13. mesuagium Willelmi de Wetacre 1340 (*RR* 65)
14. "mesuagium tenementum" Will-elmi Fraunceys, 1340 (*RR* 65)
15. Stywardes halle, 1340 (*RR* 65)
16. ten. Thome Robyn "Shipman," 1340 (*RR* 65)
17. ten. quondam Johannis de Frenge et Jacobi Wolsi, 1340 (*RR* 65)
18. Thomas de Seccheford 1355–56 (*RR* 107)
19. Johannis Ryghtwys 1355–56 (*RR* 107)
20. William de Biteryngge 1368–69 (*RR* 110)
21. Thomas de Melchebourne 1349
22. Cecilia Belyeterre and her son William, c. 1349
23. see #7
24. Walter de Biteryngge, 1340 (ten. cum kayo, etc.) (*RR* 66)
25. John de Framysdene, 1340 (*RR* 66)
26. John de Dockinge, 1340 (*RR* 66)
27. John Mafey, 1391–1402 (at least), Edmund Bonet 1425
28. William Amwyke 1391–1402 (at least), Thomas atte Lathe 1425
29. John Kempe 1425
30. John Feltewelle, litster, 1425
31. John Berwyk, bowyer (deceased), 1425
32. William Belleyeterre, merchant, 1407
33. Robert de Brunham, merchant, 1407
34. John de Brunham jr., 1413 (*Book*, App. III, 361)
35. Thomas de Banseye, 1326 (*Book of Lynn*)
36. shopkeepers and innkeepers by 16th century (Vanessa Parker, 37)
37. see #7
38. quondam William de Hautboys', 1348–49 (*RR* 92d)
39. Philip Wyth (*Book of Lynn*)
40. Priores Watergate (*Book of Lynn*)
41. John of Wyreham, 1409–17
42. Alicia de Secheford and "le Bathstowe" 1348 (*RR* 182d)

(Note: for William Amwyke, John Mafey, John Ffeltwelle [litster], and John Berwyk [bowyer], as well as Simon Kempe, see *Book* App. III 366–68.)

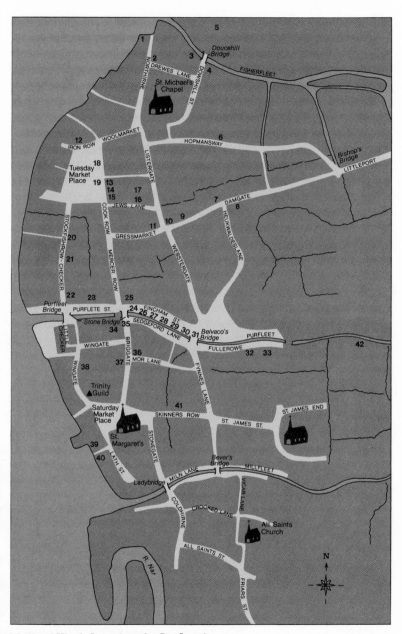

Medieval King's Lynn (map by Sue Long)

MARGERY KEMPE, ST. BRIDGET, AND MARGUERITE D'OINGT: THE VISIONARY WRITER AS SHAMAN

Nanda Hopenwasser

> As the prophet looks at the landscape of Eternity, the mystic finds and feels it; and both know that there is laid on them the obligation of exhibiting it if they can.
>
> (Underhill, "The Mystic as Creative Artist" 65)

The early twentieth-century expert on mysticism Evelyn Underhill equated mystical experiences to the creations of the artistic genius. She believed that "the mystic's personal encounter with Infinite Reality represents only one of the two movements which constitute his completed life" ("The Mystic as Creative Artist" 65). Although the visionary experience provides the raw material which the visionary writer can transmute into an expression of her identity, in order for her to fulfill the obligation of her calling she must transmit her vision to others. Otherwise she cannot provide the link between the mundane and the eternal world which is, in part, her raison d'être. "He must turn back to pass on the revelation he has received: He must mediate between the transcendent and his fellow-men" ("The Mystic as Creative Artist" 65).

The medieval visionaries Marguerite d'Oingt, St. Bridget, and Margery Kempe produced texts which support Underhill's premise that mystics are creative artists; these texts also prove that these writers adhered to the criteria set by Zev ben Shimon Halevi for the visionary in *Kabbalah: Tradition of Hidden Knowledge*. Halevi emphasizes that although "one may experience as an individual the higher landscapes of creation, glimpse the government of Heaven and even perceive angelic beings about their business," such is not the ultimate end of visionary experience (27). He, like Underhill, gives priority to sharing the vision with others for the sake of their spiritual progress. According to his interpretation of the Kabbalah, only human beings possess the free will and intelligence to employ the gifts of God within the temporal world. Only they can traverse the spiritual cosmos and perform the function of visionary artists:

> To acquire such an inner and outer faculty of sight is one of the aims of Kabbalah, for its theory and practice enable individuals to expand their consciousness down and up, and if necessary bridge the gap between the Worlds so as to bring about an increased flow of the divine and celestial influx to bear where evolution is delayed, where disorder is prevalent, or where the Presence of the Divine is to be made manifest in the midst of humanity. (Halevi 27)

Such is the work of the visionary. To employ the Jewish phrase, she is to do "the work of Creation." Despite society's frequent reluctance to accept her vocation and her own reluctance to take on the responsibility of this divine calling, the female visionary is forced to acknowledge her small but significant "participation in the Divine Plan" (Halevi 28). She has to create of her life a work of art which can help the people of her society assimilate what she herself has learned through her visions. More specifically, the female medieval visionary writer wrote to effect a change in the spiritual state of her community. Although she may well have performed functions aside from writing which contributed to her experience as a visionary artist, her textual representation of herself was the primary means by which the reader could judge the validity of her experiences.

The medieval visionary writer performed for her community many of the same functions as the modern shaman. Sociological and anthropological studies of women outside the European tradition who have undergone experiences similar to those recorded by medieval visionaries can inform our understanding of the creativity of the visionary writer. In particular, they can facilitate our understanding of the roles played by visionary women in late medieval culture through comparison with spiritual women in other communities where the official seats of power were held by men. Both the visionary and the shaman serve as bridges between the eternal and mundane spheres. Both must use knowledge derived from the spiritual world to help others. They fulfill functions often performed by psychiatrists, psychoanalysts, and priests (O'Keefe 124–26). In undertaking the roles of psychic or spiritual healers, they produce visions of reality which fuse the numinous with the commonplace for the greater good of their culture. Here the non-European shaman and the Christian visionary share a common calling with the Jewish mystic. According to Halevi, people of all cultures participate in "the Divine Plan" and are capable of experiencing a valid vision derived from God (29–30). Marguerite d'Oingt, St. Bridget, and Margery Kempe as visionaries are both paradigms for women's spiritual functions in the community and individuals who reveal their self-identities through their texts. They fulfill the measure of their self-bestowed nomens—God's "creatura"— inasmuch as they do the "work of Creation." Likewise the study of the lives and art of shamans as creatura of the higher powers of their own cultures help us to understand better the lives and art of Marguerite d'Oingt, St. Bridget, and Margery Kempe.

The anthropologist Mircea Eliade provides a detailed description of shamanistic practices. He also characterizes the shaman with great precision:

> The shaman is also a magician and medicine man; he is believed to cure like all doctors, and to perform miracles of the fakir type, like all magicians, whether primitive or modern. But beyond this, he is a psychopomp, and he may also be priest, mystic, and poet. (*Shamanism* 4)

Like the woman visionary writer, the shaman draws his inspiration from the eternal world and transfers spiritual healing to the temporal world. Female shamans practice in many parts of the world. John Grim in his work *The Shaman* cites the example of the Ojibway healer She-Who-Travels-in-the Sky (95; 125–26). And Kim Harvey devotes an entire book to the life histories of six modern Korean shamans.[1] Although Marguerite d'Oingt, St. Bridget, and Margery Kempe may not appear at first glance to fulfill the conditions of Eliade's description because they practiced their vocations within the parameters of Western Christianity, in their visions, spiritual healing, intercession with higher powers, and transmissions of divine revelations, they strongly resemble the shamans in Eliade's scholarly treatise. All are performers who use their persons to transmit information from higher authority to persons who do not possess their special gifts of privileged knowledge.

Female visionary writers, like female shamans, are conscious of their positions as women in societies which assign them functions different from those of men. The role of visionary writer or shaman opens up possibilities for personal autonomy which would not exist otherwise (Petroff 464; Harvey 235–40). Their visions permit them to stretch social boundaries and to act in ways often thought unsuitable by conservative male authorities. As Elizabeth Alvida Petroff explains, "The vision provides a creative way of relating genuinely to that world, preserving the self while crediting the world outside with power and intention" (46). Petroff stresses the medieval visionary's personal influence on her immediate environment (46–47). The visionary and the shaman imaginatively meld the spiritual and the mundane. The resulting blend gives them a sense that the everyday world includes the transcendent, providing the scope and energy to explore new options which may benefit their societies.

The visionary writer is a mirror of her two worlds; she encompasses portions of both within herself. Moreover, she is also creator of her own mirror when she constructs her art from the materials available to her. This artifacted mirror reflects realities of the commonplace as well as beauties of the transcendent. It shows how the gifts of the eternal world can be used for the spiritual enrichment of her society. Likewise, the power to transform one's environment through spiritual means is the hallmark of the shaman. She too mirrors and re-creates her two worlds in herself, and in her performance she melds both in an attempt to improve the condition of her culture.

The shaman is a creative artist who receives the capacity to heal as a function of a relationship with a higher power. Supernatural beings help the shaman to diagnose illness, heal, and cast out evil spirits. The medieval visionary writer was also a healer. Her text was the means by which she attempted to improve the spiritual health of her community. Like the shaman her medicine derived from a higher power. According to these conditions, Marguerite d'Oingt, St. Bridget, and Margery Kempe in their textual reconstructions of themselves in service of their beliefs fulfill the conditions of Eliade's restrictive definition of the shaman as well as the less restrictive definitions of most other authorities.

Eliade differentiates between the shaman and other ecstatics by pointing out that "the shaman specializes in a trance during which his soul is believed to leave his body and ascend to the sky or descend to the underworld" (*Shamanism* 5). The medieval visionary writer also often received her inspiration in the waking dream or trance (Grim 50–55). Both often meditate on some holy object or thought or undertake some prescribed system of mystical techniques (Idel 72–111; Grim 138–67; Underhill, *Mysticism* 44–94; Leuba 156–83).[2] Nevertheless, some, like Béatrix d'Ornicieux, Marguerite d'Oingt, and St. Bridget, are reported to have gone into trance unexpectedly without prior preparation (Marguerite 118–19, 146–47; Redpath 99). Visions appear to both the shaman and the visionary in dreams and occasionally manifest as auditory and visual hallucinations (Marguerite 90–91; Kempe 11). But despite such unusual physical and mental states, shamans and visionaries functioned normally most of the time. Like Marguerite, Bridget, and Kempe, who perceived themselves as God's creatura, the female shaman considered herself an insignificant member of her society.

The place of medieval visionary writers in their societies, like that of shamans, was defined by their use of sacred space in the practice of their disciplines. Joan Halifax writes that in shamanistic activity, "Psychic, cosmic and personal geography are focused on a centre" (7). Such centering focuses the visionary's and shaman's art. Moreover, it reserves for them a place where they can employ their unusual gifts without the blocking effect of society's disapproval. Often the metaphysical and geographical unite to produce a sacred space where the shaman can converse with spirit beings and learn from them (Eliade, *Myth of the Eternal Return* 6–17). For the religious Christian, God is the center; heaven is the preferred geographical locus. Yet God's heavenly city is permitted to manifest itself physically via its earthly shadows—Jerusalem and Rome (Zacher 49–50).[3] These shadows serve as beacons to the faithful, fulfilling their need to perceive the eternal within the mundane, drawing pilgrims to them like a magnet. Like the Australian shaman who draws his energy from a particular waterhole which represents the center of the world, the Christian visionary woman is often drawn to holy locations (Halifax 38–39). Such a location may be defined as any place where the presence of God or holy beings is manifest; it may be metaphorical as well as geographical. Marguerite d'Oingt felt the presence of Christ while enclosed within the walls of her cloister. St. Bridget perceived his presence in varied locations. Sometimes her visions of the holy family occurred while she remained at home; at other times she was drawn to Rome, Jerusalem, and other sites because of their spiritual power. For her, sacred space could occur either in private or as part of a public ritual in a clerically sanctioned shrine. The same was true for Margery Kempe. Both Bridget and Kempe found their visions strengthened by the special presence of God in specific geographical locations: Bridget, believing that she was guided by a revelation from Christ, chose to reside in Rome and undertook a pilgrimage to Jerusalem in her old age; Kempe also followed the pilgrim's trail and was favored with striking visionary experiences in Rome and Jerusalem which deepened her commitment to her calling.

The sacred space inhabits not only an ideal geographical region but also an ideal time. Temporal concerns often fade when the visionary or shaman is engaged in "the work of Creation." Nevertheless, she cannot forget that she is also a resident of the mundane world. The voyage to a time outside of time, a space outside of space, is the norm in visionary and shamanistic experiences, particularly when power must flow from the supernatural to the mundane world. Certain cultures believe that power is transferred when the participants in a shamanic rite take tangible items from the eternal region and transfer them into the temporal world.[4] Likewise, there exist artifacts supposedly given by the Virgin Mary or other saints to human beings as proof that their visions were valid. Nevertheless, most power transfers are psychic events and do not require concrete items which originate in the eternal world. Special information as well as special powers are usually sufficient to validate the experiences of the visionary and the shaman. They silence objections of the resistant community as well as the visionary's own internal resistance when they prove effective in bettering the spiritual health of the culture.

The sacred journey, real or metaphoric, is the means by which the medieval religious woman and the shaman replicate sacred events of their cultures. Shamans as well as visionaries make pilgrimages to contact a sacred past. For the Christian visionary the pilgrimage to Jerusalem was important because it helped re-create the historical life of Christ. The pilgrimage culminated at Calvary where the pilgrim wept at the torture and death of her God in emulation of the Virgin and the Magdalen. The graphic sight of the crucifixion often elicited fainting fits, holy tears, visions of the Passion, and even appearances of the stigmata.[5] Significantly, it was in Jerusalem that Margery Kempe was given a special gift, loud crying, as a permanent remembrance of her imaginative re-creation of the crucifixion (66–71). Kempe's pilgrimage to the holy land culminating in her visit to the site of the crucifixion was one of the signal events of her autobiography. Marguerite and Bridget also dramatically re-created this event in their writings, but whereas Bridget used the geographical locale as a stimulus to her vision, Marguerite participated in the pilgrimage only in her mind.

Sacred space allows the shaman and the medieval visionary writer to undertake emotional experiences without the negative interference of a disapproving society. There they can safely engage in the spiritual psychodramas which prepares them to serve as spokespersons for their otherworld communicants. The empathic identification with the pains of a sacrificial God aided the medieval visionary in her search for a spiritual wisdom that could only come from replicating the crucifixion within her own life. For example, Marguerite d'Oingt expressed her grief at Christ's Passion by imagining herself bathing and oiling his wounds, feeling them on her own body (149–50). In her "Speculum" she links wounds to words (92). This linkage underscores the Christian visionary writer's equation of the textual symbol with the performative action it represents. In this understanding it becomes obvious that the visionary's words to her readers serve as healing directives in the same way as the shaman's ritual methods serve as salutory procedures to her clients. Writer and reader alike learn from the heavenly message. In the change of perspective, pain is transmuted to pleasure. Both the shaman and the medieval visionary understand that pain and death can promote regeneration and life.

The transfer of power from the realm of the eternal to that of the mundane occurs in the cyclical ritual reconstruction of the signal religious events of a culture both on an institutional and on a personal level. According to Eliade, the regeneration of time also periodically takes place symbolically through the repetition of various seasonal festivals (*Myth* 49–92). Within the Christian system, such festivals are marked both by special saints' days and by the annual witnessing of the historical life of Christ through a particular sequence of holy days. These repetitive ritual events function in creating unity of purpose and subject in the revelations of many visionary writers. As in the visionary experience of sacred space, the medieval visionary artist and the shaman apply the features of the sacred reconstruction of time in their art. Korean women shamans regularly draw from their clients' personal pasts. Christian visionaries can draw from a whole host of historical and folk traditions. As prioress, Marguerite d'Oingt was familiar with the holy days throughout the year. It is significant that her conversion took place on Septuagesima Sunday, a traditional day of repentance. It also appears that St. Bridget and Margery Kempe often correlated their visionary dramas with the church calendar. Both Bridget and Kempe experienced visions of the birth of Christ at Christmas and the Passion on Good Friday. In their narration of events which took place as part of the God-drama, Bridget and Kempe believed they transferred power from the Godhead to their readers by the repetition of sacred tales.

As buffer the medieval visionary filtered the forms of heavenly power she believed she received and made them meaningful to her audience. Bridget and Kempe were received skeptically because they were neither cloistered nor in orders. Many believers felt uncomfortable in the presence of the visionary because of the holy power that clung to her. Their often ambivalent response reveals a deep-seated insecurity about personal intercourse with the divine which can mutate into violence against the visionary. Hence the visionary must always be wary of people who would do her harm; she must remain well within orthodoxy if she is to remain safe. Moreover, her role as buffer between the two worlds places her in a precarious mental state which may lead to personal exaggeration of her connection to spiritual powers or the converse desire to erase herself from power conflicts.

From the point of view of the visionary writer, apparent power masks true powerlessness. Since they perceive their spiritual and creative gifts as deriving from the otherworld, the visionary artist and the shaman alike must admit their powerlessness before forces they are unable to control. A symbolic return to infancy and temporarily to total helplessness often validates their special relationships with transcendental beings. Many times for the practicing shaman "there is a *return* to an earlier time, to Paradise, or to the womb; the theme of regression can also be reflected in the individual manifesting the behaviour of an infant" (Halifax 7). Both shaman and visionary often receive special spiritual food from the deity or deities. The nature of this food, frequently milk, oil, or other substances particularly reserved for infants, represents the total psychic dependency they must feel as a function of their liminal positions (Bynum, *Holy Feast and Holy Fast* 270–74). Both shaman and visionary are psychologically dependent upon the grace of their protectors to guard them against spiritual dangers and death. Both need special relationships to compensate for pleasures and social ties lost as a function of their special positions. Having quit the ordinary world psychologically, they cleave strongly to the eternal world (Idel 44–45). The visionary and the shaman rely on their spirit patrons much as a child relies on a parent, frequently receiving physical nourishment as well as emotional nurture. Fasting occurs as personal and public manifestations of piety. Sometimes normal eating ceases altogether. For example, Béatrix d'Ornicieux was supposed to have lived for a period of time entirely nourished by the host, and Marguerite d'Oingt in her "Meditations" alludes to possible eating problems.[6] Both St. Bridget and Margery Kempe undertook fasts, and Bridget was supposed to have ritualized her mealtimes.

Just as the shaman often draws from more than one supernatural figure, the medieval visionary artist often drew power and inspiration from various saints. Marguerite d'Oingt, St. Bridget, and Margery Kempe, like many of the women of the period, found special protection under the cloak of the Virgin.[7] Marguerite also identified with Béatrix d'Ornicieux and Mary Magdalen. Her identification with the latter was made manifest when she wrote that in spirit she washed Jesus' wounds in imitation of Mary Magdalen's actions (149–50). Kempe too seems to have identified closely with the Magdalene, a woman who in medieval tradition was both visionary and scholar.

The act of identification links the human being with the specific characteristics of the holy or supernatural personality. Under special circumstances, the human being can acquire powers or gifts specific to the personality she emulates. For example, an Ojibway shaman befriended by the spirit patron Otter gains access to the life medicine which, according to myth, Otter originally dug from the earth (Grim 151). The Korean woman shaman in trance or half-trance takes on the personality traits of the gods and ancestors who give her power (Kendall 51–61). Empowering emulation is also possible for the Christian woman visionary. For example, Béatrix d'Ornicieux closely modeled her behavior on that of the Virgin and was rewarded by the Virgin's special patronage. She received holy powers which mirrored those of the Virgin. Béatrix, who according to Marguerite's text had an intense visionary relationship with Mary, was released from captivity by a miracle performed by the Virgin herself (136–37). Marguerite in copying Béatrix's behavior established her relationship with the Virgin vicariously, mirroring her own relationship with the mother of Christ. This double identification reinforced the idea that the Christian woman who aspired to holiness nearly always mirrored the ultimate template, the Virgin Mary, even if she patterned herself after other female saints. Like Béatrix, St. Bridget and Margery Kempe appear to have derived special powers from Christ and the Virgin. According to their texts, from time to time they assumed the intercessory powers so often attributed to the Virgin (*Revelations* 50; Kempe 162). Marguerite, Bridget, and Kempe also aspired to her most appealing saintly qualities: patience, mercy, and humility. In their emulation of female saints, Marguerite, Bridget, and Kempe provided hope to their contemporary readers that in direct and indirect imitation of the Virgin they could come closer to God and, perhaps, receive some measure of empowerment.

The special relationships which the visionary writer and the shaman have with transcendent powers cause them to internalize the moral positions of those powers. Good is doing "the work of Creation" in this world by following the dictates of her higher power; Evil is ignoring the dictates of the higher power and following the urges of her lower self. The inevitable conflict results in the shaman's or visionary's strong identification with what she perceives as Good. She must battle Evil in order to help unprotected members of society benefit from the Good. The medieval woman visionary felt that it was her responsibility to help her community in its fight against Evil. Like the shaman she was an active participant in this battle, for in a dangerous world where powerful forces frequently threaten defenseless human beings spiritual guides were necessary.

Both the shaman and the active visionary guide others spiritually. In order to do this most effectively they must possess the capacity to perceive events within the spiritual world. Only then can they judge how to effect spiritual transformations in members of their communities. Shamans frequently tell their clients how to correct imbalances in their lives by means of special ceremonies where they receive the needed information from the realm of the eternal. For example, an unhappy ancestor may have to be appeased before the Korean bride can have success in her housekeeping or a member of the family can find health (Lee 110–12). According to their texts, God endowed Marguerite, Bridget, and Kempe with the gift of special sight in order to effect his purpose. They were capable of perceiving devils and angels: the former seducing people from the true faith, the latter helping people return to grace after they have strayed (Marguerite 144–45; Bridget, *Liber Celestis* 63–65, 307–09; Kempe 86–89, 144–46). They were capable of telling survivors if a beloved relative had gone to purgatory or if he or she had gone to hell. Marguerite saw the torments of everlasting perdition but was also able to tell when a loved advisor had died and gone to heaven (85–86, 153–54). Bridget observed trial scenes where negative and positive forces fought over the eventual placement of a soul and detected religious hypocrisy by means of Godly information (*Liber Celestis* 133–38, 205–07, 425–27). Kempe also commonly used her special knowledge to help those here on earth pray for those in purgatory (19–20, 172–74).

The shaman and the visionary must also possess the capacity to perceive the negative spirits which reside within human beings here on earth, for the casting out of devils can be done only by those who perceive them within the stricken soul. This ejection of negative forces permits the entry of positive forces which heal the victim, effecting at least a temporary positive change within the healed. Permanent healing can take place only where the will is strong.

Spiritual healing is one of the primary activities of the shaman and the medieval visionary writer. The efficacy of spiritual healing in the community permits the visionary and the shaman to persist in their activities despite societal disapproval because the ability to heal fulfills a needed function. In the shamanistic healing rite, the shaman transfers power from the supernatural to the commonplace world. She then releases the power within the body of the patient, loosing the bonds of illness which have kept the patient entrapped (Grim 8–11). The specific illness is often personified as a demon or demons who have to return to their rightful places in the underworld. Spiritual as well as physical transformation must follow such an exorcism. Personality is re-created and transformed as a function of the healing process. Eliade writes, "This idea that life cannot be restored but only re-created through repetition of the cosmogony is very clearly shown in curative rituals" (*The Myth of the Eternal Return* 81). Likewise, when Bridget or Kempe were purported to have healed a sick soul whose spiritual illness was manifested through mental or physical symptoms, they drew upon the same methods employed by the shaman to draw out the demons within their charges. They prayed to Jesus or Mary to release the demon from the afflicted person and asked for a spiritual as well as physical or mental transformation. The successful cure consisted of a conversion to a holy life as well as a cessation of spiritual possession.

Oftentimes will is not sufficient to withstand the power of evil, either for the Christian believer or the follower of the shaman. Evil forces always regroup and reattack the forces of Good. Discord erupts within all cultures and blocks shamans and medieval visionaries alike from healing all psychological and societal problems to their satisfaction. Shamanistic practices must often be repeated to keep the community healthy, and medieval visionaries often failed to promote permanently their message of God's love to the greater part of their audience. Moreover, despite their desire to follow the Christian message, virtually all saints and visionaries as well as serious members of the medieval Christian community were psychologically tormented and tempted at one time or another. All needed the help of positive higher powers to withstand the onslaught of negative forces. The Christian visionary believed these attacks were tests of faith which all true Christians must endure in order to achieve perfection. Although she only alludes to her own temptations, Marguerite d'Oingt writes rather graphically of those of Béatrix d'Ornicieux (108–09). St. Bridget seems to have experienced only a small number of such attacks, but according to her biographers, she suffered temptations near the end of her life (Redpath 141–44). And Margery Kempe, when tempted by devils, was plucked from the path of damnation by the grace of a healing Christ (7–8). For the medieval visionary God's power was manifest in his grace. The fact that the visionary was able to overcome negative forces validated her calling.

Resistance is the fiery forge which fashions the visionary artist. Societal resistance everlastingly plagues both shamans and medieval visionary writers. But psychological resistance also proves a stumbling block to the expression of her creativity. Internalizing society's norms, she often attempts to refuse her calling. Yet because they feel set off from the community, both shamans and visionaries often perceive themselves as specially chosen for their vocations. Consequently, after they have finally accepted their election, they feel that the fulfillment of their calling was inevitable. Yet initial resistance is common. Sometimes the visionary or shaman attempts to ignore initial visionary experiences hoping to engage in a normal secular life. Like Margery Kempe, who did not initially heed her call, Namsin-Mansin admits, ". . . that second dream was my third call from the spirits to become a mudang. But I didn't want to become one, so I resisted" (Harvey 67).

Physical or mental illness is a frequent sign that a chosen person has not yet entirely accepted her vocation. Such illness, often manifested as an attack by negative spirits, may also prove to be the visionary's initial testing. Eliade writes, "A shamanic vocation is obligatory; one cannot refuse it" (*Shamanism* 18). Indeed, many shamans in various cultures find their vocations only in illness. They are cured when they finally accept the supernatural power which flows through them (Halifax 9–10). Likewise, it is common that a person becomes a medieval visionary through illness. For example, Julian of Norwich had her guiding vision while severely ill. Margery Kempe had her premier visionary experience while suffering from postpartum depression (7–8). Marguerite d'Oingt also referred to illness that could only be cured by the deity (72). Resurgence of illness could take place at any time, particularly if the visionary slipped in her vocation. For example, Kempe suffered temporary emotional illness when she refused to accept a disappointing vision as true. According to her self-evaluation, her illness was a corrective measure taken by God to set her again to his task (144–46). Resistance is futile if God and the spirits have chosen a mortal to serve an eternal purpose; eventually the chosen one must accept her calling.

The visionary's special calling cuts her off from the normal functioning of society. Energy that would normally be allocated to her immediate family is directed to spiritual pursuits. Energy which might have been employed sexually is employed in visionary activities. The shaman and medieval visionary often counter societal resistance to their activities by withdrawing into asexuality. Sexuality is almost always problematic for the shaman and the visionary. For the Christian visionary writer abstinence and, preferably, virginity facilitate her serious commitment to her calling. Petroff argues that abstinence is even a prerequisite of women's visionary writing (5–6). Similarly, the Korean shaman often loses interest in sex (Kendall 38).

Repressed sexuality can take the form of a safe idealized figure with whom the visionary artist can identify. Halifax writes that for the shaman, "the threat of the opposite can also manifest in terms of a positive identification with one's opposite" (7). For both shaman and visionary the male who must be avoided sexually when transmuted into a transcendent figure can provide love and intimacy as well as spiritual direction to his spokespersons. They in turn tend to identify with their supernatural mentors, accepting some degree of intimacy while retaining a strong measure of awe. Halifax writes, "The transformation of the individual results in a mystical apotheosis where the experiencer becomes identified with a cosmic or royal personage" (7). This is particularly true for Marguerite d'Oingt, St. Bridget, and Margery Kempe, who fused love and awe in their relationships with Christ.

The ultimate escape from human sexuality is the sacred marriage, the culmination of the intimate connection between the woman and her deity. This emotional experience occurs both to the shaman and her medieval counterpart; it is employed as a powerful metaphor to explain the fusion between the human spirit and higher power (Halifax 7).[8] The analogy between the societal marriage of a man and a woman and the metaphysical marriage of Jesus and the woman visionary is richly complex. In part, it depends on the idea that marriage within Western medieval culture was theoretically indissoluble, and the sexual act made a permanent physical change in the maiden. Marriage transformed her from an individual, albeit one of inferior status under the power of her father, to an adjunct of her spouse. Losing her autonomy, she subordinated herself to her husband, cleaving to him for the remainder of her life.[9] Likewise, the mystical marriage to Jesus is binding and effects a permanent transformation in the bride of Christ. By its nature it supercedes all previous ties to a mortal man (Bugge 84–85).[10] Jesus can choose the widow after the death of her husband, as he did with Bridget, as well as wed the maiden, as he did with Marguerite; and in special circumstances, he can ask a woman to put aside her husband in favor of a better bridegroom, as he did with Kempe. In the spiritual intercourse between the higher power and the soul, the womanly, human part becomes infused with the light and life of the spiritual force. The heavenly bridegroom presents perfection itself to his bride (Gilson 112–18).[11]

Separation from the mundane manifests itself in all aspects of the lives of visionary artists. The existence of a disapproving external society often encourages them to invest all of their activities with sacred meaning. Such an emotional response might also quiet the visionary's internal doubts. Transmutations of ordinary actions into sacred acts are therefore the hallmark of the visionary and the shaman. Both often act as though they live in a sacred space embedded within a mundane world. They frequently ritualize common activities such as speaking, sleeping, and eating as well as the more obviously ritual action of praying. Moreover, they often react with uncommon intensity to what others perceive as ordinary events because they always see the sacred within the mundane. Uncontrollable emotion sometimes overtook the medieval visionary artist in her interaction with the eternal realm. This too sometimes led to her separation from normal society. Excessive emotion is generally distrusted by people who consider themselves normal; moreover, it is often treated as a mark of insanity. Even among the sanest of our medieval visionaries, the "raptus" caused cessation of normal activities. Marguerite d'Oingt, attempting to communicate the inexpressibility of the raptus, told her readers that her initial conversion so overwhelmed her that she desired neither food nor sleep for days afterward (70–72). St. Bridget too was rapt by her visions and wrote that it was impossible for her to explain fully her experiences in words (Noreen 67). Rarely, however, did she display overwhelming dramatic emotion within her text. On the other hand, Margery Kempe asserts in her *Book* that she was overcome by hysterical crying at the sight of the cross, even though at other times she admits that she could express her feelings more quietly (66–73). Likewise the trance can be a particularly dramatic occurrence when the shaman is possessed by her guardian spirit. Wangsimni-Mansin says, "When you are in that state of mind you cannot think of anything else" (Harvey 31). For both shaman and visionary writer the raptus results in a tighter bond between the entranced and her deity and leads to an even stronger commitment to the spiritual health of her community. It also offers the visionary some compensation for the earthly bonds she has eschewed.

After their conversion experiences, the female shaman and the medieval visionary writer appear to have died to their former lives only to be reborn as new persons totally devoted to the service of the eternal world. "A new birth is part of rebirth fantasies and experiences" (Halifax 7). The rebirth after spiritual death characterized by mutilation and ingestion by supernatural beings, often frightening and "evil," is a common experience of Siberian shamans (Eliade, *Shamanism* 43–44). Rebirth was also the experience of the medieval visionary who underwent a conversion; the qualitative change in her self-perception caused her to attempt to divorce herself psychologically from her previous mundane existence as much as possible. Yet, as she retained her mortality, complete divorce from the real world was impossible. Consequently, since she resided in both worlds, she was best able to serve as a bridge between them.

The medieval visionary writer's text and the shaman's performance validate their callings. Through her creation of her art the visionary can use her special gifts in service of her society. There she can make sense of her visions in a way which can benefit the community which would reject her and she can come to understand how she can promote the wishes of her higher power without effacing her self-identity. The mythic re-creation of historical events and the individualized reinterpretation of the religious symbols provided by her culture in dream and in trance are activities which call into being the art of the shaman and the visionary writer. Both are employed to teach spiritual lessons to their followers. For example, in one of St. Bridget's early revelations, each of Jesus' pains is utilized to present to his followers a moral lesson (*Himmelska* I, 91–92). Like the female shaman who re-creates the important events of her client's mythical and cultural history in her rituals, the visionary writer mythologizes in standard fashion the life and teachings of Jesus. The individuality of form and content corresponds to the individual performance of each shaman. Whereas distance from the subject characterizes Marguerite's writing, in Bridget's work, moderation is the norm; extreme subjectivity permeates Kempe's *Book*. Like the traditional shaman who follows faithfully the techniques of her teacher, Marguerite re-creates traditional forms which the reader easily recognizes. She paints a picture of a distant heaven which is still capable of bestowing its gifts on the favored recipient. Bridget rarely interjects her own speech into monologues delivered by holy personages. She preferred to act as translator and unobtrusive interpreter of her visions, coming as close to a purported original as is possible when one has to translate instantaneous knowledge into linear text. Kempe, on the other hand, was like the more liberal shaman who feels free to change and interpret as well as replicate the ceremonies of her master. She interjected a healthy measure of her personality into her highly subjective art.

The overcoming of her community's initial resistance to her spiritual message and its public acceptance is the final proof of spiritual power for both the medieval visionary writer and the female shaman. Her theater of action presents itself individualistically, sometimes as dramatic ceremony as in the non-Western shaman's performance and sometimes as text as in the religious writings of medieval visionaries. Medieval visionaries transcended their usual home-bound or convent-bound roles, performing as unofficial ministers to a populace which would accept their power only because it derived from the other realm—the realm of supreme power (Bynum, "Women Mystics" 193). Caroline Walker Bynum explains women's visionary activities in terms of power theaters, writing that "women's ecstasy or possession served as an alternative to the authority of priestly office" ("Women Mystics" 192). Fomenting change by their charismatic behavior and offering alternatives to intellectual priestly services which often alienated the poor and neglected the needs of the powerless, visionaries and revolutionary sect leaders such as Francis of Assisi rejuvenated the Church. They added life to institutions which might otherwise have become moribund.

The shaman and the visionary bridge the gap between the communal and individual forms of psychic experience, utilizing positive "holy magic" which derives from religion to heal the sick physically and spiritually. The Korean shaman uses the mechanisms derived from Buddhism and traditional Korean ancestor worship to effect a change in the individuals of her group (Kendall 83–85). Likewise, the medieval Christian woman visionary used her visions and the art derived from those visions to bring lapsed believers and psychically ill persons born into the culture back into the fold of traditional religion. Both infuse the majority religion with energy. As a result they make religion more palatable to those who have become estranged from more formal modes of worship.

Both the shaman and the medieval visionary writer must respond to a public which judges their self-identities and their works. In responding each overcomes the inertia and spiritual pride which may result from keeping untested revelations to oneself. Testing in a public arena also proves the validity of the visionary's message and gives ultimate worth to the visionary experience. The visionary and the shaman gain much from the testing of their revelations. In their countering of community resistance, they become stronger in their powers and surer in their practice. But, ultimately, the medieval visionary's self-identity depended on her personal interpretation of God's use for her gifts as well as the public response to her message. The visionary's life activities, and most particularly her artistic productions, like the shaman's performances, created a foundation for her sense of personal worth. She directly attributed her identity to her creator. And according to her self-attestations, her creative expressions of self both in art and life were controlled by the deity who directed her to create his works and tell his story.

Common to all visionary texts is the implied message—write. Writing serves both as a purgative and as a means by which the believer

can spread the favored words to members of the targeted readership.
They are also a means by which societal displeasure with the
visionary's activities can be countered as well as sometimes dissipated.
The medieval visionary translated her doctrinal norms into personal
visions which served a double purpose: they helped her to achieve
personal understanding of the tenets of her faith and they re-created
within her readers some measure of the personal understanding of the
personal vision she had experienced. The shaman also through her
public congress with the otherworld often achieves a personal
understanding of the interconnected aspects of her spiritual and mundane
areas of existence (Harvey 235–40; Lee 130–42, 202–03). For both the
shaman and the visionary writer work is the exemplification of the
autobiographical impulse, a true expression of self-identity.

Medieval women's dialogue offered perceptive alternatives to the
misogynistic patterns often promoted by males within the Church in
part by showing that reasonable and unreasonable women alike were
protected and loved by God. Likewise are non-Western female shamans
drawn from all levels of society and display great variety in
temperament and shamanistic powers. Nevertheless, they too in their
variety show that higher powers may light on any mortal at any time.
Even the lowly participants of a shamanistic ritual may suddenly feel
that they have been blessed by a special revelation (Lee 202–03; Harvey
109). Women's discourse promotes spiritual wisdom despite and,
perhaps, because of women's human lack of perfection. According to
medieval tradition Christianity ideally performed God's transformation
among all suspect powerless groups. The human imperfection of the
vessel proved the religious truth of a message which purported to
overshadow the reality of personality. Yet personality enriched the
message inasmuch as it made the reader of medieval visionary women's
texts realize that the message was designed for every woman. The life
and works of Marguerite d'Oingt prove that some visionary women
were models of decorum, private and demure, as well as capable
administrators of cloisters. The life and works of St. Bridget prove that
politics is not beyond the ken of visionary women and that sanctity is
possible to achieve within the mundane world. And the life and works
of Margery Kempe prove that God loves the mortal human being even
if she be feisty and unmanageable in the standard sense. In just this
manner does female discourse as well as female personality pervade the
works of female writers of periods where religious authority resides

tightly in the hands of males. Like the woman shaman who also employs many of the masculine features of her culture in service of her female clients, such women writers employ a subtext that expresses female thoughts, fears, needs, and future aspirations.

Both the female shaman and her medieval counterpart, though "defined" by male majority culture, change that culture. In providing necessary spiritual services to the community, they change the culture through social contacts and written texts. Deborah Sue Ellis writes, "Forced to perceive herself and express herself in ways shaped by male society, the medieval woman (both in literature and life) could subvert and transfigure social intercourse in a number of ways" ("The Merchant's Wife's Tale" 606–07). Employing Kempe as one of her prime figures she adds: ". . . Margery ultimately imposes most of the conditions for her transactions with males because she is in better control of crucial social interactions than are they" (607). Kempe here is powerful because she employs the male discourse to her own ends. She empowers herself and breaks the conventions of female silence in theological as well as mundane matters. St. Bridget and Marguerite d'Oingt employ text analogously. The female shaman of many male-dominated traditions does the same thing in her oral performances. Remaining within the bounds of orthodox religion, they all are able to break away from a tradition which would deny them power as well as voice.

Yet the female visionary authors of the Middle Ages, like the female visionaries of non-European cultures, hardly considered themselves subversive. From their points of view, unique power was dispensed to them by the highest religious authority: Jesus Christ. Christ made all under-authorities bow to his word. His reassurance promoted the idea on the part of each visionary writer that she was orthodox with respect to doctrinal truths. She held this belief whether or not her imaginative capacities greatly individualized her perceptions of religious reality. It occasioned self-confidence that she would not have possessed under other circumstances.

Visionary writing like the shamanistic ritual held within its province the possibility of danger. Sometimes community resistance to the woman in contact with the other world proved stronger than her circle of public supporters. For the shaman, a misstep can cause her to be considered a witch or sorcerer. This was also true for the medieval visionary. Bridget suffered from severe criticism during her lifetime, and

Kempe writes that she was imprisoned on a charge of Lollardy (Schmid 9–11; Kempe 111–17). Fears for safety as expressed by Kempe were nontrivial. Marguerite Porete and Na Prous Boneta were among the many condemned and burned for heresy and witchcraft during the later Middle Ages (Petroff 276–80). Nevertheless, the visionary artist almost always found herself forced to produce or perform whether she would or not. Her private vision could not remain private; her perceived mission was to transmit spiritual truths.

The female religious visionary artist displays a common behavior pattern in many cultures. The non-Western shaman and the medieval visionary writer are just two documented manifestations of a pattern which can arise under many cultural conditions but predominates when women do not have access to official seats of power within the mainstream religion of the culture. The religious visionary artist, having internalized her culture's ethical and spiritual norms, creates her art in order to influence others to undertake spiritually enriched lives. She attempts to heal spiritually sick members of her community, employing the metaphors powerful to her culture in her transformative art. Working within the parameters of an orthodoxy defined by ecclesiastical and secular culture, she subverts it through her art, expressing her own identity and affirming the identity of others through her "work of creation."

University of Alabama

NOTES

1. See *Six Korean Women: The Socialization of Shamans*. It is apparent from her work that their life histories closely resemble those of many medieval women visionaries who combined the "lif actif" and the "lif meditatif." Jung Young Lee's book, *Korean Shamanistic Rituals*, is also an excellent detailed study of shamanistic ritual within modern Korean culture. In addition, Laurel Kendall in her work *Shamans, Housewives and Other Restless Spirits: Women in Korean Ritual Life* discusses the value of the persistence of ancient shamanistic customs in modern Korean life. Her work informs inasmuch as her women informants live peaceful though traditional lives within the confines of a modern culture, and their position, socially,

economically, and politically, greatly resembles that of the burgher housewife in the later Middle Ages. According to Kendall, the woman shaman is an important force for cohesion in Korean society.

It is likely that the healing medieval visionary performed a similar function within her society. In fact, Atkinson in *Mystic and Pilgrim* discusses Margery Kempe as a woman who performs shamanistic activities (213–16). Defining her terms according to I.L. Lewis, she compares Kempe's characteristics and activities to those of female tribal shamans and finds them remarkably similar. I agree with Atkinson's evaluation and make that, in part, one basis for my linking Kempe and other visionary writers with shamans.

Three definitive studies of shamanism are Mircea Eliade's classic *Shamanism*, I.L. Lewis's *Ecstatic Religion*, and Roger Walsh's very recent *The Spirit of Shamanism*.

2. Moshe Idel in *Kabbalah: New Perspectives* describes in detail several techniques employed by Jewish mystics to achieve higher levels of consciousness of God. Many are quite ancient and probably date from before the birth of Christ. They may well have influenced Neoplatonic thought and practices. Of particular interest to the study of medieval women visionaries are his subsections on "Weeping as a Mystical Practice" (75–88), "Ascent of the Soul" (88–96), and "Visualization of Colors and Kabbalistic Prayer" (103–11).

3. Mircea Eliade in *The Myth of the Eternal Return* discusses the significance of cosmic geography. He writes that the symbolism of the Center has:

> survived in the Western world down to the threshold of modern times. The very ancient conception of the temple as the *imago mundi*, the idea that the sanctuary reproduces the universe in its essence, passed into the religious architecture of Christian Europe: the basilica of the first centuries of our era, like the medieval cathedral, symbolically reproduces the Celestial Jerusalem (17).

4. Thomas Overholt in *Channels of Prophecy: The Social Dynamics of Prophetic Activity* writes of such an event with regard to the followers of the Paiute shaman Wovoka, prophet of the 1890 Ghost Dance (97–99).

5. Caroline Walker Bynum in "Women Mystics and Eucharistic Devotion in the Thirteenth Century" notes that illness, mutilation, and self-torture, including the appearance of the stigmata are a significant function of the imitation of Christ, and that the miraculous and self-induced reactions to Christ's passion "were *not* an effort to destroy the body, *not* a punishment of physicality, *not* an effort to shear away a source of lust, not even primarily an identification with the martyrs" but an effort to share Christ's humanity as deeply as possible (189).

6. The relationship between food and religiosity has proven an interesting topic in recent years. Sometimes the excessive fasting of medieval female saints and holy women has been associated with anorexia nervosa (Bynum, *Holy Feast and Holy Fast* 194–202), while under other conditions it falls well within the context of the ascetic tradition (Bynum, *Holy Feast and Holy Fast* 208–12). Bridget Ann Henisch's *Fast and Feast: Food in Medieval Society* and Caroline Walker Bynum's *Holy Feast and Holy Fast: The Religious Significance of Food to Medieval Women* are excellent analyses of the role of food and its lack in the Middle Ages. The ability to live solely upon spiritual food (the host and, perhaps, some wine and/or water) is a hagiographical feature of the lives of many medieval saints including some who died young as a function of their gift. Note the hagiographical material concerning Ida of Louvain, Mary of Oignies, and Christina the Astonishing (Bynum, *Holy Feast and Holy Fast* 115–24).

7. Ute Stargardt in her article "The Beguines of Belgium, the Dominican Nuns of Germany, and Margery Kempe" places Margery within a Dominican tradition which emphasizes a systematic imitation of the Virgin Mary for the Dominican brides of Christ (291–92); Toni Schmid devotes an entire chapter of her work to Bridget's emulation of the Virgin (92–115).

8. The time-honored Christian metaphor of the mystical marriage between the human soul and a higher power derives, in part, from the biblical directive to cleave to God multiply expressed in the Pentateuch. According to Idel:

> "devekut" indicates a rather active attitude, a call upon the Jew to strengthen the bond between himself and God. The elite was supposed to cleave to God's ways or attributes by various versions of "imitatio dei," whereas the vulgus could participate in this cleaving only indirectly. (38)

Although "devekut" here is not explicitly mystical, Idel believes "it nevertheless seems to imply real contact between two entities, more than mere attachment of the devotee to God" (3839). However, "explicitly mystical interpretations occur in Jewish medieval and post medieval texts" (39). Idel speculates that the unitive state of soul and higher power evident both in Neoplatonic and later Kabbalistic texts derives from an "ancient, presumably Jewish" source; one which "might have influenced Numenius and Plotinus" (39).

Eliade links the mystical marriage to the Dionysiac Mysteries. In *A History of Religious Ideas* he writes, "In the Hellenistic period, the figure of Ariadne symbolized the human soul. In other words, Dionysus not only delivered the soul from death; he also united with it in a mystical marriage" (II, 281).

9. Weinstein and Bell emphasize the great awareness the medieval girl child had of her prospective fates; marriage or a holy life devoted to "perpetual chastity, humility and charity" (42). The young girl might well have sometimes chosen the convent over the marriage bed out of a sense of self-preservation rather than because of a genuine religious calling. To the teenager "motherhood with its disfigurement of pregnancy, screams of labor, filth of afterbirth, and early decay of beauty offered no joy that could be compared with the ethereal serenity of the Madonna" (44). It is interesting to note that Kempe's first vision occurred while she was in a postpartum depression after the birth of her first child, and that Bridget's visions of the birth of Jesus are idealized, i.e., Mary gives birth without pain.

10. According to John Bugge, "The portrayal of Jesus as the rival with other men for the affections of holy women was a unique by-product of the Anselmian atonement" (83). Anselm perceived the historical Christ as male and human; Bernard of Clairvaux and Hugh of St. Victor reaffirmed Christ's asexuality but promoted the concept of spiritual marriage (84).

11. In *The Mystical Theology of Saint Bernard,* Gilson outlines the relationships manifested in the mystical marriages between the human spirit and God and the bride of Christ and Christ, linking them to Bernard's philosophy of love (112–45). St. Bernard in his "Sermons on the Canticle of Canticles" explicates the marriage symbolism where Christ is the bridegroom of the soul (Bugge 91). For a thorough discussion of the hierarchical stages of love according to Bernard, see *Saint Bernard on the Love of God,* 23–47. By the twelfth or thirteenth century "eventually the Christian-gnostic soul marriage became almost the exclusive province of female virgins" (Bugge 92). Later, abstinent women visionaries, whether or not they had had previous sexual experience, adopted the image.

MARGERY KEMPE AND THE KING'S DAUGHTER OF HUNGARY

Alexandra Barratt

It is a commonplace of Middle English scholarship that Margery Kempe could not read, in the sense of "look over or scan (something written, printed, etc.) with understanding of what is meant by the letters or signs."[1] Paradoxically, though, she could and did "read" texts in the wider sense, in that she orally absorbed, decoded, and interpreted them, and then wove them into her own composition or "writing." This paper will look at one, relatively limited, example of Kempe's reading and rewriting (or "misreading") of another woman visionary's text. Further, it will consider what a study of this material can contribute to the vexed question of how far the priest-scribe, as distinct from Kempe herself, is the "author" of *The Book of Margery Kempe*.[2]

The priest who eventually became Margery Kempe's second and only permanent amanuensis had to overcome many difficulties, both external and internal, before he settled to his task. His first impression of the pages written by Kempe's first scribe, an English expatriate, was that the language was an English-German hybrid and the letter-forms unfamiliar (4). Indeed, he despaired of anyone making sense of what had been written so far without divine intervention, though he promised to see what he could do. At this stage, however, his charitable intentions were nearly stifled by the disrepute into which Kempe's weeping had brought her; for more than four years he prevaricated, and then referred her to an old acquaintance of the first scribe, who was familiar with his friend's script and idiolect. But this man proved useless and the priest's conscience at last began to cause him serious unease. He decided to try again. At first he had problems with his eyesight, made even worse by his spectacles, but Kempe explained that this was a diabolical impediment and finally, with the help of her prayers, he did what she wished.

The period during which the priest-scribe's faith in Kempe was seriously shaken is described in Chapter 62. A Franciscan friar famous for his preaching (possibly William Melton), who had recently arrived in Lynn (in 1420 or 1421), had banned Kempe from his sermons because of her noisy and apparently uncontrollable weeping. Even worse, he preached against her personally in pointed terms. Many of her friends, including the priest, were frightened into deserting and ostracizing her. But the priest's attitude was transformed by certain texts that both contextualized and validated her style of spirituality.[3] One of these texts, the subject of this paper, is mentioned almost as an afterthought and without further explanation: "Also, Eli3abeth of Hungry cryed wyth lowde voys, as is wretyn in hir tretys" (154) [Elizabeth of Hungary, too, cried out with a loud voice, as is recorded in her treatise].

Kempe's scribe may have thought this reference to be self-evident, but in fact there is some doubt as to the exact identification of both the "tretys" and its author. I have argued elsewhere that the text was either the Latin *Revelationes Beatae Elisabeth*, consisting of thirteen individual revelations, all dialogues between the visionary and the Virgin or Christ,[4] or one of its Middle English translations; and that the author, described in one of those versions as "Saynt Elysabeth the Kynges Doughter of Hungarye," was the Dominican nun, Elizabeth of Toess (c. 1294–1337), daughter of Andreas III of Hungary.[5] My purpose here, though, is to explore other echoes of Elizabeth's treatise in Kempe's book, and further to argue that it was Kempe herself rather than her amanuensis who was influenced by this little-known though fascinating text.[6]

Certainly several passages suggest that Elizabeth and her treatise were more than just a name to one or both of them. Significantly, the first occurs at the very beginning of Kempe's initial dialogue with Christ, in Chapter 5. When she was twenty or twenty-one years old she was miraculously cured of a post-childbirth mental illness by Christ, who appeared and spoke to her and was then taken up into Heaven (8). But Kempe was eventually converted not so much by this experience as by her worldly tribulations. She undertook many austerities and another supernatural experience, of a heavenly melody, reinforced her in her new way of life. After two years of strenuous piety, she suffered three years of sexual temptations which culminated in the fiasco of her unsuccessful attempt to commit adultery with an old friend, after which she fell "half in dyspeyr" (16) [almost into despair]. Christ himself then intervened:

> Than on a Fryday byforn Crystmes Day, as this creatur, knelyng in a chapel of Seynt Iohn wythinne a cherch of Seynt Margaret in N., wept wondir sore, askyng mercy and forȝyfnes of hir synnes and hir trespas, owyr mercyful Lord Cryst Ihesu . . . seyd on-to hir, "Dowtyr, why wepyst þow so sor? I am comyn to þe, Ihesu Cryst, that deyd on þe Crosse sufferyng byttyr peynes and passyons for þe. I, þe same God, forȝefe þe þi synnes to the vtterest poynt. And þow schalt nevyr com in Helle ne in Purgatorye but . . . þow schalt haue þe blysse of Heuyn. . . ." (16–17)

> [Then, on a Friday before Christmas, as this creature, who was kneeling in a chapel dedicated to St. John in a church dedicated to St. Margeret in N. (i.e., Lynn), wept extraordinarily bitterly, asking for mercy and forgiveness for her sins and her transgression, our merciful Lord Jesus Christ . . . said to her, "Daughter, why do you weep so bitterly? I have come to you—I, Jesus Christ, who died on the cross, undergoing harsh pains and sufferings for your sake. I, God Himself, forgive you your sins to the furthest extent. And you shall never enter hell or purgatory but . . . you will possess the glory of Heaven."]

This passage seems to be modeled on an incident from the twelfth of Elizabeth's thirteen revelations: in the words of the Wynkyn de Worde translation,

> On a daye whyles Elysabeth was lastyng in prayer and full bytterly wepte her synnes, our Lorde Jhesu Cryste, that is confortatour of theym that ben soroufull, sayde to her, apperyng, "O my dere doughter, trouble the not ne be not sory for mynde off thy synnes, forwhy all thy synnes ben forgyuen the." And whan she answeryd the contrary and sayde that she was certayn that yf he wolde doo wyth her rightfully and not mercyfully, she was worthy to be dampned to the paynes of helle; thenne our Lorde Jhesu Cryste answered and sayde, "Doughter, ryghtuosnesse is now done to God my fader for [thy] synnes and satysfaction is fully made to hym for theym all, after that ryghtuousnesse asketh. For yf thou haue

offendyd God wyth all the membrys of thy body, I was
tormentyd in all the membris of my body for thyn and all
mankindes synnes." (f. 95va)

[One day while Elizabeth was persevering in prayer and wept
most bitterly for her sins, our Lord Jesus Christ, who is the
comforter of those that are sorrowful, appeared to her and
said, "Oh my dear daughter, do not distress yourself or be
sorrowful because of the memory of your sins, for all your
sins have been forgiven you." And when she denied this in
answer, and said she was convinced that, if he were to deal
with her justly and not mercifully, she deserved to be
condemned to the pains of hell, then our Lord Jesus Christ
answered and said, "Daughter, justice has now been done to
God my father for your sins, and full recompense has been
made to him for them all, in accordance with the demands of
justice. For if you have offended against God with all the
limbs of your body, I was tortured in all the limbs of my body
for your sins and those of humankind."]

In both texts a devout woman is at prayer and weeping bitterly for her
sins; Christ appears in a vision, addresses her as "Daughter," and
comforts her. He then personally assures her that, through his
sufferings on the cross, her sins are forgiven and that she will never
suffer the pains of hell.

Such a series of coincidences is not perhaps remarkable or
unprecedented in itself. The next parallel, however, is rather more
distinctive. Chapter 14 comes between the accounts of Kempe's brush
with the monks and townspeople of Canterbury and of her interview
with Repingdon, Bishop of Lincoln (which can be dated sometime
between mid-1413 and February 1414). It was obviously inspired by her
recent experience of public hostility in Canterbury, where she had been
threatened with burning as a heretic, for in this chapter Kempe
entertains a fantasy of martyrdom:

Sche ymagyned in hir-self what deth sche mygth deyn for
Crystys sake. Hyr þowt sche wold a be slayn for Goddys lofe,
but dred for þe poynt of deth, and þerfor sche ymagyned hyr-
self þe most soft deth, as hir thowt, for dred of inpacyens, þat
was to be bowndyn hyr hed and hyr fet to a stokke and hir hed
to be smet of wyth a scharp ex for Goddys lofe. Þan seyd owyr
Lord in hir mende, "I thank þe, dowtyr, þat þow woldyst suffer

deth for my lofe, for, as oftyn as þow thynkyst so, þow schalt
haue þe same mede in Heuyn as þow þu suffredyst þe same
deth." (29–30)

[She visualized inwardly what kind of death she could die for
Christ's sake. It seemed to her that she was willing to be slain
for the sake of God's love, but she dreaded the moment of
death, and so she visualized the gentlest death for herself, as
it seemed to her, out of fear of her failure to bear suffering: and
that was that her head and her feet should be tied to a stake and
that her head should be struck off with a sharp axe for the sake
of God's love. Then our Lord said, in her mind, "I thank you,
daughter, that you would be willing to suffer death for the sake
of my love, for as often as you think like this, you shall have
the same reward in Heaven as though you had suffered that
very form of death."]

Similarly, though in dialogue with the Virgin rather than with Christ,
Elizabeth too is offered in her eighth revelation the reward of martyrdom
in return for her willingness to suffer:

"And therto," she [the Virgin] sayd, "woldest thou for the loue
of hym ben slayn, rostyd, or drynk venym?" And whan she
[Elizabeth] durst not afferme ne denye that she wolde suffre
this thynges for the name of Cryst, thenne the blyssed
mayden sayd, "In stedfastnesse I say the, doughter, yf thou
wold for loue of God be spoyled of all worldly thynges and
garmentes of thy now[n] mynde or wyll, soo that thou wyll
noo thyng haue ne coueyte in this world, I wyll procure to the
of my sonne the mede that Bartholomew hath for his fleyeng.
And yf thou bere paciently wronges and reproues, [for] all
maner of wronges born of the, thou shalte haue the mede that
Laurence had for the rostyng of his body. And whan thou art
reproued, scorned, and sette at nought of other, yf thou bere it
gladly and mekely, thou shalt haue the mede that Johan the
Euangelyst had for the drynkyng of venyme. And yf thou
wolde be trewe to me and be buxom to me, I wolde be nyghe to
the to fulfyll all that is sayd before, and I wold be wyth the,
euer helpyng the whan it is spedfull to the." (f. 94va)

["And moreover," she [the Virgin] said, "would you be
willing, for the sake of his love, to be slain, roasted, or drink
poison?" And when she [Elizabeth] dared neither assert nor
deny that she was willing to suffer these things for Christ's

name, then the Blessed Virgin said, "In constancy I say to
you, daughter, if you were willing for the sake of God's love
to be despoiled of all worldly things and the outer covering of
your own mind or will, so that you should be willing neither
to have nor desire anything in this world, I am willing to
obtain for you from my son the reward that Batholomew had
for his flaying. And if you patiently endure injustices and
reproaches, for all the kinds of injustices endured by you, you
shall have that reward that Lawrence had for the roasting of
his body. And when you are reproached, mocked, and despised
by others, if you endure it cheerfully and humbly, you shall
have the reward that John the Evangelist had for his drinking
of poison. And if you were willing to be faithful to me, and
obedient to me, I would be willing to be with you, always
helping you when it is expedient for you."]

Kempe has clearly both read and responded to the passage from the
Revelations.[7] She has considered her ability to undergo the three forms
of martyrdom offered Elizabeth by the Virgin, and has silently decided
that she is not capable of such heroism. (Elizabeth herself
circumspectly "durst not afferme ne denye" her willingness to suffer
such deaths.) Instead, Kempe concentrates on and elaborates the idea of
decapitation as the only kind of martyrdom she could support (a death
very different from burning, the usual form of capital punishment for
women in the Middle Ages, with which she was threatened on several
occasions). But in her attention to this literal and arresting aspect of the
text she seems to have missed the Virgin's point—that each mode of
martyrdom, however spectacular or grotesque, has its precise moral
equivalent in everyday life.

One of the most striking of Elizabeth's revelations is the first.
The visionary, in a state of spiritual dryness, is forestalled from seeking
advice and comfort from a male religious by the appearance of the
Virgin, who proposes herself as a more reliable teacher: "Thenn she [the
Virgin] sayde, 'Ther is noo brother in the worlde that may better
enforme the of thy spouse than I maye'" (f. 91va) [Then she [the
Virgin] said, "There is no friar in the world who is able to instruct you
better about your spouse than I"]. Kempe too seems to have been struck
by the passage, but thought it could be improved. In Chapter 64, it is
Christ who offers himself to her in an identical capacity: "Þer is no
clerk in al this world þat can, dowtyr, leryn þe bettyr þan I can do"
(158) [There is no cleric in all the world, daughter, that knows how to

teach you better than I]. Immediately after this passage, Elizabeth falls
to her knees and places her hands between the Virgin's in the traditional
gesture of feudal homage. The Virgin then demands that the visionary
enter her service:

> And eftsonys Our Lady sayde, "If thou wylt be my doughter,
> dyscyple and seruaunt, I wolde be thy moder, ladye, and
> maystresse. And when thou art of me suffycyently enfor[m]ed
> and taught, I wolde lede the to th[y] louyd spouse, my sone,
> whiche wol receyve the in to hys hondes as I now have
> receyved the."

> [And afterward Our Lady said, "If you are willing to be my
> daughter, disciple, and servant, I would be willing to be your
> mother, lady, and mistress. And when you have been
> sufficiently instructed and taught by me, I would conduct you
> to your beloved spouse, my son, who will accept you into his
> hands as I have just accepted you."]

In a dialogue in Chapter 21, which relates to an early phase of Kempe's
spiritual life, before she and her husband had taken vows of chastity and
she was still bearing children (i.e., before 1414), Christ assures her that
he loves wives as much as virgins and calls on his own mother to
assure Kempe of his love. Immediately following, the Virgin speaks to
her directly in terms that seem influenced by this passage:

> "Dowtyr, I am thy modyr, þi lady, and thy maystres for to
> teche þe in al wyse how þu schalt plese God best." Sche tawt
> þis creatur and informyd hir so wondyrfully þat sche was
> abaschyd to speke it or telle it to any, þe maters wer so hy and
> so holy. (50)

> ["Daughter, I am your mother, your lady, and your mistress to
> teach you in every respect how you must best please God."
> She taught this creature and instructed her so marvelously that
> she (Margery) was abashed to speak of it or tell it to anyone,
> the subjects were so lofty and so holy.]

The idea of the Virgin as a teacher or "maystresse," and of the visionary
as her disciple, clearly derives from Elizabeth. It is perhaps more
significant, because it is more unusual, than the shared but not
uncommon idea of the Virgin as "mother," and also as "mistress" in the

domestic rather than educational sense, which Hope Emily Allen in a note also traces to the *Revelations* of St. Elizabeth (265, n. 18/31).

There are further signs of Elizabeth's influence in the next chapter of Kempe's book. She is again lamenting her lost virginity, and Christ is moved to say, "A, dowtyr, how oftyn-tymes haue I teld þe þat thy synnes arn forȝoue þe & þat we ben onyd to-gedyr wyth-owtyn ende?" (50) [Ah, daughter, how many times have I told you that your sins are forgiven you, and that we are eternally united?] Like Kempe, Elizabeth has to be personally assured of forgiveness—no fewer than three times in her *Revelations*. On the last occasion, in the thirteenth and final revelation, Christ says: "This thyrde tyme I saye to the, thy synnes ben fo[r]gyuen, and thou hast my grace" (f. 95vb) [For this third time I say to you, your sins are forgiven and you have my grace.]

On Kempe's return from her pilgrimage to Jerusalem, probably in late 1414 or early 1415, she stayed in Rome at the Hospital of St. Thomas of Canterbury, but was expelled because of the slanders of a hostile priest. As she describes it in Chapter 32:

> Whan þis creatur sey sche was forsakyn and put fro among þe good men, sche was ful heuy, most for sche had no confessour ne myth not be schrevyn þan as sche wolde. . . . Than owyr Lord sent Seynt Iohn þe Evangelyst to heryn hir confessyon. . . . Than sche teld hym alle hir synnes and al hir heuynes wyth many swemful teerys, and he herd hir ful mekely and benyngly. (80–81)
>
> [When this creature saw that she was abandoned and ejected from the company of the good, she was very unhappy, most of all because she had no confessor and could not then be confessed as she would like. . . . Then our Lord sent St. John the Evangelist to hear her confession. . . . Then she told him all her sins and all her sorrows, with many sorrowful tears, and he listened to her very humbly and kindly.]

As Hope Allen points out in the Notes (299, 81), this motif, which appears in the lives of several holy women, occurs first in the *Revelations* of St. Elizabeth, specifically in the tenth revelation:

> It happened that Elysabeth was mornyng in a spyrytuall dysese duryng thre yere. And that was for thought that she myght not haue her confessour as ofte as she wolde bee confessyd. Wherfore God hauyng compassyon of her

desolacyon, he assygned Saynt Johan the Euangelist to be her
confessour, commaundynge that soo ofte as she wolde be
shryuen, he sholde besely here hir and assoyle her by his
auctoryte. (f. 95ra)

[It happened that Elizabeth was mourning, in a state of
spiritual distress, for three years. And that was because of the
thought that she could not have her confessor as often as she
wanted to make her confession. For this reason God, taking
pity on her desolation, delegated St. John the Evangelist to
be her confessor, commanding that as often as she wanted to
be confessed, he should carefully listen to her and absolve her
by his authority.]

However, the two accounts diverge significantly. Kempe in a lengthy
and detailed passage (81) stresses the way in which confession to St.
John exactly parallels normal confession to a human priest—she says
"Benedicite," he says "Dominus"; he gives her a penance, speaks words
of comfort, bids her receive communion, and goes on his way.
Elizabeth, on the other hand, emphasizes the supernatural nature of the
experience and its superiority to the sacrament of penance as usually
mediated through the Church:

And it shop soo by Goddis grace, that whan she shroue her to
ony other confessour, she hadde unnethes mynde what she
sholde saye; she was not glad and iocunde after her assoyling
as whan she shroue her to Saynt Johan. (f. 95va–b)

[And it so came about through God's grace that when she made
her confession to any other confessor, she could scarcely
remember what she had to say; she was not happy and cheerful
after her absolution as she was when she made her confession
to St. John.]

What is one to make of these parallels? It is clear that Kempe
had a suggestible sensibility, a receptive mind, and a memory both
capacious and tenacious. We also know that, as she could not read
herself, she had heard read various standard devotional classics (see, e.g.,
Book 276, n. 39/23–25). Her ability to retain effortlessly what she had
thus absorbed is characteristic of those who come from an oral rather
than literate culture. Her amanuensis became aware of Elizabeth's
treatise sometime between 1424 (four years after the arrival of the

Franciscan friar who shook his faith in Kempe) and 1436 (when he began to revise Book I). But Kempe, if her memory is accurate—and all the evidence suggests that it was—showed signs of Elizabeth's influence earlier, possibly as early as the birth of her first child (say, about 1394), and well before 1413 when she and her husband started to "live chaste." Unless the priest-amanuensis was putting words into Kempe's mouth, or unless she substantially re-phrased and re-shaped her experiences in retrospect, it seems that it was initially Kempe who had heard read, and was influenced by, a version of Elizabeth's *Revelations*.

There are two Middle English translations of the *Revelations* extant, apparently independent. One was printed by Wynkyn de Worde around 1492 and we have no evidence as to its previous existence. The other version is extant in a fifteenth-century manuscript, Cambridge University Library Hh.1.11, which from the contents appears to have belonged to a house of women religious. A number of scribes contributed to the volume and some of their dialects can be localized to various parts of East Anglia (Essex, Norfolk, and East Norfolk). Possibly it belonged to the Augustinian Canonesses at Campsey in Suffolk, or to the Franciscan nuns at Bruisyard in Suffolk or at Denney in Cambridgeshire.[8] It is presumably not sheer coincidence that Kempe too came from East Anglia (Lynn is in Norfolk) but it is not possible to say definitely that it was the version witnessed by the Cambridge manuscript which she knew.[9]

Margery Kempe, then, seems to have known the *Revelations* in the last decade of the fourteenth century or the first decade of the fifteenth, and it may have been she who drew the text to the attention of her future amanuensis. The aspects of the text that impressed him, however, were different from those that had caught her imagination. He was comforted by its stress on the tears wept by the visionary. The *Revelations* is a relatively brief text (the Middle English translations both run to about 6,000 words), but within its modest compass it contains no less than nine references to weeping. Seven of these concern Elizabeth herself, one the Virgin, and one any devout soul. Of the seven references to Elizabeth's weeping, all but one link tears and prayers. One example, the earliest in the treatise, is representative: "Elysabeth, Goddes seruaunt, in prayeng wepte full bitterly . . ." (f. 91vb) [Elizabeth, God's servant, wept very bitterly while praying . . .]. Two passages also make it clear that Elizabeth's weeping was noisy, though not perhaps as "bowystows" as Kempe's: "soo bytterly she weped that she myght not wyth-holde her from vtterly sobbynges and cryenges wyth voyce . . ." (f. 91vb) [she wept so bitterly that she could not restrain herself from outward sobs and vocal cries] and "she was prayeng . . . wyth hye voyce and moche deuocion and shedyng of teres . . ." (f. 92ra) [she was praying . . . with a loud voice and much piety and shedding of tears]. It is interesting that the Virgin also models this form of behavior.[10] She explains to the visionary that her sanctification in the womb did not exempt her from the need to work for God's grace, and describes her habitual spiritual practices, which include weeping and prayer: "Alle other grace I hadde wyth moche trauell of soule and body, contynually pray[y]ng daye and nyght, wyth full brennyng desyre, and wepyng with full bytter mornyng . . ." (f.93vb) [All other grace I gained with great exertion of soul and body, praying unceasingly day and night, with most ardent desire, and weeping with most bitter lamentation . . .]. The Virgin also implies that such behavior might be manifested by other devout persons when she goes on to describe how a person dedicated body and soul to God enjoys special favors such as spiritual inebriation, and how the soul characteristically behaves after such an experience of ecstasy or rapture:

> Buth qwan swych a sowle comth aȝen to hereself, yt schal þanne ȝeldyn thankyngys and louengys to God wyt al þe deuociown and affeccyown of here soule, and oldyn here vnworthy all grace, and wepe and sorwe wyt mich dred þat yt ys so vnkende to swych a benefyce. (C.U.L. Hh.1.11, f.125ʳ: the Wynkyn de Worde version here omits the reference to tears.)

> [But when such a soul returns to herself (i.e., recovers consciousness), she must then render thanks and praise to God with all the devotion and love of her soul, and must consider herself unworthy of all grace, and must weep and sorrow with much fear that she is so unfit by nature for such a blessing.]

Finally, Margery Kempe might well have felt that she had even more in common with the visionary Elizabeth than a certain style of spirituality. Although I have argued that the *Revelations* originate with Elizabeth of Toess, O.P., daughter of King Andreas III of Hungary, and not with St. Elizabeth of Thuringia, the daughter of King Andreas II of Hungary, it is undeniable that the later Middle Ages universally attributed them to the latter. St. Elizabeth of Hungary, canonized shortly after her death in 1231, was a popular figure throughout Europe, including England. Her life is often included in hagiographical collections; for instance, there is an Anglo-Norman version in the volume of saints' lives, formerly belonging to the Duke of Portland, now in the British Library, that in the Middle Ages belonged to the nuns of Campsey, and a Middle English version in the East Anglian Osbert Bokenham's *Legends of Holy Women*. But, like Kempe herself, St. Elizabeth had been a married woman and a mother (she bore three children); although widowed young, she did not become an enclosed nun, but joined the Third Order of St. Francis. Franciscan tertiaries shared the Order's commitment to poverty but continued to live in the world (though wearing a distinctive habit) and engaged in works of mercy (Elizabeth worked among the poor and the sick). St. Elizabeth then, at least as evidenced by the misattributed *Revelations*, provided a model of ecstatic piety and of copious and noisy weeping. But she was also an early exemplar of the mixed life of action and contemplation that Kempe pursued,[11] and shining proof that Christ, as he told Kempe in Chapter 21, loved wives as well as virgins. In these respects, as also in her aristocratic background, St. Elizabeth was a precursor of the much more recent figure of St. Bridget of Sweden.

There is one final irony. The friar who attacked Kempe for her noisy weeping was a Franciscan, if the medieval marginal note identifying him with William Melton has any authority. But it was also an ostensibly Franciscan text (for the Latin *Revelationes Beatae Elisabeth* almost always circulated with texts of genuinely Franciscan origin) which helped give Kempe's future amanuensis the courage to defy him and help her.

University of Waikato

NOTES

1. See *The Oxford English Dictionary*, 2nd edition, Oxford, 1989, entry for "read," *v*. Its apparently literal and specific meanings are not historically anterior to the more general and metaphorical.

2. On this subject, see John C. Hirsh, "Author and Scribe in *The Book of Margery Kempe*," who concludes, "it may be confidently stated that the second scribe, no less than Margery, should be regarded as the author of *The Book of Margery Kempe*" (150).

3. For a detailed discussion of these texts, which argues that the priest himself "misread" them, see Roger Ellis, "Margery Kempe's Scribe and the Miraculous Books."

4. For a discussion of the textual tradition of the Latin, and an edition of one Latin version and of the Catalan translation, see P.L. Oliger, "Revelationes B. Elisabeth: Disquisitio Critica cum Textibus Latino et Catalaunensi."

5. See "*The Revelations of Saint Elizabeth of Hungary*: Problems of Attribution," forthcoming in *The Library*.

6. Contrast Hirsh's remark (in connection with *Book* I, Ch. 28, and its use of one of the Meditations on the Passion ascribed to Richard Rolle), "In articulating what Margery must have seen, the second scribe fell back . . . on *his own* [my emphasis] devotional reading in order to make the significance of the event clear to the reader" ("Author and Scribe" 149).

7. The parallel with Elizabeth's text is much closer than Hope Allen's citation of a passage from Mechtild of Helfta's *Liber Specialis Gratiae* (*Book* 271, n. 30/12).

8. For further details on C.U.L. Hh.1.11, see Barratt, "*The Revelations of Saint Elizabeth of Hungary*." Sarah McNamer is preparing an edition of the manuscript version for publication in the Heidelberg Middle English Texts series.

9. In this paper most of the quotations are taken from the Wynkyn de Worde version, as the orthography of the Cambridge University Library version is somewhat eccentric.

10. On this aspect of the text, see Barratt, "The Virgin and the Visionary."

11. See Susan Dickman, "Margery Kempe and the Continental Tradition," especially 156–57.

BRIDE, MARGERY, JULIAN, AND ALICE: BRIDGET OF SWEDEN'S TEXTUAL COMMUNITY IN MEDIEVAL ENGLAND

Julia Bolton Holloway

Margery Kempe of Lynn, in the fifteenth century, both had a book written, beginning it on St. Bridget's day, July 23, 1436,[1] and carried out pilgrimages, as we see on the accompanying map, reaching Jerusalem in Asia by way of Venice (1413), and crisscrossing the continent of Europe, journeying to Assisi and Rome in Italy (1414–15), Compostela in Spain (1417), perhaps Trondheim and Munkaliv in Norway, certainly Gdansk in Poland, and Aachen in Germany (1433), finally visiting Carthusian Sheen and Brigittine Syon in London (1434) (*Book* xlviii–li). In doing so, she was clearly imitating Saint Bridget of Sweden, who likewise had written a book, the *Revelations*, pairing and validating that book with her pilgrimages, which we see upon the same map, to Trondheim in Norway, Compostela in Spain (1342), Cologne, Aachen (1349), Rome, Farfa (1350), Assisi, Naples (1365), Bari, Ancona (1369) and elsewhere in Italy, and Jerusalem in Asia (1372) (*Bride* xii–xiv). Kempe not only replicates Bridget's book and pilgrimages with her own; she also takes pains to visit Brigittine houses, the Hospice in Rome near the English College where Bridget wrote so much of her *Revelations* and other books and where she died, perhaps the Norwegian Brigittine convent of Munkaliv, almost cer-tainly the Brigittine convent of Marienbrunn at Gdansk,[2] and also English Brigittine Syon and Carthusian Sheen, founded in 1415 by King Henry V.

Pilgrimage gave women equality with men, as on a pilgrimage all were to be theocratically equal, whether they were beggars or kings.[3] Book writing, which was typical of pilgrims who shaped their texts in time to maps in space, especially granted women, as well as men, access to power. Such had already occurred with the pilgrimage writings of Egeria from Spain and Paula from Rome in the fourth century.[4] Because women—according to Paul—were forbidden to preach, they were driven to quest attention through visions, which were really not so much hallucinations as they were devotional exercises, the "revisioning" of sacred dramas, especially when experienced *in situ*, in their appropriate Holy Places, in which these women "saw in their ghostly sight," in their imagination, what male guides and priests were reading and preaching to them, as their "reception aesthetic," and which they in turn could write or have written down. Especially after the coming of the universities in the twelfth century women were further marginalized. They could through visions, pilgrimages, and books enter into theology, the universities' "Queen of Sciences." These women and their male scribes/advisors created a powerful theological "textual community," to use Brian Stock's term, that has transcended time and space. St. Bridget's life and her *Revelations* were especially studied and imitated by women in Italy, where she is known as "Santa Brigida," and in England, where her name became "Bride," as in "Bride of Christ," and this is the form used by Margery Kempe of Lynn, and, more rarely, "Bridget," even "Brigypt," echoing the name of the Irish saint.[5] Both her life and her book were studied and emulated by women seeking power and respect. It is possible that Chaucer's English Wife of Bath parodies such women and their pilgrimages and writings, in his desire to unravel their textual powerfulness.[6] This essay will map out the lives, texts, and pilgrimages these factual and fictional women shaped.

Saint Bride

Bride's position in Sweden and abroad was one of great status. She was born to Birger Persson, Lawman of Uppland, in 1303. The position of Lawman in Sweden is analogous to that of the Icelandic Lawspeaker, the one who codified and interpreted the law of the land. Birger Persson had so codified the Uppland laws for the King of Sweden in 1296. Bride's mother, Ingeborg, died when she was young and the child was raised by her aunt Catherine. The girl read the legend of Saint Cecilia and likewise wanted to be a virgin,[7] but her family insisted upon her marriage at twelve, in 1316, to Ulf Gudmarson, who was to be Lawman of Nericia. She became the mother of eight children, named Martha, Ingeborg, Cecilia, Catherine, Benedict, Birger, Charles, and

Gudmar. Of these Ingeborg, Benedict, and Gudmar died young, while Cecilia contrarily left her convent and married several times. In 1335, King Magnus married the twelve-year-old Blanche of Namur and Bride became their governess, teaching the young queen Swedish and holding an important position at court. Earlier, Ulf and Bridget pilgrimaged to Trondheim in Norway. In 1342, Ulf and Bridget pilgrimaged to Compostela, Ulf dying on their return in the Cistercian abbey of Alvastra in 1344. This and her later pilgrimages would crisscross all of Europe and reach Asia (*Bride* 3–5), as seen on the map.

Bride's life was marked by her visions, which prompted her pilgrimages and her writings, and which granted her even greater access to power than she already had as a Swedish noblewoman. Bride had had visions since she was a child: the first, of the Virgin crowning her; another, in which Christ called her his spouse, his bride (*Bride* 33–35; cf. Kempe 31); several concerning the founding of her Order of the Most Holy Saviour; a grim one indeed of Christ coming as Ploughman to plough under the realm of Sweden with the Black Death to punish King Magnus for his wickedness, which came to pass two years following that revelation (*Bride* 12–13, 37); later, many more concerning the various popes of her day and the emperor Charles of Bohemia.

Her teachers had included Sweden's best scholar, Master Mathias, who had studied under the converted Jew, Nicholas of Lyra, in Paris, and who translated the Pentateuch for her, rendering it in medieval Swedish (*Bride* 9). In visions Christ and the Virgin also enjoined her to pay heed to Prior Petrus Olavsson of the Cistercian monastery at Alvastra as well as Master Peter Olavsson of Linköping, these two men remaining with her for the rest of her life. In Sweden she and her sons studied Latin under Nicholas Hermansson, who would later write the hymn *Rosa rorans bonitatis* to honor the translation of her relics to Sweden, while in Rome she continued to be taught Latin, this time in visions, she said, by Saint Agnes. Her entourage, in Italy, would come to include a Spanish bishop turned hermit, Alfonso de Jaen, who would edit her *Revelations*' almost final version. Care was always taken by Bride and her circle that her writings be authorized and orthodox (*Bride* 9). However, that never prevented them from being powerful, subversive, and feminist. Her role came to be seen as that of sibyl and prophet to medieval Europe. Her writings presented her as the Bride of Christ, blending the Song of Song's Queen of Sheba and Revelations'

Woman Clothed with the Sun (*Bride* 121–22). Margery Kempe would adopt that stance in her *Book* as well. Bride's writings would in turn influence, with their images of the Brides of Christ and Christ as the Ploughman, important English texts such as *Pearl* and *Piers Plowman*.

Bride left Sweden in 1349, reaching Rome in 1350 for its Jubilee year. She would be joined there by three of her children, Catherine, Birger, and Charles. Her chief aim in life would be to found the Order of the Most Holy Saviour, consisting of double monasteries, for women first and foremost and also for men, ruled by abbesses and prioresses as well as having a confessor general. During Bride's lifetime she would fail at this task of establishing her monastic Rule and Order, though King Magnus had already given to her the royal castle at Vadstena for the new monastery. The Rule was eventually approved by Urban VI in 1379, then confirmed in 1419 by Martin V at the request of King Henry V of England, but always as an addition to the Augustinian Rule (Deanesly 92). Another goal was to have the popes return from Avignon to Rome. In this she succeeded twice, even having the pope and the emperor meet in Rome and, after Bride's death, Catherine of Siena, copying her, would achieve this same triumph.

Despite the power and wealth of the royal households of Sweden and Naples with which she was associated, Bride and her household encountered financial difficulties. She first lodged in a cardinal's palace off Saint Lawrence in Damaso. But in 1354 she was evicted for nonpayment of rent. Francesca Papazuri took her into her own palace in the Piazza Farnese. At times, to keep her household from penury, with advice from Christ to do so, Bride would go and sit among the beggars outside the church of Saint Lawrence in Panisperna, run by the Poor Clares. Her patched and mended mantle in which she so begged still exists (Andersson and Franzen 18–29, 33–44). Interestingly, the image of a humble mantle, such as would have been worn by the Virgin and under which Christians could take umbrage, keeps recurring in Bride's writings. Bride succeeded in deliberately dramatizing her poverty, becoming the princess turned beggar maid of fairy tales. To do so she borrowed from Cistercian simplicity and Franciscan poverty. This model of pious poverty would be effectively copied in turn by Margery Kempe during her sojourn in Rome. In Kempe's case the copy is inverted, having the beggar become as if a princess (*Bride* 5; Kempe 92–95).

To understand Bride's visions, which influenced Kempe's, it is important to survey the modes of writing which she cultivated and which partly came to her from her Cistercian and Hieronymite spiritual confessors and advisors. The use of theatrical modes had been practiced in monastic writings through time and especially in connection with women, largely to compensate them for the Pauline prohibition against their preaching. Paula and Jerome had described how, in Paula's mind's eye, she had perceived the sacred dramas that had occurred at Bethlehem and upon Calvary when they were carrying out their pilgrimages. A Franciscan friar, known now as Pseudo-Bonaventure, wrote for a Franciscan nun a book that influenced many medieval women, including Margery Kempe, the *Meditations on the Life of Christ*, which further dramatized with feminine details episodes of Jesus' childhood and adulthood. Bride's spiritual advisor, and after her, Catherine of Siena's, was the Spanish bishop and Hieronymite hermit, Alfonso of Jaen. The Hieronymites, commenced as an Order of Hermits by Alfonso's brother, were followers of St. Jerome, continuing his devotional practices. Such practices had already been recommended to women anchoresses by St. Anselm and by Aelred of Rievaulx.[8] They consisted of revisioning the Gospel narrative with oneself as witness and participant, transcending both time and space. Rather than as hallucinations, it could be wise to perceive Bride's and Kempe's visions (*Bride* 18–19, 130–31; *Book* 68–75, 139–49, 190–98, and *passim*) as such spiritual exercises, such sacred conversations, and such participatory "devotional theaters" of the past's sacred drama.[9] In Margery Kempe's case, we even find Jerome in a vision in Rome at his tomb endorsing her behavior (*Book* 99), just as we will also find Paul later apologizing to her for his prohibition against the preaching of women (*Book* 160).

Bride, when married to Ulf, had traveled with him first to Trondheim in Norway, then to Compostela in Spain. As a widow, Bride pilgrimaged everywhere, visiting the places sacred to St. Francis in Assisi, the shrine to St. Nicholas in Bari, and many more. Years before, it had been prophesied to her that she would see Bethlehem and Jerusalem before her death. In 1372, at almost seventy, she journeyed there.[10] Then, in 1373, she died in Rome, her body being carried from her room in Francesca Papazuri's house (a room Margery Kempe would later visit) to lie in state in the church of Saint Lawrence in Panisperna, outside of which she had begged in her patched and mended mantle. (It was likely in this year that Margery Kempe was born. It was in this year that Julian had her vision.) Miracles occurred and were carefully recorded, Bridget's bones next being taken from Rome, by way of

Gdansk, to Vadstena. By 1391, with powerful lobbying by Queen Margaret of Sweden, Queen Joan of Naples, the emperor Charles of Bohemia (Richard II's wife's father) and several popes, the princess turned beggar maid was made a saint (*Bride* 20–21).

Dame Margery and Dame Julian

André Vauchez has called for renewed study of canonization materials as a mode for historical investigation.[11] In these materials we can find illuminating vignettes and anecdotes, stories of people of actual flesh and blood, especially of the lives of women and peasants, material generally passed over or censored as of no consequence or as of too much danger, for sainthood and its miracles are not unlike heresies and its rebellions, and often similarly contain forms of opposition to authority, which were to be controlled by being paradoxically authorized.[12] In the canonization materials concerning Saint Bride we meet vividly with one Catherine of Flanders, a marginalized servant girl, and the account given, in her own words and those of others, now translated into Latin, of her serious illness and Bride's miracle of healing concerning it. We meet her again in the pages, this time, of Margery Kempe's *Book* concerning her pilgrimages and visions, modeled in turn upon those of Saint Bride, and here validated by Kempe's actual conversation at the Casa di Santa Brigida in Rome with a major witness at Bride's trial or *processus* for sainthood, Bride's personal maidservant, now grown old, this same Catherine of Flanders.

In the process for canonization it is clearly stated that Catherine of Flanders, Bride's maidservant, fell gravely ill while they were returning from Bari, likely with appendicitis, with a fever and a puncture on the left side, and so was given extreme unction, the others asking Peter Olavsson to ask Bride to pray for her, believing that her prayers would cure Catherine. Which he did, Bride then prostrating herself on the floor where she prayed, and Catherine of Flanders was immediately freed from the illness and rose up cured and was able to journey on horseback quickly to Rome.[13] The passport for this journey to Bari and Ancona was written out in 1369.

In 1415, nearly half a century later, Margery Kempe, the mother of not eight but fourteen children (*Book* 115), on her pilgrimage modeled on that of Saint Bride, stopped in Rome, staying at the English College, then the Hospital of St. Thomas of Canterbury (*Book*

80, 94), adjacent to the Casa di Santa Brigida (Redpath 90–91), and asked Bride's now very elderly servant, Catherine of Flanders, about her mistress, and was told through an interpreter that she was "Seynt Brydys mayden," Saint Bride's maid, and that Bride "was goodly and meke to euery creatur & þat sche had a lawhyng cher" (95) [had been gentle and kind to everyone and always shown a smiling face].[14] The host agreed with the maid, saying that Saint Bride was so humble he did not even realize that she was a great saint. Dame Margery visited the chamber in which Saint Bride wrote her books and died, made into a chapel, and she heard a Dutch priest preach there concerning her. On St. Bride's day, Dame Margery kneeled upon the stone upon which Saint Bride was said to have kneeled when she had her vision of Christ telling her of her death (95). Margery, already in Rome, had been asked to be godmother to a child, named by the parents after Saint "Brigypt," because they had known her when she was alive (94). We learn too of Margery, in Rome, as emulating Saint Bride's poverty and being given charity for this by a Dame Margarete Florentyn who had known her on her pilgrimage from Assisi to Rome (93). It was in Rome also, at the Lateran, that Margery had her Brigittine vision of her marriage to God—but in Margery's case not to God the Son, but to God the Father (86–87). Her ring had already been engraved with, "Ihesus est amor meus" [Jesus is my love] (76, 161), which was more in consonance with the Brigittine espousal, and also with the motto of the Brigittine Order, "Amor meus crucifixus est" [My love is crucified]. Carolyn Walker Bynum has told us much about the erotic spirituality practiced by women in this period, and her thesis is strongly borne out by the Brigittine manuscripts confiscated at the Reformation and now preserved in the Lambeth Palace Library.[15]

What had drawn Margery Kempe of Lynn to her book writing and pilgrimage *imitatio Brigidae*?[16] The East Anglian region is the port area for the Baltic and Scandinavian routes. Already, by the 1370's, literary traces of Bride's writings were to be found in English texts, their importance being especially stressed in the East Anglian region about Cambridge University.[17] Adam Easton, a Benedictine monk of Norwich Priory, like Master Mathias, was a scholar of Hebrew, trained in the mode of Nicholas of Lyra. He may have taught Julian of Norwich some of her theology. In 1386, as cardinal, he vowed to work for Bride's canonization if he were to be saved from execution for his alleged conspiracy against the pope. In 1389, Cardinal Adam Easton of

England, whose Roman church was that of St. Cecilia, was reinstated by the new pope and in 1391, on October 7, Bride was canonized, Boniface IX's bull of October 9 granting both the canonization of Saint Bride and the Portiuncula and St. Peter in Chains indulgences for Vadstena Bride had so strongly desired. Interestingly, in the following year, 1392, Julian of Norwich completed the longer version of her *Revelations*.[18]

In 1406, Eric, King of Sweden, Norway, and Denmark, married Philippa, daughter of Henry IV and sister of Henry V. Her royal party returned to England after visiting Vadstena and Henry Lord Fitzhugh, strongly recommended to leprous Henry IV that he found a similar house in penance for his murders of King Richard II and Archbishop Richard le Scrope.[19] In that same year, Henry Fitzhugh donated Hinton-Upperhall, or Cherry Hinton, near Cambridge in the diocese of Ely, to the Brigittines, when he was present at the nuptials of Henry IV's daughter, Philippa, to King Erik of Denmark, Norway, and Sweden, at their royal visit to Vadstena, and in 1407 the *Vadstena Diary* wrote of Brigittine brothers being sent to East Anglia to establish a monastery (Nyberg, *Birgittinische Klostergründen* 70). We also know of their presence in Yorkshire. Moreover, Lord Fitzhugh himself owned a copy, perhaps even the holograph, of Yorkshire Richard Rolle's *Incendium Amoris*, one of Margery Kempe's favorite texts, bequeathed to him in 1415 by Henry Lord Scrope "for a remembrance" (Deanesly 96). Thus it is clear that the area around Cambridge, Ely, Lynn, and Norwich, as well as Yorkshire, was deeply affected by Saint Bride and the Brigittines, that influence being associated with the writings of the Yorkshire mystics.

Henry V brought the body of Richard II for burial in Westminster Abbey and founded Syon Abbey, in London instead of East Anglia, in April 1415, simultaneously with the Charterhouse of Jesus of Bethlehem at Sheen, ordering prayers for his father, ". . . for the souls of John, late Duke of Lancaster, our grandfather, and Blanche, his late wife, our grandmother" (elegized in Chaucer's *Book of the Duchess*). Henry declared before Agincourt, according to Shakespeare, "I have built/Two chantries, where the sad and solemn priests/Sing still for Richard's soul" (*Henry V* 4.1.317–19). In the King's Charter for Syon it is stated that whichever kingdom has within it a Brigittine monastery, "there peace and tranquillity, by meditation of the same, should be perpetually established" (*Mirrour of oure Lady* 61). Margaret

Deanesly tells us of the founding of Syon Abbey: "The little party of Brigittines [from Sweden] arrived at King's Lynn [August 26, 1415], proceeding to the building at Twickenham, which had been begun in February, five months before" (107; also Nyberg, *Birgittinische Klostergründen* 74). Pope Martin V approved the English Brigittine Rule in 1419.[20] Then, in 1430, Queen Philippa, sister to Henry V, died and was buried at Vadstena in the Brigittine garb.

In the 1430's Margery Kempe visited the English Brigittine Monastery, Syon, to attain the Pardon at Sheen (245–46),[21] and earlier had also visited Julian of Norwich, following the cessation of her childbearing travails, discussing that visit in her *Book* within a few pages of mentioning "Bride's book." She enjoyed many days of "holy dalyawns" and "comoyning in þe lofe of owyr Lord Ihesu Crist" (42–43) [of holy conversation and communion in the love of Christ], with Julian. The anchoress Julian of Norwich likewise wrote down her *Revelations*, her *Showings*, of her vision which came to her on May 13, at four in the morning, in 1373, in the Short and Long Texts. The Westminster Cathedral manuscript of her text, though written out around 1500, gives its date as 1368, and, while it includes most of Julian's theology (all that is created is like a hazelnut in the palm of her hand; God as "I it am"; Jesus as Mother), it nowhere includes any materials concerning her 1373 version, giving one to believe that its original text had indeed been written in 1368 when Julian was twenty-five and Margery not yet to be born for another five years. It perhaps should be called the First Text. Illiterate Dame Margery also was to dictate and have her revelations written down as the 1436 *Book of Margery Kempe*, imitating that of Bride's 1373 *Revelations* and Julian of Norwich's 1373 *Showings*. Interestingly, one manuscript, that of Julian's Short Text, and the earliest extant manuscript of her *Showings*, brings together Julian's and Bride's texts, with those of Richard Rolle, the Yorkshire mystic, while also stressing the legend of St. Cecilia: British Library, Add. 37,790. It was written by the Carthusian from Sheen, who had very close associations with Syon, one James Grenehalgh.[22] Margery, who was illiterate, spoke often of the books read to her, which include Hilton's book, "Bride's book," the *Stimulus Amoris*, the *Prick of Love*, and the *Incendium Amoris*, the *Fire of Love*, of Richard Rolle of Hampole.[23] It is clear that the program in which she participated, of the reading of holy books and the writing of her own, mirrored that of Saint Bride.[24] We recall that Kempe's own manuscript was to come into the possession of the Carthusians at Mount Grace Priory in Yorkshire, folio 3, stating, "Liber Montis Graciae. This boke is of Mountegrace," it being carefully annotated by these same Carthusians (*Book* xxxii), with which James Grenehalgh had associations.

Aristocratic Bride, who was willing to break down social barriers by becoming a beggar and a pauper, gave to two other very disparate women, the hysterical Margery of Lynn and the quiet Julian of Norwich, a pattern for their lives and for their books, a model for marginalized women of whatever social class who could thereby attain praise and respect—what Bride's text calls "worship"—through visions, writings, and, in two cases, pilgrimages, though not the third. Margery Kempe, we recall, had married beneath her, had experienced mental illnesses following her many childbirths, and had ignominiously failed at the businesses she had attempted. To then model her life and her book writing concerning her visions and pilgrimages upon that of the influential and powerful figure of St. Bride would be restorative and healing (*Book* 219). Another aspect to that healing, beyond the eroding of social boundaries, was that of the eroding of sexual boundaries. Women were either virgins and saintly, or mothers or whores and not so. Bride was of both spheres, being a mother of eight children who had desired to be a virgin, and who successfully became a saint. This second aspect to Bride as model validated Margery's former sexuality and her bearing of many children, permitting her, too, to quest, though not attain, canonization.

What drew women, especially those who were secular, to Bride was that she was a mother who had travailed in a near fatal childbirth. This obstetrical obsession in connection with Margery Kempe has been noted by Gail McMurray Gibson in "St. Margery: *The Book of Margery Kempe*," a chapter in her book, *The Theater of Devotion*. Women were clearly attracted by Bride's linking of the body and the book, defying the requirement that for access to Latin one had to be virgin or celibate, giving up the body for the book. The canonization materials giving testimony presented by women frequently stress miracles in connection with women, their bodies, and childbearing. A major vision and miracle concerning Bride herself as childbearer was that of the Virgin helping Bridget in her perilous childbirth with Cecilia (*Bride* 4).[25] One later story is of a woman in Rome whose seven previous pregnancies had all miscarried. She requested that Catherine of

Sweden give her something of her mother Bride's clothing, and wore this for the rest of the pregnancy. The living child who was born was named Bridget.[26] Later, Margery would be godmother to another child in Rome named "Brigypt," the *Book* observing that the child's parents had known Saint Bride (*Book* 94). They clearly saw the analogy between Bride and Margery in making these choices of name and godparent.

A further miracle was given in the Middle English life of Saint Bride, taken from the canonization bull, and likely to have been read in some similar form to Margery Kempe:

> and after the sayde Bonys and Relykes of seynt Birgette were translatyd from Rome to the sayde Monasterye of Watstenes in swecia . . ./and after this blessyd woman seynt Birgette was canonyzed by pope bonyface of that name the nynth/the yere of our Lord god a thousande .CCC.lxxxi. as in the Bull of hyr canonyzation apperyth/A woman of the dyocesse of Lyncopence callyd Elseby Snara with great peyne/and sorowe was delyuered of a deed Chylde/and when she was after her great peyne come to hyr perfyte remembraunce with humble prayer she besoughte almyghtye god that by the merytes of his gloryiouse espouse seynt Birgette the Chylde myghte be restoryd to Lyfe and made a vowe that if the Chylde came to lyfe that she wolde vysyte the sepulcre of Seynt Birgette/And anon the Infaunte beganne to waxe hote/and to take Brethe and afterwarde it was restoryed to full Lyfe wherfore the Moder with great deuocyon/and gladnes fullfyllynge hyr auowe/vysyted the Relykes of Seynt Birgette in the Monasterye of watzstenes aboute the Natyuyte of oure Lorde. (*Mirrour of oure Ladye* lviii)

St. Margaret was the patron saint of childbirth. Women named Margaret particularly cultivated Saints Margaret and Bride, Margery of Lynn among them, as Gail McMurray Gibson has shown.[27] In connection with that material we could give the story from the canonization documents concerning a woman in Trondheim in Norway named Margaret who had been paralyzed and mute but to whom came a vision of a lady who said, "I am Bride of Vadstena who will cure you of your terminal illness, and you will go healed to my place and proclaim publicly what grace has been done to you" (*Acta et Processus* 117). Which Margaret of Trondheim did.[28] Such a story, coupled with Bride's

earliest pilgrimage to Trondheim, and the founding in Norway of the
Brigittine monastery, Munkaliv, could help explain Margery Kempe's
pilgrimage to Norway in 1433, though this visit may have been due to
her ship being driven off course in a storm (*Book* 230–31). Another
pilgrimage goal for Kempe was Gdansk (*Book* 231–32). Gdansk was an
important Brigittine site, the body of Saint Bride having passed that
way on its return to Sweden from Rome and a Brigittine monastery,
Marienbrunn, being established there during Henry IV's exile from
England as Earl of Derby and sojourn in that city (Nyberg, "Klasztor
Brygidek" 53–77). In turn his son, Henry V, would carry out his
father's wishes in founding Brigittine Syon and Carthusian Sheen to
atone for his murders of Richard II and Archbishop le Scrope of York.
Kempe took pains to visit Brigittine Gdansk and Brigittine Syon and
Carthusian Sheen (*Book* 245–47). It is likely that the miracles of
healing given in the life and the canonization process, which generally
occur with women, are an endorsement and participatory proof by these
women concerning the empowerment they felt Bride gave them. Both
Bride and Margery Kempe had to combat Paul's dictate against the
preaching of women (*Book* 126, 140). Both Bride and Margery Kempe
had to combat men's criticism of them for not spending their time
spinning and carding wool (*Book* 129). Both Bride and Margery Kempe
finally got their husbands to permit them to make vows of chastity, in
Bride's case, all her life having longed to be like St. Cecilia, in
Margery's case, likely prompted by fears of the postpartum psychosis
to which she was so prone (*Book* 23–25).[29] Both women had had many
children and experienced serious complications in childbirth, Margery
finding in Bride a therapeutic model (*Bride* 4; *Book* 6–9). Both were told
by Christ they were his spouse (*Bride* 33–35; *Book* 31). Other
analogies exist, besides those of childbirth. Bride wrote to Nicholas
Acciaiuoli's widow and his sister Lapa that he was in purgatory.
Margery dictated to a Master of Divinity a letter to a widow, saying her
husband was in purgatory (*Bride* 54–62; *Book* 45–47). Both women
knew of the coming deaths and the dispositions of souls of others (*Bride*
52; *Book* 53–55). Both Bride and Margery had visions in which they
saw names written in the Book of Life (*Bride* 67–97, 113–19, 126,
129; *Book* 206–07). Both Bride and Margery use a feminine pantheon,
Margery having the "Qwen of Mercy, Goddis Modyr," and Saints
Katherine, Margaret, Barbara, and Mary Magdalen among her patrons
(*Book* 50–52). Bride's daughter, Catherine, stopped a flood of the Tiber

in Rome by her prayers (Gregersson and Gascoigne 18–19); similarly, Margery Kempe stopped a fire in Lynn (*Book* 162). Bride accurately prophesied, through Christ, the coming of the Black Death to King Magnus within two years; similarly did Margery, through Christ, prophesy the coming of a pestilence within a year (*Bride* 12–13, 37; *Book* 185–86). Both were reduced to theatrical begging in the city of Rome (*Bride* 15; *Book* 92–95). Thus Margery can be seen to model her life, her book, the cessation of her childbirths, her miracles, and her pilgrimages upon Bride's. As a grace note to the anxiety of influence of Bride upon Margery, we even find Margery one-upping Bride by having "owyr Lord Ihesu Crist" [our lord Jesus Christ] grant to Margery a vision he had withheld from Bride, of the sacrament flickering in the priest's hands like a flying dove and likewise the chalice moving, and his stating to Margery, "My dowtyr, Bryde, say me neuyr in þis wyse" (47) [My daughter, Bride, never saw me in this manner].

It is clear, in turn, that Margery's book, like Julian's *Showings*, is created in the image of Bride's book, her *Revelations*, and that these shared in a powerful woman's textual community, fostered by the men who were their spiritual advisors and who were willing to be their amanuenses, and that the manifest piety of these women's visions, pilgrimages, and writings were frequently sanctioned by the Church in its nervousness about the imminent Reformation.[30] Similarly would the Church foster the writings of the nun of Canterbury, Dame Elizabeth Barton, the Maid of Kent, on the very eve of that Reformation (*Book* lxvii–lxviii).

Saint Catherine and Dame Alys

In 1378 Chaucer was carrying out secret diplomacy in Lombardy on behalf of England with Sir John Hawkwood, the English *condottiere* in Italy, and Bernabo Visconti (Crow and Leland xxi), and would have heard of both St. Catherine of Siena and Bridget of Sweden at that time, as well as knowing of St. Bride from Richard Lavenham, King Richard II's confessor, who had lectured on Bride's *Revelations* at Oxford in 1370.[31] For Bride's life and her *Revelations* had been much studied and imitated by women in Italy, as well as in England. St. Catherine of Siena closely modeled her *acta*, her deeds, upon those of St. Bride of Sweden, and who similarly wrote letters to figures in power, for instance, to Sir John Hawkwood, or Gianni Acuto, as the Italians called him, around 1375, ordering him to go on crusade to the Holy Land rather than ravage her Tuscany (Luttrell 188).[32] For in 1373, following the death of Saint Bridget, the pope had given to Saint Catherine, as her spiritual advisor, the bishop hermit, Alfonso de Jaen, who knew very well how to make use of such women and their writings for political purposes. St. Catherine even sought to outdo St. Bride, in having her marriage to Christ take place through the use of the strange relic then preserved in Rome of Christ's foreskin, which is not a detail St. Bride would have employed. Likewise Margery jealously would seek to outdo Bride, in having Christ award her the privilege of seeing the Host flutter in the priest's hands. The Brigittines were to publish the account of St. Catherine of Siena in their book, *The Orcherd of Syon*, in 1475. Margery Kempe was likewise to have some of her account be published, and by the same printer, Wynken de Worde of Fleet Street, London, in 1521.[33] However, Catherine of Siena, Margery Kempe of Lynn, and Julian of Norwich followed reverently in St. Bride's physical and spiritual footsteps, each carrying out an *imitatio Brigidae*, an imitation of Bride. Chaucer, I believe, satirized Bride outrageously in his portrait of the Wife of Bath, patriarchally subverting her matriarchal liberation.

It is possible that Chaucer's fictional Wife of Bath, whose pilgrimages are likewise those of Bride and Margery, the journeying to Compostela, Rome, and Jerusalem, as seen in the accompanying map, was created by that male poet to deconstruct the games of power these flesh-and-blood women played with male figures of authority, in Bride's case, dialoguing with popes and emperors, kings and princes, in Catherine's with popes and knights of Fortune, in Margery's with bishops and pilgrims, merchants and priests, in Julian's, with difficult, troubled women like Margery. All four flesh-and-blood women formed an important textual community that has succeeded in transcending space and time.

Let us ask why Chaucer, writing the *Canterbury Tales*, might have been moved to undercut the Brigittine model? My own hypothesis is that Chaucer was a Wycliffite, a member of the Gaunt faction, whose friends were the Lollard Knights, for which he was in exile from court during much of the writing of the *Canterbury Tales*, and that the *Canterbury Tales* is his Wycliffite, Lollard satire against the institution of pilgrimage. For John Wyclif and his followers it was not necessary to perform physical pilgrimages or to give rich gifts to shrines, but instead to quest God within. The most famous pilgrim of Chaucer's century was Saint Bride, who journeyed to Compostela, Cologne, Rome, and Jerusalem, as we see on our map. Her canonization in 1391 was used by Rome to counter Wycliffism. If Chaucer could create a fictional *contrefait* to her figure he could undercut and propagandize against orthodoxy. With the western Wife of Bath, rather than of eastern Lynn, in Alys's scarlet, rather than in bridal or pilgrim white or widow's black of Bride and Margery, the *Canterbury Tales' contrefait* similarly journeys to Compostela, Cologne, Rome, and three times, not just once, to Jerusalem, but she is lecherous, rather than taking vows of chastity as the Bride of Christ, and, paradoxically, she has no children, instead of Bride's eight or Margery's fourteen. She is, as if it were, Bride and Margery and Julian turned inside out and upside down.

Thus to the flesh-and-blood women, Bride, Margery, and Julian, should be added the glorious fourth whose existence is only a fiction, of words penned on parchment, Alys of Bath. I think of her as created by Chaucer like those transvestite heroines, Defoe's Moll Flanders, Flaubert's Madame Bovary, Tolstoy's Anna Karenina, and Joyce's Molly Bloom who exemplify their authors' *anima* and *id.* And I think of her as created by Chaucer like that fictional, pirated Don Quixote, mirrored in yet another character, "The Knight of Mirrors," who encounters the true one in the pages of Cervantes's continuation of his great novel, *Don Quixote*, Part II. For in Dame Alys of Bath we meet refracted images of Saint Bride, Saint Catherine, Dame Margery, and Dame Julian.[34] In this way Hopi clowns mimic white women in "Cross Your Heart" bras, tottering on high heels, carrying handbags with mirrors and cosmetics, warding off what they fear. "Increase and multiply" became the Wife of Bath's text to justify sex (III.28–29). But Margery Kempe replies to her persecutors, explaining that text spiritually, not physically (*Book* 121). "Experience, thogh noon auctoritee/Were in this world, is right ynogh for me" [Experience, though no authority were in this world, is good enough for me], proclaims Chaucer's Alice, while Bride, Catherine, Julian, and Margery instead quest authorization.

University of Colorado, Boulder

NOTES

1. ". . . in þe 3er of our Lord am.cccc.xxxvi on þe day next aftyr Mary Maudelyn" (*Book* 6). Page references for Bride are from *Saint Bride and Her Book*, trans. Holloway, as *Bride*.

2. Henry IV of England, when he was Henry, Earl of Derby, visited Gdansk, August 1390 and September 1392, when Marienbrunn was being founded. See Nyberg, "Klasztor Brygidek" 53–77 and Tait 83.

3. Turner 94–203; Holloway 18 and *passim*.

4. See Egeria, "*Peregrinatio Aetheriae*"; Paula and Eustochium, *The Letter of Paula and Eustochium to Marcella*; Jerome, *The Pilgrimage of Holy Paula*; Jerome and Paula, *Epistolae*.

5. William Patterson Cumming, in *The Revelations of Saint Birgitta*, notes Irish *brighid* derives from *brigh*, virtue, strength (xxiii).

6. Holloway 180–88.

7. See *The Life of Christina of Markyate* for similar instance; Chaucer's *Canterbury Tales*' "Second Nun's Tale" also gives the legend of St. Cecilia.

8. See Jantzen 57 and Elizabeth Robertson, "An Anchorhold" 171–76.

9. See Gail McMurray Gibson's book *Theater of Devotion* for a fuller discussion of this concept.

10. The manuscript notebook, Uppsala (Uppsala University Library C86) likely written by Bishop Alfonso, gives Bride's itinerary: March 11, Naples; March 14, sails to Messina from Naples, reaching Messina March 19; March 26, Cyprus; March 30, Cephalonia in great tempest; April 1–4, comes to Cos, is greeted by Master of the Order of St. John Hospitaller; April 8, Cyprus, Paphos, then, with good wind, Famagusta.

11. Emmanuel LeRoy Ladurie and Natalie Zemon Davis have already successfully quarried Inquisition documents for their glimpses of medieval lives.

12. This has been especially noted by Peter Brown and Victor Turner in numerous studies, among them, Brown, *The Cult of the Saints* and Turner, *The Ritual Process*. Fatima Mernissi (10–12) and Vincent Crapanzano note the same phenomenon concerning women and pilgrimage in Islam.

13. ". . . quod Katerina de Flandria, ancilla dicte domine Brigide infirmata fuit graviter ad mortem de febribus et de punctura lateris sinistri taliter, quod tractabant ei facere extremam unccionem . . . supplicavit eidem domine Brigide matri sue, quod oraret pro illa infirma credens quod oracionibus illius curaretur et fieret sana, et tunc dominus Petrus confessor predictus eidem mandavit, et tunc ipsa extendit se totam in pavimento et ibi oravit pro illa, et statim in momento liberata fuit illa infirma et surrexit

illico sana et equitavit et arrivet iter versus Romam" (*Scriptorum rerum svecicarum* 3: 226).

14. Jørgensen 2:299; *The Book of Margery Kempe* (ed. Meech and Allen), here, notes that "S. bridis madyn" is rubricated in red in the margin of the text. It is interesting that Swedish wood sculptures of St. Bride so show her with laughing eyes and maternally plump while Italian frescoes and manuscripts depict her as spare and stern.

15. See *Holy Feast and Holy Fast*. For the Brigittine manuscripts: Lambeth Palace 432: Bride on Jerome and Eustochium, Richard Rolle, miracles at Lichfield, Norwich, Westminster, associated with Margaret, Duchess of Clarence; Lambeth 545, Lewkenor Hours, Brigittine material, drawings of Bromholme Cross, Christ's Wound; Lambeth 546, "IHS/MARIA/BIRGITTA," manuscript owned by Syon Sister EW, all being texts for women's devotions. Syon Abbey manuscript 1 gives "Amor meus crucifixus est," among others.

16. Gibson especially discusses Kempe's identification with Bride (47–56).

17. *Liber Celestis* xii; Roger Ellis, "Flores ad fabricandum" 183.

18. Jantzen discusses the influence of Adam Easton's preaching in Norwich on Julian, his knowledge of Greek and Hebrew, and his cardinalship of St. Cecilia in Rome (17).

19. Archbishop Richard le Scrope had connections to both Henry Lord Fitzhugh and to Thomas Gascoigne. Lord Fitzhugh, Richard le Scrope's nephew, sought to donate Cherry Hinton in East Anglia for the Brigittines, that letter of donation dated 1406 being at Uppsala, the Syon Martiloge, British Library Add. MS 22,285, fol. 14, noting he was "primus hanc religionem in regnum Anglie" [the first to introduce the order into England]. Closely associated with both Henry IV and Henry V, he became Constable of England. Thomas Gascoigne, whose uncle, William Gascoigne, refused to preside over Richard le Scrope's trial, traveled to both Sweden and Rome, visiting Brigittine houses, became Chancellor of Oxford, and likely translated the *Life* of St. Birgitta, printed by Pynson, 1516.

20. *ASS* Oct 4:477C, E, Martin V's bull dated Florence, April 6, 1419 (Sargent, "The Transmission" 228).

21. The unique manuscript notes in red in the margin, beside "Schene" in text, "syon" (*Book* 245; Redpath 178).

22. Bride is at fol. 97, Julian, fol. 237. It is the earliest Julian manuscript. A manuscript that came to Vadstena, Uppsala, Uppsala University Library, C159, written by Clement Maidstone for Syon Abbey, includes Walter Hilton's and Richard Rolle's writings, while C631 includes Richard Rolle's and Bonaventure's writings. Ann Warren notes similar patronage for Brigittines, Julian of Norwich, and recluses of Lynn, *passim*.

23. "Neyþyr Hyltons boke, ne Bridis boke, ne Stimulus Amoris, ne Incendium Amoris" (39). Christ tells her, "I telle þe trewly, it is trewe euery word þat is wretyn in Brides boke" (47). Also, "as þe Bybyl with doctowrys þer-up-on, Seynt Brydus boke, Hyltons boke, Boneventur, Stimulus Amoris, Incendium Amoris, & swech other" (143); and "He red also of Richard Hampol, hermyte, in Incendio Amoris" (154).

24. The therapeutic quality of Kempe's book writing is noted on 219, which is true also of Hildegard of Bingen. The serial quality to Kempe's book writing (220–21) is found in Bride's *Revelations*, likewise written at different stages and with different amanuenses during her life.

25. *ASS* Oct 4:469E; *SRSMA* 192.

26. *ASS* Mar 3:515C.

27. Lynn's church is St. Margaret's Church; Norwich Cathedral has a fine fifteenth-century painting of St. Margaret in one of its chapels. See Gibson, especially 178–79.

28. Bride had pilgrimaged to Trondheim on foot from the region around Vadstena. It took me a night and half a day to travel from Stockholm to Trondheim by train, the distance being so great.

29. Elizabeth M. Makowski ably discusses the meaning of the payment of the marriage debt, relevant to Bride, Kempe, and Alice of Bath.

30. Kempe even mentions the mystical writings of the Carthusian Mary of Oignies and Elizabeth of Hungary (153). It should be stressed that British Library, Add. 37,790, containing both Julian and Bridget, was written by James Grenehalgh, who customarily wrote books at Carthusian Sheen for the Brigittines at Syon.

31. Richard Lavenham, Richard II's confessor and Professor of Theology at Oxford, owned an early version of Bride's *Revelations* and was teaching that text at Oxford: "revelationes in scholis Oxoniensibus et in cathedris publicis magistralibus exposuerunt magni sua aetate doctores Thomas Stubbes, Dominicanus, Ricardus Lavynham, Carmelita, et adhunc alii ejus generis multi circa annum domino MCCCLXX" (*ASS* Oct 4:409A) [the *Revelations* were being much taught at that time in the schools at Oxford and from public lectures, the Dominican Thomas Stubbs, the Carmelite Richard Lavenham, and others reaching many people around the year 1370]; British Library MS Royal 7 C IX; Cumming xxix; Bodleian MS 169. Later Hoccleve, Audelay, and Gascoigne wrote about Bride. In wills we find Elizabeth Sywardby, 1468, Margaret Purdawnce, 1481, Cecily, Duchess of York, 1495, leaving copies in English of St. Bridget's *Revelations* (Cumming xxxviii; Gibson 21, 78).

32. In connection with Luttrell see *Book* 58–60 as both involve requesting the pope to grant equivalent privileges at churches which, in both cases, was denied.

33. See *The Orcherd of Syon*: "Here begyneth a shorte treatyse of contemplacyon taught by our lord Ihesu cryst out of the boke of marguerite Kempe of lynn. . . . Here endeth a shorte treatyse of a devoute ancres called margerye kempe of Lynn" (London: Wynken de Worde, 1521).

34. For instance, Chaucer takes pains to place her within the landscape of pilgrimage in the holy places, at Jacob's Well (Holloway, *Pilgrim and Book* 181–95).

Map of Saint Bride's pilgrimages, those of Margery Kempe's *imitatio Brigidae* (imitation of Bridget), and Brigittine convents.

MARGERY AND ALISON: WOMEN ON TOP

Janet Wilson

There is no more telling comment on the limited representation given to women writers in the Middle Ages than the fact that the first professional female writer, Christine de Pisan, in her celebrated defense of women's status in *The Treasure of the City of Ladies* (1405), does not include learning and knowledge and certainly not her vocation of writing among the pursuits she recommends for women (Bell 173–84). Christine no doubt recognized that her aristocratic birth granted her privileged access to the world of learning whereas for the average laywoman, however articulate, illiteracy was an overwhelming obstacle to written communication. The lack of formal education underlies just one of many points of collision that a contemporary of Christine, the fifteenth-century mystic Margery Kempe, found with the lay and ecclesiastic societies to whom she announced, often inarticulately— through gesture, noise, or clothing—her spiritual experiences; for how could an illiterate woman, however blessed with revelatory visions and the gift of tears hope to authenticate her experiences in print and so communicate them to a wider audience? Yet this was precisely Kempe's ambition, accomplished against the odds through the mediation of masculine clerical authorities in what is now recognized as the first autobiography in English. *The Book of Margery Kempe* in its very genesis and construction reflects the deep-seated conflict with patriarchy which dogged the last twenty years of her life, for the scribal intermediaries who arbitrate between the spoken word and its literary expression create a tension between the surface and deep structures which gives the work "the stamp of clerical analysis and controversy" (Goodman 349). We might reconstruct a less controversial image of Kempe, however, by a semiotic reading of her text, that is, by using the discourse of carnival to align her behavior with that of the carnivalesque woman. Reading the figure of the marginal woman in relation to the prior scribal text may then enable her to be defined as a dynamic model who helped create space for women outside patriarchy.

Although the complex textual history of Kempe's *Book* problematizes her visibility in the literary sense, her account leaves us in no doubt about her powerful presence and the reality for her of her visionary experiences. Kempe's refusal to be silenced is the most enduring feature of her extraordinary personality and she was further driven to justify her revelations by popularizing them in written form. The very theatricality of her devotions—the tears, the twisting of her neck, her roaring like a bull—suggest at one level a consummate actor living out her mystical experiences in a mode of self-dramatization which is close to mime. Kempe may have believed that her emotional excesses validated her mystical experiences, but her contemporaries regarded her skeptically. Her biography shows that her persistent hyperbolic behavior, resisting any easy social or religious definition, triggered off her interminable conflicts with ecclesiastical authorities. This extremism, stemming from the concrete, physical nature of her identification with Christ's Passion, has also confounded critics who earlier in this century compared her unfavorably with mystics of the negative way such as Julian of Norwich and Richard Rolle.[1] But if Kempe's hysteria and her gift of tears do not conform to the conventional expectations of piety, they can be located within the parameters of an alternative symbolic order, that is, an order which is situated within the existing social and political system but symbolically at its edges. Her eccentric conduct shows affinities with the categories of speech and spectacle which Bakhtin (5–17) and subsequent critics have identified as belonging to the world of carnival: "The masks and voices of carnival resist, exaggerate, and destabilize the distinctions and boundaries that mark and maintain high culture and organized society" (Russo 218).

Only fifty years earlier Chaucer's most famous creation, the Wife of Bath, anticipated Kempe's dramatic self-presentation and the ambivalent challenge to religious and social orthodoxies which insured her notoriety. Alison's flamboyant appearance, extravagant claims of domestic and marital supremacy, and lengthy diatribe in favor of women's wiles make her resemble the carnival figure of the "unruly woman," a multivalent image which, according to Natalie Davis, operated not only to reinforce female subordination but also potentially to subvert existing social options (126–31). Her extraordinary personality emerges principally through her celebrated marital exploits. These do not merely rebound from her status of widowhood and her claim to have had five husbands, for they originate in Chaucer's symbolically locating her on top of the first three husbands, thus inverting the social and domestic hierarchy. In her Prologue (WBP) she defines her expertise in marriage as, "This is to seyn, myself have been the whippe" (175). This upside-down vision which the assertion of female domestic superiority creates, differs in degree but not in kind from Kempe, whose greater vocation in Christ to which she was called after twenty years of marriage and fourteen children, forced her to take the reins of marriage into her hands and make her husband agree to a relationship of celibacy (Ch. 11).

Although both Kempe and Alison can be seen as figures of excess, capable of dislocating social boundaries and of disrupting society's norms, such an interpretation must take into account the fact that some gender asymmetry and distortion in medieval texts are inevitable given the circumstances of literary production and composition in the Middle Ages. In both accounts the representation of the feminine is mediated and hence vindicated by a masculine consciousness. Chaucer consciously contrives and masks his depiction of exaggerated bourgeois feminism under the guise of confessional autobiography: he impersonates Alison's spoken voice by an act of ventriloquism just as he conjures up her tyrannical nature from the stereotype of the virago or the shrewish, nagging wife. Margery Kempe's voice, which her male clerical scribes filter to us, poses an equally intransigent problem of authentication. Her account involves both a deliberate rhetorical strategy as the mediating scribes provide a textual layering which simultaneously transform it into a clerical response, and self-reflexivity as Kempe attempts to accommodate that response. On occasion the scribal opinion becomes explicit as, for example, in her second scribe's decision to renounce her after the famous friar, William Melton, bans her from his preaching at Lynn because of her crying and interruptions of his sermons.

> And þan many of hem þat pretendyd his frenschep turnyd a-
> bakke for a lytyl veyn drede þat þei haddyn of hys wordys &
> durst not wel spekyn wyth hir, of þe whech þe same preyste
> was on þat aftirward wrot þis boke & was in purpose neuyr to a
> leueyd hir felyngys again. (152)

[And then many of those who pretended friendship to her
hung back out of a little vain dread that they had of his words,
and dared not very well speak with her. Among these people
was the same priest who afterward wrote down this book, and
he was resolved never again to believe her feelings.] (191)

Some reference to the discourse of carnival may partially redefine
the problems of visibility which these sociolinguistic constructions of
Margery and Alison pose, for this discourse replaces authoritarian
modes with models of transformation and counterproduction and
"translocates issues of bodily exposure and containment, disguise and
gender masquerade, abjection and marginality, parody and excess, to the
field of the social constituted as a symbolic system" (Russo 214). In
the late sixties anthropologists and social historians interpreted the
upside-down world with its reversals of role and status as evidence for
the reinforcement of social structures and order. But the motif of the
woman on top as a symbolic model of transgression is not necessarily a
closed one, capable only of reversal, for recent feminist scholarship has
suggested that there is a connection between symbology and social
change. The options which the alternative world of carnival presents,
whether in fiction or in real life, might be seen as belonging to the
conflict over efforts to change the basic distribution of power within
society, as Natalie Davis surmised in 1975:

> The image of the disorderly woman did not always function to
> keep women in their place. On the contrary, it was a
> multivalent image that could operate, first, to widen
> behavioral options for women within and even outside
> marriage, and second to sanction riot and political
> disobedience for both men and women in a society that
> allowed the lower orders few formal means of protest. (131)

If this is the case then we may approach Alison and Kempe from the
perspective of Irigaray's account of feminism which insists on
inscribing the female body outside and beyond phallocentrism and
scrutinizing cultural representations of femininity to the point where
women may achieve representation and recognition on their own terms
(*Speculum* 142–43; Grosz 109–10). Do the clerical representations of
Kempe's account provide sufficient space for her outside patriarchy to
show an essential difference from masculine constructions of the
feminine? Does Chaucer's portrait of Alison allow for an authentic

female voice and position when answering the question of her tale: What is it that women most desire? In order to compare the two texts from this perspective the generic distinctions of the different discourses which they contain—fictional autobiography and Arthurian romance in the case of Alison, and non-fiction in the case of Kempe—will be deliberately conflated under the genre of autobiography.

We can loosely view Kempe and Alison within the descriptive category of grotesque realism which Bakhtin defines as vital to the carnival spirit (18–30). Crucial is the focus on the body as a continuous process or in its state of becoming: its imperfections, its excrescences, its instinctive and purely functional condition. Kempe's many pregnancies, the first of which led to postpartum psychosis causing delirium and near-madness, others of which distorted her shape, the very physicality of her sufferings—the crying, sobbing, roaring to convey her frustrations—portray the body in an extreme state. These symptoms of hysteria—convulsive, repetitive gestures and sounds, which provoked such ambivalent responses—may also be associated with the carnivalesque, for the cultural category of hysteria has variously been identified with the repression of sexuality, with language not yet at the point of verbal expression but confined within the bond of the body, with things heard but not understood, with an audience which sees but does not hear (Weissman, "Margery Kempe" 202; Russo 222).[2] In the General Prologue portrait Alison's florid complexion and capacious hips exemplify the irregular body; the description of her attire adds figurative and parodic dimensions to an already strident appearance by metaphorically projecting her preoccupation with "maistrye." The martial overtones of her hat "as brood as is a bokeler or a targe" (471) and the sharp spurs (473) construct an image of her as a mock knight about to enter battle. By these means Chaucer also develops his portrayal into a parody of the Virtuous Woman from Proverbs 31:10– 31 ("mulier fortis"), who was celebrated as a figure of the Church and of the New Woman Mary triumphant (Boren 247–56; Weissman, "Antifeminism" 105). By contrast, when Alison poignantly reflects on the passing of her youth, her body, now worn and used, becomes the site of her losing battle against time:

> But age, allas, that al wole envenyme,
> Hath me biraft my beautee and my pith.
> Lat go. Farewel! The devel go therwith!

> The flour is goon; ther is namoore to telle;
> The bran, as I best kan, now moste I selle. (WBP 474–78)

Chaucer also links the Wife's self-presentation with the General
Prologue portrait by noting the distinguishing features—the birthmarks
planted in "privee" places and her gaptooth (GP 468; WBP 603–04,
619–20)—which, according to physiognomical lore, make her conform
to that familiar stereotype of fabliau and antifeminist satire: the woman
whose insatiable sexual appetite exceeds her powers of discrimination
and whose inexhaustible energies make her disorderly when let loose in
a public sphere:

> For, God so wys be my savacioun
> I ne loved nevere by no discrecioun;
> But evere folwede myn appetyt,
> Al were he short, or long, or blak, or whyt;
> I took no kep, so that he liked me,
> How poore he was, ne eek of what degree. (WBP 621–26)

Also relevant to the category of grotesque realism is the
conspicuous hubris which both women display as part of their wish to
be noticed; the Wife's determination to be first in the parish to the
offering on Sundays (GP 449–50), the flamboyant, outsized coverchiefs
which she wears to church (GP 453–55), and her pride in her weaving
(GP 447–48) have their counterpart in Kempe's descriptions of her
elaborate dress and her ambitious business ventures, designed to attract
the attention of her society before her conversion. Kempe, however,
unlike the Wife, redefines this antifeminist stereotype in her attempt to
gain "absolute perfection" (Weissman, "Margery Kempe" 216). After
her conversion she wears a hair shirt; in Rome as Christ's bride and as a
symbol of virginity she begins to wear white clothes (Chs. 2, 3, 30).[3]

Alison's and Kempe's over- or under-dressing in order to create a
public spectacle of themselves is equally matched by their compulsion
to speak out in order to be heard. The exhibitionism which leads them
to transgress social and ethical boundaries is nowhere more evident than
in their violation of the taboo against female preaching, a clerical
prohibition which was strongly reinforced in the fourteenth and fifteenth
centuries due to its association with fears of Lollard insurgency (Lochrie
42–46). Kempe's mission as a mystic—to live in the world to help and
instruct men and women rather than to retreat into solitude, meditation,

and prayers—was in itself unconventional, and the clerical authorities who probably felt she did not deserve the holy reputation she claimed for herself objected to it. Accusations of Lollardy or heresy, some of which led to imprisonment, were frequent. The Mayor of Leicester called her ". . . a fals strumpet, a fals loller, & a fals deceyuer of þe pepyl, & þerfor I xal haue þe in preson" (112) [a false strumpet, a false Lollard, and a false deceiver of the people, and therefore I shall have you in prison (149)]; and members of Archbishop of York's household: "þer comyn . . . despisyng hir, callyng hir 'loller' & 'heretyke,' & sworyn many an horrybyl othe þat sche xulde be brent" (123–24) [came there, scorning her, calling her "Lollard" and "heretic," and swore many a horrible oath that she should be burned (162)]. Chaucer anticipated this conflict with the Church and the challenge Kempe posed to its authority, for Alison's prologue opens with a discourse, which has been described as a mock Lollard sermon, directed against the Church's views of marriage (D.W. Robertson, "And for my land" 415). In fact, the Wife's very raison d'être begins as a comic travesty of the clerical belief, sanctioned by St. Paul, that women should not teach and preach, and her theme is another tenet of antifeminist satire: the misery that women inflict on their husbands in marriage. Chaucer resurrects the antifeminist arguments of Jerome, Theophrastus, and the Gospel authorities through her voice and she misquotes, distorts, and partially suppresses them in order to fuel her heterodox interpretation of marriage. He later uses this rhetorical strategy to make Alison speak against herself in a way which is appropriate for masculine contrived discourses, mockingly "vindicating" her shameless and outrageous character by making her denigrate women as fickle, treacherous, devious, willful, and perverse, using the same arguments by which clerical misogyny sustained its condemnation of them. "Deceite, weping, spinning God hath yive/To wommen kindely, whil that they may lyve" (WBP 401–02).

Kempe also represented to her clerical interlocutors a living reincarnation of the apostolic prohibition against female preaching because she freely and publicly proclaimed her visions. But she is equally capable of self-defense and to the Archbishop of York's clerk who accused her of preaching the Gospel she replied: "I preche not, ser, I come in no pulpytt. I vse but comownycacyon & good wordys, & þat wil I do whil I leue" (126) [I do not preach, sir; I do not go into any pulpit. I use only conversation and good words, and that will I do while

I live (164)], and she then impressed her interrogators with a pleasing story about an errant priest. Unlike the Wife who draws exclusively on literary and scriptural authorities Kempe's responses to men's accusations are divinely inspired by Christ who tells her: "I schal ȝeue þe grace j-now to answer euery clerke in þe loue of God" (17) [I shall give you grace enough to answer every cleric in the love of God (51)]. The Holy Ghost also empowers her to quote from the Gospels, so that she confounds a monk of Lincoln: "Eyþyr þow hast þe Holy Gost or ellys þow hast a devyl wyth-in þe, for þat þu spekyst her to vs it is Holy Wrytte, and þat hast þu not of þiself" (28) [Either you have the Holy Ghost or else you have a devil within you, for what you are speaking here to us is Holy Writ, and that you do not have of yourself (63)]. Furthermore the Spirit's inspiration enables her to tell in English "a story of Holly Writte" to her German confessor who could not understand English, but who nevertheless miraculously comprehends it, then repeats it in Latin.[4] Her account, fluctuating between the perspectives of the marginal woman and the masculine literary consciousness, also exposes misogynistic clerical responses. The ecclesiastical authorities of Lynn evidently came to link female eccentricity and hysteria with familiar antifeminist charges of deception, deviousness, and dishonesty; but Kempe is able to repudiate them and to vindicate herself by her verbal dexterity and evidence of irreproachable piety—such as her knowledge of the Articles of the Faith—thus disassociating herself from overt antifeminist sentiment in a way that Alison does not.

    The phenomenon that both women represent in speaking out forthrightly and critically is magnified by their interactions with the audiences they address who either mirror or subvert their theatricality. Chaucer, in comically dramatizing the impact of Alison's revelations on his three scurrilous ecclesiastics—the friar, pardoner, and summoner—anticipates the potential threat which the shameless yet verbally adroit woman poses to masculine clerical authority. But he continues his masquerade by making Alison collude in the reception of her performance and so avoids any conflict. The Pardoner interrupts her discourse on marriage saying: "Ye been a noble prechour in this cas" (WBP 165); but she chooses to echo his later definition of her discourse as a fiction, a "tale" and, moreover, accommodates his discomfort by redefining her "learned" pronouncements on the institution of marriage as a jest: "As taketh nat agrief that I seye,/For myn entente nys but for to pleye" (WBP 192).

Kempe's peculiar form of affective piety led to her identify with Christ's Passion to the point of subjecting herself to persecution of a similar kind; and she overturns her domestic woman-on-top image by casting herself into social role of the abject or victim (Natalie Davis 140; Russo 216). The element of stage management in her melodramatics is mirrored by the violence and theatricality of her audiences' responses which range from astonishment to outright hostility or compassion. Her form of crying, writhing, and wresting her body, holding in the tears and turning the color of lead, "enduryd many ȝerys . . . & þerfor sufferyd sche mych despyte & mech reprefe. Þe cryeng was so lowde & so wondyrful þat it made þe pepyl astonyd . . ." (68) [lasted for many years . . . and she suffered much contempt and much reproof for it. The crying was so loud and so amazing that it astounded people . . . (104)]; "many man & many woman wondyrd up-on hir, skornyd hir & despised hir, bannyd hir & cursyd hir, seyde meche euyl of hir, slawndryd hir, & born hyr on hande þat sche xulde a seyd thyng whech þat sche seyd neuyr" (107) [many men and women were astonished at her, scorned her and despised her, cursed her, spoke much evil of her, slandered her, and accused her of saying something she never said (144)]; on one occasion she is reduced to silence and forced to act the part of a fool:

> They cuttyd hir gown so schort þat it come but lytil be-nethyn hir kne & dedyn hir don on a whyte canwas in maner of a sekkyn gelle, for sche xuld holdyn a fool & þe pepyl xuld not makyn of hir ne han hir in reputacyon. Þei madyn hir to syttyn at þe tabelys ende be-nethyn alle oþer þat sche durst ful euyl spekyn a word. (62)

> [They cut her gown so short that it only came a little below her knee, and made her put on some white canvas in a kind of sacking apron, so that she would be taken for a fool, and people would not make much of her or hold her in any repute. They made her sit at the table below all the others, so that she scarcely dared speak a word.] (98)

Kempe willingly suffered humiliation and persecution, however, since abjection validated her relationship with Christ. He tells her in visions, "Þow xalt ben etyn & knawyn of þe pepul of þe world as any raton knawyth þe stokfysch. . . . I swer to þe be my mageste þat I schal neuyr forsakyn þe in wel ne in wo" (17) [You shall be eaten and gnawed by the people of the world just as any rat gnaws the stockfish. . . . I swear to you by my majesty that I shall never forsake you whether in happiness or in sorrow (51)]. By enduring worldly shame she will be assured of his grace: "Dowtyr . . . þe mor schame & mor despite þat þu hast for my lofe, þe mor joy schalt þu haue wyth me in Heuyn, and it is rithful þat it be so" (185) [Daughter . . . the more shame and more contempt that you endure for my love, the more joy shall you have with me in heaven, and it is just that it should be so (225)].

Kempe denies antifeminist stereotypes and Chaucer reincorporates Alison into his satire of them; to see their apparently subversive behavior in relation to the perceivable norms of society (upon which the satiric model is based) urges some consideration of the potential of the symbolic model of transgression for effecting social change. Striking is the paradox that despite their interruption of patriarchal discourses and their intrusion on the margins of moral and religious orthodoxies both women seek some form of masculine approval and by implication a restoration of social structures. Chaucer deconstructs his act of ventriloquism when he attempts to resolve her conflicting desires for power and love. In suggesting that she compromises her "maistrye" and becomes conciliatory toward her fifth husband, he reinscribes her into the very system he makes her mock.

> After that day we hadden never debaat.
> God helpe me so, I was to him as kynde
> As any wyf from Denmark unto Ynde,
> And also trewe, and so was he to me. (WBP 822–25)

The conclusion of Alison's tale further echoes the reversal of the position of marital and domestic supremacy from which she had launched her "apologia pro vita sua." Chaucer silently reinterprets the answer to the question of what it is that women most desire because the knight finally discovers that the ugly hag, transformed into a beautiful princess, is desirable; ironically it is because "she obeyed hym in every thyng/That myghte doon him plesance or liking" (WBT 1255–56).

This recipe of comradely reciprocity for domestic happiness and the suggestion of her Tale's conclusion that women want to be young and beautiful illustrate Irigaray's definition of masquerade as the false position of women experiencing desire only as male desire for them

(*This Sex* 84–85). Chaucer reinforces this shift in focus by deploying a rhetorical strategy of silence to accommodate the position where a "real" female voice may be heard.[5] As Alison's Prologue draws to a close, so her "identifiable" voice disappears. By allowing her no part in the Friar and Summoner's squabbling and by resolving the impasse through the host's intervention, Chaucer implies that her voice does not exist outside male discourses. To that extent patriarchal ideology both defines and contains her point of view.[6] His masquerade can only recommence by means of a transition to another discourse—the romance mode of her tale—requiring another narrative "voice" and a further "resolution" which will reinforce the norms of gender and society.

The provisional loss of distinctions or boundaries in liminal states (that is, states which inititate a process) usually leads to a redefining of social structures. Chaucer rightens his upside-down world and sets it back on course in a neat schematization which enables him to celebrate and expose the vices of the bourgeois woman. Chaucer's uneasy attempts at closure in the Wife's Prologue and Tale—as in the discordant reintroduction of Alison's radical voice at the conclusion of her tale, demanding new, young husbands and denigrating old and miserly ones (WBT 1259–64)—suggest that he backed away from the temptation to open up new behavioral options for women just as he avoided any redefinition of the relationships of social and political power.

In *The Book of Margery Kempe* no such tidy reversal as Chaucer achieves is possible. Instead Kempe attempts to redefine her behavior against the boundaries that she has transgressed. She, too, seeks and usually acquires the approval of masculine clerical authorities both to validate her piety and to record her story. To the extent that her *Book* records these attempts and the acquiescence of her detractors, it is a justificatory treatise. For example, her second scribe is restored to faith in her after reading that the gift of tears was possessed by another mystic, St. Bridget of Sweden (Ch. 62). But the scribal collaboration also implies a clerical shaping of Kempe's point of view which potentially reinscribes a patriarchal ideology and reduces her radicalism (Goodman 349). And for the reason that her verbal performance is controlled by a literary, masculine representation, the surface level of her text is not the most comprehensive guide to the complex mystical experiences which she seeks to convey. Instead it is in the elements of masquerade which characterize her non-verbal behavior—the hysteria that her mimesis of Christ's Passion produces in her—that the potential

for a feminine subversion of masculine stereotypes of the feminine
might be found.

In psychoanalytic theory of hysteria the body is usually seen as
the site of insurgence not withdrawal. Margery's hysterical behavior is a
form of erotic expression, attributable to the very subjective nature of
her identification as a woman with Christ's Passion, birth, and
childhood, and with the Blessed Virgin's responses, all of which create a
pathology of vulnerability: victimization, passivity, and suffering.
Through her violently empathetic mimesis she projects various forms
of sexual or sex-related sensations associated with the female body, as
when witnessing a vision of the crucifixion in Jerusalem, her body
expresses the movements both of crucifixion and of childbirth
(Weissman, "Margery Kempe" 210–12):

> þan sche fel down & cryed wyth lowde voys, wondyrfully
> turnyng & wrestyng hir body on euery syde, spredyng hir
> armys a-brode as ȝyf sche xulde a deyd, & not cowde kepyn hir
> fro crying, and þese bodily mevyngys for þe fyer of lofe þat
> brent so feruently in hir sowle wyth pur pyte & compassyon.
> (70)

> [then she fell down and cried with a loud voice, twisting and
> turning her body amazingly on every side, spreading her arms
> out wide as if she would have died, and could not keep herself
> from crying and these physical movements, because of the
> fire of love that burned so fervently in her soul with pure pity
> and compassion.] (106)

Reminders of Christ and his mother at the time of his Passion come
from seeing a child being suckled (Ch. 34); and of Christ's manhood
from seeing women in Rome bearing children: "ȝyf sche myth wetyn
þat þei wer ony men children, sche schuld þan cryin, roryn, & wepyn as
þei sche had seyn Crist in hys childhode" (86) [if she could discover that
any were boys, she would cry, roar, and weep as if she had seen Christ
in his childhood (123)]. These responses are reinforced by the physical
nature of the revelations she receives from Christ in the course of their
spiritual marriage:

> Dowtyr, thow desyrest gretly to se me, & þu mayst boldly,
> whan þu art in þi bed, take me to þe as for þi weddyd husbond,
> as thy derworthy derlyng, & as for thy swete sone, for I wyl

> be louyd as a sone schuld be louyd wyth þe modyr & wil þat þu
> loue me, dowtyr, as a good wife owyth to loue hir husbonde.
> & þerfor þu mayst boldly take me in þe armys of þi sowle &
> kyssen my mowth, myn hed, & myn fete as swetly as thow
> wylt. (90)

[Daughter, you greatly desire to see me, and you may boldly,
when you are in bed, take me to you as your wedded husband,
as your dear darling, and as your sweet son, for I want to be
loved as a son should be loved by the mother, and I want you
to love me, daughter, as a good wife ought to love her
husband. Therefore you can boldly take me in the arms of your
soul and kiss my mouth, my head, and my feet as sweetly as
you want.] (126–27)

Kempe's overpoweringly subjective identification with all aspects of
Christ's life and suffering meant that she was unable to achieve that
transcendental union which would have released her from the corporeal;
she continuously redirected her sexual energies into public areas,
reenacting them through repetitive gesture and emotion. Incapable of
breaking away from this mold in which she physically sublimated her
identity in an intensely imagined relationship with Christ, she
effectively reinforced the traditional patriarchal conception of the
feminine as the object of man's desires, a conception which equates the
female body with debasement, passivity, and victimization. In this she
is no different from other women mystics and saints, her
contemporaries and models, in whose hagiographies the representation
of pain is crucial. As Sarah Beckwith says:

> It is clear that women's access to the visionary, far from
> deriving from their place outside representation, in patriarchy
> derives instead from the very specific representative function
> given to them in medieval culture, the very representation of
> themselves as associated with the debased matter of the flesh,
> which they see valorised and redeemed in Christ's torture on
> the cross, a redemption through physicality. (47)

Her hysteria, that is, at its most transparent, has the negative function
of reinforcing the masculine prejudice that the feminine is inextricable
from the material—the world, the flesh, and the devil—and it does so
even more thoroughly than Chaucer does in his treatment of Alison

because of the validating influence of the spiritual, visionary medium which inspires it.

Insofar as Kempe reinforces existing social structures and a patriarchal ideology rather than creating any space out of which women might construct an identity that will lead to recognition on their own terms, she as a symbolic model of transgression does not meet the demands of Irigaray's program for feminism. Despite her affinity with continental secular women mystics such as St. Bridget of Sweden, the Blessed Dorothea of Montau, and Angela of Foligno, she seems to have remained an isolated figure within the English mystical tradition. Yet her hyperbolic, theatrical behavior does suggest some ways in which women might potentially subvert masculine discourses. For the hysterical or mimed performance which precedes speech and is a substitute for it can make visible experiences that are foreign to the realm of public discourse, and thereby give them potential for verbal expression; that is, hysteria might be one way of using the body to create the distance necessary for articulation. Irigaray says:

> To play with mimesis is thus, for a woman, to try to recover the place of her exploitation by discourse, without allowing herself to be simply reduced to it. It means to resubmit herself . . . to "ideas," in particular to ideas about herself, that are elaborated in/by a masculine logic, but so as to make "visible," by an effect of playful repetition, what was supposed to remain invisible: the cover-up of a possible operation of the feminine in language. (*This Sex* 76)[7]

Kempe was a phenomenon who created more mystification than revelation; yet she projected into the public sphere in an incoherent and inchoate fashion, destabilizing those who guarded public morals, the erotic and private areas of women's experience for which no rhetorical dimension, no literary tradition or even language existed in the fifteenth century. Expressing through bodily gesture an extreme form of affective piety (which insisted on the physical as the legitimate means to the spiritual) she remained as trapped within her subjectivity as firmly as Alison was within the masculine modes of discourse. But to the extent that she was unable to restore herself to the existing norms of gender and society as completely as Chaucer restores Alison, she might be seen to have created space for the subversive potential of the disorderly woman.

University of Otago

NOTES

1. On the distinction between negative and positive mysticism see Sarah Beckwith, 37–41. For a critique of male writers on Margery Kempe see Eluned Bremner's essay in this volume.

2. For links between the carnivalesque and the hysterical crisis see Hélène Cixous and Catherine Clément, *The Newly Born Woman* 46. Freud identifies the hysterical crisis as "a pantomime of sexual pleasure," for "what is played out in the body, takes the place of a discourse that cannot be uttered"; see the rereading by Monique David-Ménard, *Hysteria from Freud to Lacan* 3, 105.

3. Sheila Delany points out these and other parallels between Alison and Margery in "Sexual Economics, Chaucer's Wife of Bath, and The Book of Margery Kempe" 104–15. See also Karma Lochrie 41–42.

4. David Lawton, in his discussion of Margery's linguistic abilities, says of this incident: "Divine grace bestows upon Margery's English an honorary Latinity" (see above, 98). See also Margery's response, citing Matt. 10:19–20, to the Lincoln men of law (Ch. 55).

5. For the view that verbal omissions and repressions in the Wife's Prologue voice the values that Chaucer's culture inscribed in him see Sheila Delany, "Strategies of Silence in the Wife of Bath's Recital" 112–29. According to Elizabeth Grosz in *Sexual Subversions*, "Irigaray thus seeks out the residues, the remains or traces of female eroticism and corporeality which exceed patriarchal representations. . . . They indicate points of 'repression' and sites of symptomatic eruption of femininity" (109).

6. For similar readings see Lee W. Patterson, "'For the Wyves Love of Bathe'"; Hope Phyllis Weissman, "Antifeminism and Chaucer's Characterization of Women"; and Arthur Lindley, "'As Clerkes': Alice's Absence in the Wife of Bath's Prologue and Tale" (unpublished paper).

7. See also *Speculum of the Other Woman* 59–61, 71–72 and Grosz 135–36.

LIST OF REFERENCES CITED

Primary

Acta et Processus Canonizaciones beate Birgitte. Ed. Isak Collijn. Uppsala: Almqvist, 1924–31.

Acta Sanctorum quotquot toto coluntur (ASS). Brussels: Greuse, 1857.

Aelred of Rievaulx. *De vita eremetica ad sororem liber.* Ed. J.P. Migne. PL 32. 1451–74.

Bernard of Clairvaux. *Saint Bernard on the Love of God.* Trans. Terence Connolly. New York: Spiritual Book Assn., 1937.

Birgitta of Sweden. *The Book of St. Bride: Birgitta of Sweden's Revelations.* Trans. Julia Bolton Holloway. Newburyport: Focus, 1992.

———. *Himmelska Uppenbarelser.* Ed. and trans. Tryggve Lunden. Vols. 1–4. Malmo: Allhems, 1957.

———. *The Liber Celestis of St. Bridget of Sweden.* Ed. Roger Ellis. EETS 291. London: Oxford University Press, 1987.

———. *Life and Selected Writings.* Ed. Marguerite Tjader Harris, Albert Ryle Kezel, and Tore Nyberg. New York: Paulist, 1990.

———. *The Revelations of Saint Birgitta.* Ed. William Patterson Cumming. EETS 178. London: Oxford University Press, 1929.

A Calendar of the Freemen of Lynn 1292–1836. Norwich: Norfolk and Norwich Archaeological Society, 1913.

Chaucer, Geoffrey. *The Riverside Chaucer.* Ed. Larry D. Benson. Boston: Houghton, 1987.

The Cloud of Unknowing and the Book of Privy Counseling. Ed. Phyllis Hodgson. EETS 218. London: Oxford University Press, 1944.

Egeria. "*Peregrinatio Aetheriae.*" *Egeria: Diary of a Pilgrimage.* Trans. George E. Gingras. New York: Newman, 1970.

Ephraem Syri. *Hymni et Sermones.* Mechlin: Archiepiscopal Press, 1982.

Hilton, Walter. *The Scale of Perfection.* Trans. Dom Gerard Sitwell. London: Burns, 1953.

Jerome. *The Pilgrimage of Holy Paula.* London: Palestine Pilgrim's Text Society, 1896.

————— and Paula. *Epistolae*. Ed. J.P. Migne. PL 22. 325–1224.

Joseph of Arimathea. Ed. David A. Lawton. New York: Garland, 1983.

Julian of Norwich. *A Book of Showings to the Anchoress Julian of Norwich*. Ed. Edmund Colledge and James Walsh. 2 vols. Toronto: Pontifical Institute of Medieval Studies, 1978.

—————. *Revelations of Divine Love*. Trans. Clifton Wolters. Baltimore: Penguin, 1966.

The Life of Christina of Markyate, A Twelfth-Century Recluse. Ed. and trans. C.H. Talbot. Oxford: Oxford University Press, 1959

Kempe, Margery. *The Book of Margery Kempe*. Ed. Sanford Brown Meech and Hope Emily Allen. EETS 212. London: Oxford University Press, 1940. Rpt. 1961.

—————. *The Book of Margery Kempe*. Trans. B[arry] A. Windeatt. London: Penguin, 1989.

—————. *The Book of Margery Kempe, 1436, A Modern Version*. Trans. W. Butler-Bowden. Intro. R.W. Chambers. London: Cape, 1944.

Love, Nicholas. *The Mirrour of the Blessed Lyf of Jesu Crist, translated by Nicholas Love*. Ed. Lawrence F. Powell. London: Methuen, 1908.

Marguerite d'Oingt. *Marguerite d'Oingt: édition critique de ses oeuvres*. Ed. A.P. Durdilly, P. Duraffour, and P. Gardette. Paris: Belles Lettres, 1965.

Mirrour of oure Ladye. Ed. John Henry Blunt. EETS 19. London, 1873.

The Orcherd of Syon. Ed. Phyllis Hodgson and G.M. Liegey. EETS 258. London: Oxford University Press, 1966.

Langland, William. *Piers Plowman by William Langland: An Edition of the C-Text*. Ed. Derek Pearsall. Berkeley: University of California Press, 1978.

—————. *Piers Plowman: The B-Text*. Ed. A.V.C. Schmidt. London: Dent, 1978.

—————. *Piers Plowman: The B-Version*. Ed. George Kane and E.T. Donaldson. London: Athlone, 1975.

Paula and Eustochium. *The Letters of Paula and Eustochium about the Holy Places (363 AD)*. Trans. Aubrey Stewart. London: Palestine Pilgrims' Text Society, 1896.

Pseudo-Bonaventure. *Meditations on the Life of Christ: An Illustrated Manuscript of the Fourteenth Century*. Ed. Isa Ragusa and Rosalie B. Breen. Princeton: Princeton University Press, 1967.

The Reuelacions of Saynt Elysabeth the kynges doughter of Hungarye, in The Lyf of Saint Katherin of Senis, printed by Wynkyn de Worde, ?1492, ff. 91v⁻96; ed. C. Horstmann, *Archiv* 76 (1886), 392–400.

Rolle, Richard. *The Incendium Amoris of Richard Rolle of Hampole*. Ed. Margaret Deanesly. Manchester: Manchester University Press, 1915.

Scriptorium rerum svecicarum medii aevi (*SRSMA*). Ed. Claudius Annerstedt. Vol. 3. Uppsala: Berling, 1876.

Teresa of Avila, St. *The Collected Works*. Vol. 1. Ed. and trans. K. Kavanaugh and O. Rodriguez. Washington, D.C.: Institute for Carmelite Studies, 1976.

———. *The Life of St. Theresa of Avila by Herself*. Trans. J.M. Cohen. Harmondsworth: Penguin, 1957.

Secondary

Abell, Troy D. *Better Felt Than Said: The Holiness-Pentecostal Experience in Southern Appalachia*. Waco, Tex.: Markham Press, 1982.

Aers, David. *Community, Gender, and Individual Identity: English Writing 1360–1430*. London: Routledge, 1988.

Allen, Hope Emily. Prefatory Note. *The Book of Margery Kempe*. Ed. Sanford Brown Meech and Hope Emily Allen. EETS 212. Oxford: Oxford University Press, 1940. liii–lxviii.

Allen, Prudence. *The Concept of Woman: The Aristotelian Revolution 750 B.C.–A.D. 1250*. Montreal: Eden, 1985.

Anderson, Aron. *St. Birgitta and the Holy Land*. Trans. Louise Setterwell. Stockholm: Museum of National Antiquities, 1973.

——— and Anne Marie Franzen. *Birgittareliker*. Stockholm: Almqvist, 1975.

Anson, Peter F. *The Call of the Desert: The Solitary Life in the Christian Church*. London: SPCK, 1964.

Aston, Margaret. *Lollards and Reformers: Images and Literacy in Late Medieval Religion*. London: Hambledon, 1984.

Atkinson, Clarissa W. *Mystic and Pilgrim: The "Book" and the World of Margery Kempe*. Ithaca: Cornell University Press, 1983.

Auerbach, Erich. *Mimesis: The Representation of Reality in Western Literature*. Trans. Willard Trask. Princeton: Princeton University Press, 1953.

Bakhtin, Mikhail. *Rabelais and His World*. Trans. Helene Iswolsky. Cambridge: MIT Press, 1968.

Barratt, Alexandra. "*The Revelations of Saint Elizabeth of Hungary*: Problems of Attribution." *The Library*, forthcoming (?March 1992).

———. "The Virgin and the Visionary in *The Revelations* of Saint Elizabeth." *Mystics Quarterly* 42 (1991): 125–36.

Bataille, Georges. *Eroticism*. Trans. Mary Dalwood. New York: Calder, 1962.

Bateson, Mary. *Catalogue of the Library of Syon Monastery, Isleworth*. Cambridge: Cambridge University Press, 1898.

Beckwith, Sarah. "A Very Material Mysticism: The Medieval Mysticism of Margery Kempe." *Medieval Literature. Criticism, Ideology & History.* Ed. David Aers. New York: St. Martin's, 1986. 34–57.

Belenky, Mary Field, Blythe McVicker Clinchy, Nancy Rule Goldberger, Jill Mattuck Tarule, eds. *Women's Ways of Knowing: The Development of Self, Voice, and Mind.* New York: Basic, 1986.

Bell, Susan Groag. "Christine de Pizan (1364–1430): Humanism and the Problem of a Studious Woman." *Feminist Studies* 3 (1975): 173–84.

Belsey, Catherine. *Critical Practice.* New Accents. London: Methuen, 1980.

Bennett, J.A.W. *Chaucer at Oxford and at Cambridge.* Oxford: Clarendon, 1974.

———. *Piers Plowman: The Prologue and Passus I–VII of the B Text.* Oxford: Clarendon, 1972.

Blofield, Francis, and Charles Parkin. *An Essay Towards a Topographical History of the County of Norfolk.* 11 vols. London, 1805–1810.

Boren, James L. "Alysoun of Bath and the Vulgate 'Perfect Wife.'" *Neuphilologische Mitteilungen* 76 (1975): 247–56.

Boswell, James. *Life of Johnson.* Ed. R.W. Chapman. London: Oxford University Press, 1976.

Bouyer, Louis, and Dom Jean Leclerq, eds. *A History of Christian Spirituality: The Spirituality of the Middle Ages.* New York: Seabury, 1961.

Brown, Peter. *The Cult of the Saints: Its Rise and Function in Latin Christianity.* Chicago: University of Chicago Press, 1981.

———. "Society and the Body: The Social Meaning of Asceticism in Late Antiquity." First Plenary Address, 21st International Congress on Medieval Studies, Kalamazoo, May 1986.

Bugge, John. *Virginitas: An Essay in the History of a Medieval Ideal.* The Hague: Nijhoff, 1975.

Burns, George. "Margery Kempe Reviewed." *The Month* 171 (1938): 238–44.

Bynum, Caroline Walker. "'. . . And Woman His Humanity': Female Imagery in the Religious Writing of the Later Middle Ages." *Gender and Religious: On the Complexity of Symbols.* Ed. Caroline Walker Bynum, Stevan Harrell, and Paula Richman. Boston: Beacon, 1986. 257–88. Rpt. Caroline Walker Bynum. *Fragmentation and Redemption: Essays of Gender and the Human Body in Medieval Religion.* New York: Zone, 1991. 151–79.

———. *Holy Feast and Holy Fast: The Religious Significance of Food to Medieval Women.* Berkeley: University of California Press, 1987.

———. "Women Mystics and Eucharistic Devotion in the Thirteenth Century." *Women's Studies* 11 (1984): 179–214.

Chambers, R.W. Introduction. *The Book of Margery Kempe, 1436*. Trans. William Butler-Bowden. London: Cape, 1944. xv–xxiii.

Christ, Carol P. *Diving Deep and Surfacing: Women Writers on Spiritual Quest*. Boston: Beacon, 1980; 2nd ed. 1986.

Chodorow, Nancy. *The Reproduction of Mothering: Psychoanalysis and the Sociology of Gender*. Berkeley: University of California Press, 1978.

Cholmeley, Katherine. *Margery Kempe: Genius and Mystic*. London: Longmans, 1947.

Cixous, Hélène. *La Jeune Née*. Paris: Union Générale, 1975.

———, and Catherine Clément. *The Newly Born Woman*. Trans. Betsy Wing. Intro. Sandra M. Gilbert. Minneapolis: University of Minnesota Press, 1986.

Clarke, Helen, and Alan Carter. *Excavations in King's Lynn, 1963–70*. Society for Medieval Archaeology, Monograph No. 7. London, 1977.

Clay, Rotha M. *The Hermits and Anchorites of England*. 1914. Rpt. Detroit: Singing Tree Press, 1968.

Coleman, Thomas W. *English Mystics of the Fourteenth Century*. London: Epworth, 1938.

———. "Margery Kempe: Medieval Mystic, Evangelist and Pilgrim." *London Quarterly and Holborn Review* 162 (1937): 498–502.

Colledge, Edmund. "Epistola Solitarii ad reges: Alphonse of Pecha as Organizer of Brigittine and Urbanist Propaganda." *Mediaeval Studies* 18 (1956): 19–49.

———. "Margery Kempe." *Pre-Reformation English Spirituality*. Ed. James Walsh. New York: Fordham University Press, 1965. 210–23.

Cozens-Hardy, Basil. *Norwich Consistory Court Depositions, 1499–1512 and 1518–1530*. Norfolk Record Society 10. Norwich, 1938.

Crapanzano, Vincent. *The Hamadsha: A Study in Moroccan Ethnopsychiatry*. Berkeley: University of California Press, 1973.

Cross, Claire. *Church and People, 1450–1660: The Triumph of the Laity in the English Church*. Atlantic Highlands, N.J.: Humanities, 1976.

Crow, Martin M., and Virginia E. Leland. "Chaucer's Life." *The Riverside Chaucer*. Ed. Larry D. Benson. Boston: Houghton, 1987. xv–xxvi.

Cumming, William Patterson. Introduction. *The Revelations of Saint Birgitta*. Ed. William Patterson Cumming. EETS 218. London: Oxford University Press, 1944. xi–xxxix.

Cutts, Edward L. *Scenes and Character of the Middle Ages*. London: Virtue, 1902.

David-Ménard, Monique. *Hysteria from Freud to Lacan*. Trans. Catherine Porter. Ithaca: Cornell University Press, 1989.

Davis, Natalie Zemon. *Society and Culture in Early Modern France.* Stanford, Calif.: Stanford University Press, 1975.

Davis, Norman, ed. *Paston Letters and Papers of the Fifteenth Century.* 2 vols. Oxford: Oxford University Press, 1971, 1976.

De Lauretis, Teresa. *Alice Doesn't: Feminism, Semiotics, Cinema.* Bloomington, Ind.: Indiana University Press, 1984,

Deanesly, Margaret. Introduction. *The Incendium Amoris of Richard Rolle of Hampole.* Ed. Margaret Deanesly. Manchester: Manchester University Press, 1915,

Delany, Sheila. "Sexual Economics, Chaucer's Wife of Bath, and *The Book of Margery Kempe.*" *Minnesota Review* 5 (1975): 105–15. Rpt. in Sheila Delany. *Writing Woman: Women Writers and Women in Literature, Medieval to Modern.* New York: Schocken, 1983.

———. "Strategies of Silence in the Wife of Bath's Recital." *Medieval Literary Politics: Shapes of Ideology.* Manchester: Manchester University Press, 1990. 112–29.

Delasanta, Rodney M. "Sacrament and Sacrifice in the Pardoner's Tale." *Annuale Medievale* 14 (1973): 43–52.

Despres, Denise L. "The Meditative Art of Scriptural Interpolation in *The Book of Margery Kempe.*" *Downside Review* 106 (1988): 253–63.

———. *Ghostly Sights: Visual Meditation in Late-Medieval Literature.* Norman, Okla.: Pilgrim, 1989.

Dickman, Susan. "Margery Kempe and the Continental Tradition of the Pious Woman." *The Medieval Mystical Tradition in England: Papers Read at Dartington Hall, July 1984.* Ed. Marion Glasscoe. Cambridge: Brewer, 1984. 150–68.

———. "Margery Kempe and the English Devotional Tradition." *The Medieval Mystical Tradition in England: Papers Read at the Exeter Symposium, July 1980.* Ed. Marion Glasscoe. Exeter: Exeter Medieval English Texts and Studies, 1980. 156–72.

Duby, Georges. *Medieval Marriages: Two Models from Twelfth-Century France.* Trans. Elborg Forster. The Johns Hopkins Symposia in Comparative History 11. Baltimore: Johns Hopkins University Press, 1978.

Eberly, Susan. "Margery Kempe, St. Mary Magdalene, and Patterns of Contemplation." *Downside Review* 107 (1989): 209–23.

Eliade, Mircea. *A History of Religious Ideas.* Trans. Willard Trask. Vols. 2 and 3. Chicago: University of Chicago Press, 1982.

———. *The Myth of the Eternal Return.* Trans. Willard Trask. New York: Pantheon, 1954.

———. *Shamanism: Archaic Techniques of Ecstasy.* Trans. Willard Trask. New York: Pantheon, 1964.

Elliott, Alison Goddard. *Roads to Paradise: Reading the Lives of the Early Saints*. Hanover and London: University Press of New England, 1987.

Ellis, Deborah S. "The Image of the Home in Early English and Spanish Literature." Diss. University of California, Berkeley, 1981.

———. "Margery Kempe and the Virgin's Hot Caudle." *Essays in Arts and Sciences* 14 (1985): 1–11.

———. "The Merchant's Wife's Tale: Language, Sex and Commerce in Margery Kempe and in Chaucer." *Exemplaria* 2 (1990): 595–626.

Ellis, Roger. "'Flores ad fabricandum . . . coronam,' An Investigation into the Uses of the Revelations of St. Bridget of Sweden." *Medium Aevum* 51 (1982): 163–86.

———. "Margery Kempe's Scribe and the Miraculous Books." *Langland, the Mystics and the Medieval English Religious Tradition*. Ed. H. Phillips. Woodbridge: Suffolk, 1990. 161–75.

Erb, Peter C. "Pietist Spirituality: Some Aspects of Present Research." *The Roots of the Modern Christian Tradition*. Ed. E. Rozanne Elder. Kalamazoo, Mich.: Cistercian, 1984. 249–70.

Faulkner, P.A. "Domestic Planning from the 12th to the 14th Centuries." *Archeological Journal* 115 (1958): 150–83.

Fienberg, Nona. "Thematics of Value in *The Book of Margery Kempe*." *Modern Philology* 87:2 (1989): 132–141.

Freud, Sigmund. *Beyond the Pleasure Principle*. Ed. and trans. James Strachey. New York: Norton, 1961.

Fries, Maureen. "Margery Kempe." *An Introduction to the Medieval Mystics of Europe*. Ed. Paul E. Szarmach. Albany: State University of New York Press, 1984. 217–35.

Furnivall, Frederick J., ed. *The Fifty Earliest English Wills*. EETS 78. London, 1882.

Fuss, Diana. *Essentially Speaking: Feminism, Nature and Difference*. New York: Routledge, 1989.

Gibson, Gail McMurray. *The Theater of Devotion: East Anglian Drama and Society in the Late Middle Ages*. Chicago: University of Chicago Press, 1989.

Gillis, John R. *For Better, For Worse: British Marriages, 1600 to the Present*. New York: Oxford University Press, 1985.

Gilson, Etienne. *The Mystical Theology of Saint Bernard*. Trans. A.H.C. Downs. New York: Random, 1955.

Goodman, Anthony. "The Piety of John Brunham's Daughter, of Lynn." *Medieval Women*. Ed. Derek Baker. Oxford: Blackwell, 1978. 347–58.

Gregersson, Birger, and Thomas Gascoigne. *Life of Saint Birgitta*. Trans. Julia Bolton Holloway. Toronto: Peregrina, 1991.

Grim, John. *The Shaman: Patterns of Siberian and Ojibway Healing.*
    Norman: University of Oklahoma Press, 1983.
Grosz, Elizabeth. *Sexual Subversions: Three French Feminists.* Sydney:
    Allen, 1989.
Gurevich, Aron. *Medieval Popular Culture: Problems of Belief and
    Perception.* Trans. J.M. Bak and P.A. Hollingsworth. Cambridge
    Studies in Oral and Literature Culture 14. Cambridge University
    Press, 1988.
Halevi, Zev ben Shimon. *Kabbalah: Tradition of Hidden Knowledge.*
    London: Thames, 1988.
Halifax, Joan. *Shaman: The Wounded Healer.* London: Thames and Hudson,
    1982.
Harvey, Youngsook Kim. *Six Korean Women: The Socialization of
    Shamans.* New York: West, 1979.
Henisch, Bridget Ann. *Fast and Feast: Food in Medieval Society.* University
    Park: Pennsylvania State University Press, 1976.
Herlihy, David. *Medieval Households.* Cambridge: Harvard University
    Press, 1985.
Hilton, Walter. *The Scale of Perfection.* Trans. Dom Gerard Sitwell. London:
    Burns, 1953.
Hirsh, John C. "Author and Scribe in *The Book of Margery Kempe.*"
    Medium Aevum 44 (1975): 145–50.
———. "Margery Kempe." *Middle English Prose: A Critical Guide to Major
    Authors and Genres.* Ed. A.S.G. Edwards. New Brunswick, N.J.:
    Rutgers University Press, 1984. 109–19.
———. *The Revelations of Margery Kempe: Paramystical Practices in Late
    Medieval England.* Leiden: Brill, 1989.
Hogg, James. "Mount Grace Charterhouse and Late Medieval English
    Spirituality." *Analecta Cartusiana* 82 (1980): 1–43.
Holbrook, Sue Ellen. "Order and Coherence in *The Book of Margery
    Kempe.*" *The World of Medieval Women.* Ed. Constance H. Berman,
    C.W. Connell, J.R. Rothschild. Morgantown, W.Va.: West Virginia
    University Press, 1985. 97–110.
Holdsworth, Christopher J. "Christina of Markyate." *Medieval Women.* Ed.
    Derek Baker. Studies in Church History. Subsidia I. Oxford:
    Blackwell, 1978. 185–204.
Holloway, Julia Bolton. *The Pilgrim and the Book: A Study of Dante,
    Langland and Chaucer.* New York: Lang, 1987.
Howard, Donald R. *Writers and Pilgrims: Medieval Pilgrimage Narratives
    and Their Posterity.* Berkeley: University of California Press, 1980.
Hutchison, Ann M. "Devotional Reading in the Monastery and in the Late
    Medieval Household." *De Cella in Seculum: Religious and Secular*

Life and Devotion in Later Medieval England. Ed. Michael S. Sargent. Cambridge: Brewer, 1989. 215–27.

Idel, Moshe. *Kabbalah: New Perspectives.* New Haven: Yale University Press, 1988.

Ingleby, Holcombe, ed. *The Red Register of King's Lynn.* King's Lynn, 1919, 1921.

Irigaray, Luce. *Speculum of the Other Woman.* Trans. Gillian C. Gill. Ithaca: Cornell University Press, 1985.

———. *This Sex Which Is Not One.* Trans. Catherine Porter with Carolyn Burke. Ithaca: Cornell University Press, 1985.

———. "When Our Lips Speak Together." Trans. Carolyn Burke. *Signs: Journal of Women in Culture and Society* 6 (1980): 69–79.

Jantzen, Grace M. *Julian of Norwich: Mystic and Theologian.* London: SPCK, 1987.

Jelinek, Estelle C. *The Tradition of Women's Autobiography: From Antiquity to the Present.* Boston: Twayne, 1986.

Jørgensen, Johannes. *Saint Bridget of Sweden.* Trans. Ingeborg Lund. London: Longmans, 1954.

Kendall, Laurel. *Shamans, Housewives, and Other Restless Spirits: Women in Korean Ritual Life.* Honolulu: University of Hawaii Press, 1985.

Kieckhefer, Richard. *Unquiet Souls: Fourteenth-Century Saints and Their Religious Milieu.* Chicago: University of Chicago Press, 1984.

Knowles, David. *Bare Ruined Choirs: The Dissolution of English Monasteries.* Cambridge: Cambridge University Press, 1976.

———. *The English Mystical Tradition.* London: Burns, 1961.

———. *The Religious Orders in England.* 2 vols. Cambridge: Cambridge University Press, 1950, 1955.

Kolodny, Annette. "A Map for Rereading: Gender and the Interpretation of Literary Texts." *The New Feminist Criticism. Essays on Women, Literature, and Theory.* Ed. Elaine Showalter. New York: Pantheon, 1985. 46–62.

Ladurie, Emmanuel LeRoy. *Montaillou: The Promised Land of Error.* Trans. Barbara Bray. New York: Braziller, 1978.

Lagorio, Valerie L. "Defensorium contra oblectratores: A 'Discerning' Assessment of Margery Kempe." *Mysticism: Medieval and Modern.* Ed. Valerie M. Lagorio. Salzburg: Institut für Anglistik und Amerikanistik, 1986. 29–48.

———. "The Medieval Continental Women Mystics: An Introduction." *An Introduction to the Medieval Mystics of Europe.* Ed. Paul E. Szarmach. Albany: State University of New York Press, 1984. 161–93.

Lawless, Elaine J. *God's Peculiar People: Women's Voices and Folk Tradition in a Pentecostal Church.* Lexington, Ky.: University Press of Kentucky, 1988.

Lawton, David. *Chaucer's Narrators.* Cambridge: Brewer, 1985.

———. "The Unity of Middle English Alliterative Poetry." *Speculum* 58 (1983): 72–94.

———. "The Voices of Margery Kempe." Paper read *in absentia* at MLA International Meeting, New Orleans, 1988.

Lee, Jung Young. *Korean Shamanistic Rituals.* The Hague: Mouton, 1981.

Leuba, James. *The Psychology of Mysticism.* New York: Harcourt, 1926.

Levy, Leonard W. *Treason Against God: A History of the Offense of Blasphemy.* New York: Schocken, 1981.

Lewis, I. L. *Ecstatic Religion: An Anthropological Study of Spirit Possession and Shamanism.* Baltimore: Penguin, 1975.

Lindley, Arthur. "'As Clerkes': Alice's Absence in the Wife of Bath's Prologue and Tale." Unpublished article.

Lochrie, Karma. "*The Book of Margery Kempe*: The Marginal Woman's Quest for Literary Authority." *Journal of Medieval and Renaissance Studies* 16 (1986): 33–55.

Lucas, Elona K. "The Enigmatic, Threatening Margery Kempe." *Downside Review* 105 (1987): 294–305.

Luttrell, Anthony. "Englishwoman to Jerusalem: Isolda Parewastell, 1365." *Equally in God's Image: Women in the Middle Ages.* Ed. Julia Bolton Holloway, Joan Bechtold, and Constance Wright. New York: Lang, 1990. 184–97.

Maclean, Ian. *The Renaissance Notion of Woman: A Study in the Fortunes of Scholasticism and Medical Science in European Intellectual Life.* Cambridge Monographs on the History of Medicine. 1980. Cambridge: Cambridge University Press, 1987.

Maisonneuve, Roland. "Margery Kempe and the Eastern and Western Tradition of the 'Perfect Fool.'" *Medieval Mystical Tradition in England: Papers Read at the Exeter Symposium, July 1982.* Ed. Marion Glasscoe. Exeter: University of Exeter, 1982. 1–17.

Makowski, Elizabeth M. "The Conjugal Debt and Medieval Canon Law." *Journal of Medieval History* 3 (1977): 99–111.

Mann, Jill. *Chaucer and Medieval Estates Satire.* Cambridge: Cambridge University Press, 1973.

Mason, Mary G. "The Other Voice: Autobiographies of Women Writers." *Life/Lines.* Ed. Bella Brodzki and Celeste Schenck. Ithaca: Cornell University Press, 1988. 19–44.

McEntire, Sandra J. "The Doctrine of Compunction from Bede to Margery Kempe." *Medieval Mystical Tradition in England. Exeter*

Symposium IV, Papers Read at Dartington Hall, July 1987. Ed. Marion Glasscoe. Cambridge: Brewer, 1987. 77–90.

———. *The Doctrine of Compunction in Medieval England. Holy Tears*. Lewiston, N.Y.: Mellen, 1990.

———. "Walter Hilton and Margery Kempe: Tears and Compunction." *Mysticism: Medieval and Modern*. Ed. Valerie M. Lagorio. Salzburg: Institut für Anglistik und Amerikanistik, 1986. 49–57.

McNamara, Jo Ann. "The Need to Give: One Aspect of Voluntary Suffering Among Holy Women of the High Middle Ages." Paper delivered at 22nd International Congress on Medieval Studies, Kalamazoo, May 1987.

Medcalf, Stephen. "Inner and Outer." *The Later Middle Ages*. Ed. Stephen Medcalf. The Context of English Literature. London: Methuen, 1981. 108–71.

———. "Medieval Psychology and Medieval Mystics." *The Medieval Mystical Tradition in England: Papers Read at the Exeter Symposium, 1980*. Ed. Marion Glasscoe. Exeter: University of Exeter Press, 1980. 120–55.

Mernissi, Fatima. "Women, Saints and Sanctuaries." *Signs: Journal of Women in Culture and Society* 3 (1977): 101–12.

Miller, Gayle Houston. "Imagery and Design in Julian of Norwich's *Revelations of Divine Love*." Diss. University of Georgia, 1988.

Minnis, Alastair. *Medieval Theory of Authorship*. London: Scolar, 1985.

Mitchell, Jerome. *Thomas Hoccleve. A Study in Early Fifteenth-Century English Poetic*. Urbana: University of Illinois Press, 1968.

Moi, Toril. *Sexual/Textual Politics*. London: Methuen, 1985.

Morey, G.E. "East Anglian Society in the Fifteenth Century: An Historio-regional Survey." Diss. London University, 1951.

Mueller, Janel M. "Autobiography of a New 'Creatur': Female Spirituality, Selfhood, and Authorship in *The Book of Margery Kempe*." *Women in the Middle Ages and the Renaissance*. Ed. Mary Beth Rose. Syracuse: Syracuse University Press, 1986. 155–71.

Murphy, J.J. *Three Medieval Rhetorical Arts*. Berkeley: University of California Press, 1971.

Noreen, Eric. "Heliga Birgitta som svensk författare." *Birgittaboken*. Ed. Yngve Brilioth, Carl Hamilton, Selma Lagerlöf, Andreas Lindblom, and Eric Noreen. Stockholm: Nordisk, 1954. 61–70.

Nyberg, Tore. *Birgittinische Klostergründen des Mittelalters*. Leiden: Gleerup, 1965.

———. "Klasztor Brygidek w Gdansku i jego najwczesniejsze kontakty z krajami Skandynawskimi na przelomie XIV i IV wieku/The Bridgettine Abbey of Gdansk and Its Earliest Contacts with

Scandinavian Countries in the Fourteenth and Fifteenth Centuries."
Zapiski Historycnze 27 (1962): 676–80.

O'Connell, John R. "Mistress Margery Kempe of Lynn." *Downside Review* 55 (1937): 174–82.

O'Keefe, Daniel Lawrence. *Stolen Lightning: The Social Theory of Magic.* New York: Continuum, 1982.

Oliger, P.L., "Revelationes B. Elisabeth: Disquisitio Critica cum Textibus Latino et Catalaunensi." *Antonianum* 1 (1926): 24–83.

Overholt, Thomas. *Channels of Prophecy: The Social Dynamics of Prophetic Activity.* Minneapolis: Fortress, 1989.

Owen, Dorothy M. "White Annays and Others." *Medieval Women.* Ed. Derek Baker. Studies in Church History. Subsidia I. Oxford: Blackwell, 1978. 331–46.

The Pageant of the Birth, Life and Death of Richard Beauchamp, Earl of Warwick. Ed. Viscount Dillon and W.H. St. John Hope. London: Longmans, 1914.

Pantin, W.A. "Adam Easton's *Defensorium.*" *English Historical Review* 51 (1936): 676–80.

———. "Medieval English Town-house Plans." *Medieval Archaeology* 6–7 (1962–63): 202–39.

———. "The Merchants' Houses and Warehouses of King's Lynn." *Medieval Archaeology* 6–7 (1962–63): 173–81.

Parker, J.H., and T.H. Turner. *Domestic Architecture of the Middle Ages.* Oxford, 1853.

Parker, Vanessa. *The Making of King's Lynn: Secular Buildings from the 11th to the 17th Century.* London: Phillimore, 1971.

Partner, Nancy. "'And Most of All for Inordinate Love': Desire and Denial in *The Book of Margery Kempe.*" *Thought* 64 (1989): 254–67.

———. "Reading the Book of Margery Kempe." *Exemplaria* 3 (1991): 29–66.

Patterson, Lee W. "'For the Wyves Love of Bathe': Feminine Rhetoric and Poetic Resolution in the *Roman de la Rose* and *The Canterbury Tales.*" *Speculum* 58 (1983): 656–95.

Pearsall, Derek, ed. *Piers Plowman by William Langland: An Edition of the C-Text.* York Medieval Texts. Berkeley: University of California Press, 1978.

Pelikan, Jaroslav. *Jesus Through the Centuries.* New York: Harper, 1987.

Petroff, Elizabeth Alvida. *Medieval Women's Visionary Literature.* New York: Oxford University Press, 1986.

Power, Eileen. *Medieval Women.* Ed. M.M. Postan. Cambridge: Cambridge University Press, 1975.

Propp, Vladimir. *Morphology of the Folktale.* Trans. Laurence Scott. Austin: University of Texas Press, 1968.

Redpath, Helen. *God's Ambassadress: St. Birgitta of Sweden.* Milwaukee: Bruce, 1946.

Riehle, Wolfgang. *The Middle English Mystics.* Trans. Bernard Standring. London: Routledge, 1981.

Robertson, D.W., Jr. "'And for my land thus hastow mordred me': Land Tenure, the Cloth Industry and the Wife of Bath." *Chaucer Review* 14 (1980): 403–20.

——. *A Preface to Chaucer.* Princeton: Princeton University Press, 1962.

Robertson, Elizabeth. "An Anchorhold of Her Own: Female Anchoritic Literature in Thirteenth-Century England." *Equally in God's Image: Women in the Middle Ages.* Ed. Julia Bolton Holloway, Joan Bechtold, and Constance Wright. New York: Lang, 1990. 170–83.

——. *Early English Devotional Prose and the Female Audience.* Knoxville: University of Tennessee Press, 1990.

——. "The Rule of the Body: The Feminine Spirituality of the *Ancrene Wisse.*" *Seeking the Woman in Late Medieval and Renaissance Writings.* Ed. Sheila Fisher and Janet Halley. Knoxville: University of Tennessee Press, 1989. 109–34.

Rosenberg, Charles E. "Introduction: History and Experience." *The Family in History.* Ed. Charles E. Rosenberg. Philadelphia: University of Pennsylvania Press, 1975. 1–11.

Rosenthal, Joel T. Introduction. *Medieval Women and the Sources of Medieval History.* Ed. Joel T. Rosenthal. Athens: University of Georgia Press, 1990.

Russo, Mary. "Female Grotesques: Carnival and Theory." *Feminist Studies, Critical Studies.* Ed. Teresa de Lauretis. Bloomington: Indiana University Press, 1986. 213–29.

Sargent, Michael S. *James Grenehalgh as Textual Critic.* 2 vols. Salzburg: Institute für Anglistik und Amerikanistik, 1984.

——. "The Transmission by the English Carthusians of Some Late Medieval Spiritual Writings." *Journal of Ecclesiastical History* 27 (1976): 225–40.

Scase, Wendy. *Piers Plowman and the New Anticlericalism.* Cambridge: Cambridge University Press, 1989.

Schiller, Gertrud. *Iconography of Christian Art.* Trans. Janet Seligman. 2 vols. London: Lund, 1972.

Schmid, Toni. *Birgitta och hennes Uppenbarelser.* Lund: Gleerup, 1940.

Shahar, Shulamith. *The Fourth Estate: A History of Women in the Middle Ages.* London: Methuen, 1983.

Sherbo, Arthur. *Christopher Smart. Scholar of the University.* East Lansing, Mich.: Michigan State University Press, 1967.

Showalter, Elaine. "Feminist Criticism in the Wilderness." *The New Feminist Criticism*. Ed. Elaine Showalter. New York: Pantheon Books, 1985. 243–70.

Sizer, Sandra S. *Gospel Hymns and Social Religion: The Rhetoric of Nineteenth-Century Revivalism*. Philadelphia: Temple University Press, 1978.

Smith, Sidonie. *A Poetics of Women's Autobiography: Marginality and the Fictions of Self-Representation*. Bloomington, Ind.: Indiana University Press, 1987.

Smyser, H.M. "The Domestic Background of Troilus and Criseyde." *Speculum* 31 (1956): 297–315.

Stanton, Domna C. "Autogynography: Is the Subject Different?" *The Female Autograph*. Ed. Domna C. Stanton. Chicago: Chicago University Press, 1987. 3–20.

Stargardt, Ute. "The Beguines of Belgium, the Dominican Nuns of Germany, and Margery Kempe." *The Popular Literature of Medieval England*. Ed. Thomas J. Heffernan. Tennessee Studies in Literature 28. Knoxville: University of Tennessee Press, 1985. 277–313.

Stock, Brian. *Implications of Literacy: Written Language and Models of Interpretation in the Eleventh and Twelfth Centuries*. Princeton: Princeton University Press, 1983.

Stone, Robert Karl. *Middle English Prose Style: Margery Kempe and Julian of Norwich*. The Hague: Mouton, 1970.

The Story of English. Ed. Robert McCrum, William Cran, and Robert McNeil. New York: Penguin, 1986.

Tait, Michael Beckwith. "The Brigittine Monastery of Syon (Middlesex) with Special Reference to Its Monastic Usage." D.Phil. Thesis, Oxford, 1975.

Tanner, N.P., ed. *Heresy Trials in the Diocese of Norwich, 1428–31*. Camden Society 4, series 20. London, 1977.

Thornton, Martin. *Margery Kempe: An Example in the English Pastoral Tradition*. London: Talbot, 1960.

Thrupp, Sylvia. *The Merchant Class of Medieval London*. Ann Arbor: University of Michigan Press. Rpt. 1968.

Thurston, Robert. "Margery the Astonishing." *Month* (1936): 446–56.

Trinterud, Leonard. "Origins of Puritanism." *Church History* 20 (1951): 35–57.

Turner, Victor. *The Ritual Process: Structure and Antistructure*. Chicago: Aldine, 1969.

Underhill, Evelyn. "The Mystic as Creative Artist." *The Essentials of Mysticism and Other Essays*. London: Dent, 1920. 64–85.

———. *Mysticism*. New York: Dutton, 1961.

Unity Song Selections. Summit, Mo.: Unity School of Christianity, 1955.

Vauchez, André. *La sainteté en occident aux derniers siècles du Moyen Age d'après les procès de canonisation et les documents hagiographiques.* Rome: Ecole Française, 1981.

Wallace, David. "Mystics and Followers in Siena and East Anglia: A Study in Taxonomy, Class, and Cultural Mediation." *Medieval Mystical Tradition in England: Papers Read at Dartington Hall, July 1984.* Ed. Marion Glasscoe. Cambridge: Brewer, 1984. 169–91.

Walsh, Roger. *The Spirit of Shamanism.* Los Angeles: Tarcher, 1990.

Watkin, E.I. "In Defence of Margery Kempe." *Downside Review* 59 (1941), 243–63.

Warren, Ann. *Anchorites and Their Patrons in Medieval England.* Berkeley: University of California Press, 1985.

Weinstein, Donald, and Rudolph Bell. *Saints and Society: The Two Worlds of Western Cristendom 1000–1700.* Chicago: Chicago University Press, 1982.

Weissman, Hope Phyllis. "Antifeminism and Chaucer's Characterization of Women." *Geoffrey Chaucer.* Ed. George D. Economou. New York: McGraw-Hill, 1975. 93–110.

———. "Margery Kempe in Jerusalem: *Hysteria compassio* in the Late Middle Ages." *Acts of Interpretation: The Text in Its Contexts 700–1600.* Ed. Mary J. Carruthers and Elizabeth D. Kirk. Norman, Okla.: Pilgrim, 1982. 201–17.

Wesley, Charles. *The Journal of Charles Wesley.* Vol. 1. Grand Rapids, Mich., 1980.

Wilson, R.M. "Three Middle English Mystics." *Essays and Studies* n.s. 9 (1956): 87–112.

Windeatt, B[arry] A. Introduction. *The Book of Margery Kempe.* Trans. B[arry] A. Windeatt. New York: Penguin, 1985.

Wood, Margaret. *The English Mediaeval House.* London: Phoenix, 1965.

Woolf, Virginia. *A Room of One's Own.* New York: Harcourt, 1929.

Wunderli, Richard M. *London Church Courts and Society on the Eve of the Reformation.* Speculum Anniversary Monographs 7. Cambridge, Mass.: Medieval Academy of America, 1981.

Zacher, Christian K. *Curiosity and Pilgrimage: The Literature of Discovery in Fourteenth Century England.* Baltimore: Johns Hopkins University Press, 1978.

INDEX

absolution 86, 197
Aelred of Rievaulx 207
Alfonso de Jaen 207, 216
amanuensis 3, 44, 98, 189, 197–198; see also scribe(s)
anchoress/anchorite xiii, 7–8, 11, 37–39, 76, 112, 207, 211
anchor-hold xiii, 37
Angela of Foligno 20, 40, 236
Anselm 207
antifeminism 228–229
Arianism 109
Ars praedicandi 47
Atkinson, Clarissa xii, 19, 94, 139
autobiography 18, 74, 94, 104, 170, 223, 225
autohagiography 78

Béatrix d'Ornicieux 169, 173, 176
Blanche of Namur 205
blasphemy xiv, 93–96, 106, 109–110, 113–114
bride of Christ 84, 217; see also spiritual marriage
Bridget (Bride) of Sweden xii, xv–xvi, 17–19, 23, 99–100, 148, 165, 167–176, 178–180, 182–183, 200, 203–205, 206–213, 215–218, 233, 236
Brigittines 210–211, 216

carnival 223, 226–227
Casa di Santa Brigida 209

Catherine of Flanders 208–209
Catherine of Siena 17–20, 23, 103, 206–207, 215–217
Cecilia 204, 211–212, 214
celibacy 11, 38, 148, 212, 221
charismatic 30
Charles of Bohemia 205
chastity 195, 217
Chaucer xv, 4–6, 9, 25, 96, 108–111, 114, 204, 210, 215–217, 224–230, 232–233, 235, 237; *Canterbury Tales* 4, 6, 25, 110; Alison of Bath xiii, xvi, 3–9, 14, 19, 27, 82, 95, 146147, 203–204, 214–217, 223–230, 232–233, 235–237; General Prologue 25; Miller's Tale 9; Nun's Priest's Tale 6; Pardoner's Tale 109–111
childbearing 22, 57, 60, 59, 64, 190, 212, 214215
Christina of Stömmeln 41
Christine de Pisan 223
Clare, St. 153
Cleanness 107
Cloud of Unknowing 139
Compostela 216–217
confession 76, 86, 197; see also absolution; penance
conversion 24, 52, 56, 179

devotion 18, 20, 30, 34
devotional theater 207

Dorothea of Montau 19, 101, 236
double monastery 206

Egeria 204
Elizabeth of Hungary xvi, 40,
    189–200
Elizabeth of Schönau 41
Elizabeth of Toess 190, 199
Eucharist 26–27, 33, 110, 130

feudalism 5
flagellants 120
Francis of Assisi 20–21, 24, 28–
    29, 181, 207
Freud, Sigmund xiv, 86

gender 11, 34, 65, 76, 84, 87,
    105, 236

hagiography 19, 83–85, 200, 235
Halle, Heinrich 101
Handlyng Synne 107
heresy 13, 17, 26, 95, 121–122,
    229
Hieronymites 207
Hilton, Walter 17, 18–19, 54, 98,
    104–105, 211
homage 195
hysteria x, xi, xv, 17, 51, 94,
    126, 130–133, 179, 212,
    224, 227, 230, 233–236

illiteracy 81, 95, 102, 139, 211,
    223
Irigaray, Luce 117–118, 126–127,
    132–133

Jacques de Vitry 20, 101
Jerome 207, 229
Johnson's Creek 30, 31, 33
journey 15, 51–52, 65–66, 68,
    170

Julian of Norwich xii–xiii, xvi, 3–
    4, 7–11, 13–14, 17–18, 24,
    38, 41, 47, 76, 85, 113,
    125, 144, 153, 177, 203,
    207–212, 215–217, 224

King's Lynn xv, 3, 15, 37, 46,
    76, 127, 140–142, 147,
    190, 198, 217, 225
Knowles, Dom David xi, 125, 131

Lagorio, Valerie 17
Langland, William xv, 96, 109,
    111, 114, 144; *Piers
    Plowman* 106–109, 206
Latin 19, 25, 43, 47, 96–100,
    106–109, 112, 190, 200,
    205, 208, 212, 230
Lollard 17, 26, 47, 75, 78, 106,
    183, 216, 228
Love, Nicholas 18, 100
Luther, Martin 24

Margarete Florentyn 209
Marguerite d'Oingt xv, 112–113,
    165, 167–171, 173–74,
    176–180, 182–184, 216
Marguerite Porete 112
martyrdom 194
Mary: see Virgin Mary
Mary Magdalene 17, 60, 99–100,
    173, 214
Mary of Oignies 19–20, 40, 101
Master Mathias 205, 209
Mechthild of Magdeburg 101, 112
Meditations on the Life of Christ
    xiii, 17–18, 27, 99, 112,
    207
Melton, William 190, 200, 225
midwifery 60
Mirror for Simple Souls 113
Monk of Farne 113
motherhood 57, 85

Mount Grace Priory 94, 111–113, 212
mystic/mystical ix–xi, 4, 10, 18, 51, 53, 58, 68, 74, 94–95, 102, 105

Nicholas of Lyra 205

Oldcastle 122–123
Orcherd of Syon 103, 216
Order of the Most Holy Saviour 205–206
orthodoxy xii, 84, 96, 108–109, 183, 217, 232

paramystical 30
Passion, of Christ 22, 62, 66, 99–100, 104, 113, 127, 170–172, 224, 231, 233–234; cult of 112
patriarchal ideology 233, 236
Paula 204
Pearl 206
penance 9, 19–20, 40–41, 197, 210; Sacrament of 197; see also absolution; confession
Pentecostal xi, 30–33, 76
phallocentrism 226
pilgrimage xvi, 27, 43, 76–77, 79, 82, 98, 170–171, 196, 203–204, 207–209, 212–217; to Jerusalem 196
postpartum illness 214, 227
preaching 46–47, 214, 229; forbidden 204, 207
pregnancy 9, 57, 59
Pseudo-Dionysius 52

Raymond of Capua 20
Richard of Caister 13
role reversal 226
Rolle, Richard 17, 18, 98–99, 113, 210–211, 224

scribe(s) 79–80, 82, 98, 100–102, 124–125, 189–190, 233; see also amenuensis
sexuality 57, 60–65, 78, 83, 118–119, 127, 133, 177, 212, 227, 235
shaman xvi, 165–166, 168–169, 171
spiritual dryness 194
spiritual marriage 23, 61, 95, 105, 107, 145, 148, 178, 209, 216, 234
Suso, Heinrich 27
Syon Abbey 210–211, 214

tears ix, xiii–xiv, 17, 31, 34, 37, 39–43, 49, 118, 120, 127, 130, 132, 198, 223–224, 231
Teresa of Avila 21, 27, 33–34, 100, 104
textual community xv–xvi, 215
Theophrastus 229
Thomas à Kempis 19, 27
Thomas Camperis 20

victimization 235
virgin/virginity xiv, 57, 60, 65, 78, 87, 119, 177, 196
Virgin Mary 17, 24, 33, 58–59, 84, 99–100, 170, 173–175, 223
vocation 4–7, 9, 13–14, 131, 176
voice xii, 8, 13, 19, 29, 40, 44, 46, 52, 55–56, 64–65, 68, 84–85, 93, 99, 101–103, 105–106, 110–111, 114, 118–119, 123–124, 126, 130, 132, 183, 190, 199, 225, 227, 229, 233–234

weeping 24, 34, 37, 39–43, 61, 76, 80, 82, 100–101, 103,

105, 111, 124, 126–127,
153, 169, 189–190, 192,
198–200
Wenslawe 76
white clothes 39, 59, 63, 65–66,
77–78, 83, 85, 120–121
Windeatt, Barry 46 94, 99, 102,
123
Wyclif, John 216
Wynkyn de Worde 94, 191, 198,
216

DATE DUE